Constructing Danger

Constructing Danger

the mis/representation
of crime in the news

Chris McCormick

Fernwood Publishing
Halifax

The cover photo is a detail from a mural painted by Alex Runt on Lee's Palace, 529 Bloor West, Toronto, Ontario.

Editing: Douglas Beall
Cover photo and design: Chris McCormick
Design and production: Beverley Rach
Printed and bound in Canada by: Hignell Printing Limited

A publication of:
Fernwood Publishing
Box 9409, Station A
Halifax, Nova Scotia
B3K 5S3

Fernwood Publishing Company Limited gratefully acknowledges the financial support of The Ministry of Canadian Heritage.

Every reasonable effort has been made to acquire permission for copyright material used in this text, and to acknowledge such indebtedness accurately. Any errors or ommissions called to the publisher's attention will be corrected in future editions.
Newspaper articles have been reprinted with the gracious permission of Associated Press, Canadian Press, The Chronicle-Herald and The Mail-Star, The Daily News, The Evening Telegram, The Globe and Mail, Globe International, The Ottawa Citizen, Reuter News Service and Southam News.

Canadian Cataloguing in Publication Data
McCormick, Christopher Ray, 1956-
Constructing danger

Includes bibliographical references.
ISBN 1-895686-45-8

1. Crime and the press -- Canada. 2. Crime in mass media -- Canada. 3. Journalism -- Canada -- Objectivity. I. Title.

PN4914.C74M33 1995   070.4'49364971   C95-950067-7

Contents

Figures and Tables

"THE GENERAL APPROACH I'M TAKING
SEEMS TO ME RATHER SIMPLE-MINDED
AND UNSOPHISTICATED,
BUT NEVERTHELESS CORRECT."

Noam Chomsky, Royaumont France, 1975.

Manufacturing Consent: Noam Chomsky and the Media
National Film Board 1992

Contributors

Anne Derrick is a feminist lawyer with the all-women's law firm of Buchan, Derrick and Ring in Halifax. Since her admission to the Nova Scotia Bar in 1981, she has been engaged in a practice involving public-interest litigation. She has represented women working as prostitutes against a civil injunction brought by the provincial Attorney General in 1984, Donald Marshall Jr. before two royal commissions, Dr. Henry Morgentaler and a women's newspaper whose policy to publish material only by women made it the subject of a human rights complaint.

Debi Forsyth-Smith was president of the Nova Scotia Advisory Council on the Status of Women from 1987 to 1993 and is currently chief of staff for the Leader of the Official Opposition in Nova Scotia. She has served on the Dalhousie University's Medical School task force on violence against women, children and the elderly; and on the boards of MediaWatch and the Service for Sexual Assault Victims.

Sharon Fraser is a freelance journalist and broadcaster. She is a regular participant on CBC Radio Morningside's political panel and on CBC TV's (Maritime) Saturday Edition. She contributes to various regional, national and international publications with stories on current affairs, women's issues, the fishery, culture and politics. She has taught at the university level in women's studies and journalism.

Gary Kinsman received his doctorate from the Ontario Institute for Studies in Education, in Toronto. He has taught sociology at Memorial, Acadia and Laurentian Universities. He is the author of *The Regulation of Desire* and numerous articles and book chapters on sexual and gender relations. He is also a gay, AIDS and socialist activist.

Paul MacDonald is a constable in the Halifax Police Department, was formerly the media relations officer and currently works in the community policing office.

Joy Mannette is an associate professor in the Department of Social Science at the University College of Cape Breton. She is the author of *Elusive Justice*, a book on the Marshall Inquiry.

Chris McCormick is an assistant professor in the Department of Sociology (Criminology Certificate Program) at Saint Mary's University in Halifax.

Darrel Pink is the executive director of the Nova Scotia Barrister's Society. He received undergraduate degrees from Acadia and Dalhousie, and a Master's in Law from the London School of Economics in 1979. He is a lecturer at the Dalhousie Law School, on the board of directors of the Metro United Way, past president of the Children's Aid Society of Halifax and has served on several committees of the Canadian Jewish Congress.

Eric Smith fought a long but ultimately unsuccessful battle to regain his post as a teacher after his confidentiality as an HIV-positive person was violated. He often represents the Persons Living with Aids Coalition.

Tony Thomson is a professor in the Department of Sociology at Acadia University. He has done research on policing, young offenders and child abuse.

Deborah Woolway is the executive producer for News and Current Affairs at CBC Radio in Halifax. She has an undergraduate degree from the University of Toronto and a Bachelor's in Journalism from Carleton University in Ottawa. In 1988 she won a Canadian Bar Association Scales of Justice Award for her work on the Donald Marshall Inquiry.

Acknowledgements

A book is a solitary project involving long hours and late nights, based on individual inspiration and perspiration. Thus, the first person I want to acknowledge is myself. However, I am enough of a sociologist to realize that a book involves the efforts of more than one person. Therefore, I want to thank the various people who helped make this project a reality; they are not responsible for what appears here, as I did pretty much as I wished, but they are due thanks nonetheless.

First of all, I would like to acknowledge Dr. Don Clairmont and the Atlantic Institute of Criminology (AIC) for funding the "Crime, Social Problems and Moral Panics" conference in 1991, and Donna Matheson for taping the proceedings. The AIC generously allowed me to use the recording, and they are not responsible for what I did after that point.

I thank the participants who gave their time to speak at the conference and allowed me to use their words in this text. I have tried not to change the words they spoke, only to squeeze them into a smaller space. I hope they are intrigued with how I built on their thoughts and expanded them in these chapters.

I thank the students in various courses I have taught who told me which of my media examples they found interesting, and especially the students in a seminar called "Crime and the Media" I developed at Saint Mary's University in 1993–94. They engaged issues with passion, insight and genuine dialogue. Students in succeeding generations of that course helped to modify some of the ideas that appear here, and they continue to surprise me with new ways of looking at the media.

I also thank Errol Sharpe for encouraging me in this project. I had been toying with several ideas about crime and the news, which I put to him, and he simply said it would be nice to do a book that put an analysis of the news alongside actual news articles. Somewhere in there the project took shape. I especially appreciate the close editing of Douglas Beall and the close communication with Bev Rach. The people at Fernwood did an excellent job producing this text.

Finally, I thank my partner Amani Wassef, who put up with my stacks of newspapers, read and commented on this text, made excellent suggestions and told me not to do another book for a while.

Introduction

Ideology refers to the ideas people have about the world and to the possibility that these ideas can be false. For example, crime is reported in the media in a way that doesn't adequately reflect reality. People come to believe what they read and, in a sense, it is irrelevant whether what they believe is true or not, for their ideas affect how they live their lives. However, people can also develop an exaggerated and distorted fear of crime from the media. This book is not based on the assumption that the media cannot do a good job of reporting crime, for much of what we learn about the world comes from television, newspapers, magazines and so on. My analysis is based on our need to question the view of the world we get from the media.

This book is based on ideas which appeared first as examples in my criminology classes. I have long been interested in how crime is reported in the news and have often used newspaper articles to present topics in "current affairs" format. I have come to see that crime is more than simply reported by the news; it is constructed, distorted and manipulated as well. So what started out as a teaching aid has expanded to a field of research, and I now teach an advanced seminar course devoted solely to the topic of crime in the news. I have never found the "perfect" book for that course, although I have used some that have come close, and so I have decided to write my own. I suspect many books stem from similar beginnings. I wanted a book that showed how analysis was done rather than one that simply summarized the results of research after the fact.

In 1991 I had a chance to organize a conference at Dalhousie University called "Crime, Social Problems and Moral Panics: How the Media Deals with Social Issues." At the time I had applied for a research grant to study the way newspapers report crime. The funding body, the Atlantic Institute

1

of Criminology, asked me if I was interested in organizing a conference on the topic and offered to sponsor it.

The resulting conference drew thirteen presenters from various backgrounds—university academics, lawyers, police, civil servants, journalists and broadcasters. Everybody was local, providing a chance to look at common issues from different points of view. There were two workshops in the morning, "The Media and the Legal System" and "Inquiries and Commissions," and a roundtable on "Social Issues" in the afternoon.

This book strongly retains the flavour of the conference in scope and organization. With the gracious permission of the speakers, I have selected some of the presentations from the sessions and edited and condensed them. Each selection provides a preamble for one chapter and briefly introduces some crime and the media issues in a clear and straightforward way from a professional point of view. For example, one speaker pointed out that the media is male-centred, that women are not in the news except when they are crime victims or beauty contest winners; another presenter pointed out the difficulty of dealing with the press on a regular basis when reporters are not trained to understand how the criminal justice system works.

Following each talk, some actual news articles that embody the point made by the speaker are provided in a section called "Reading the news." These examples may be reports on young offenders, Crime Stoppers articles or examples of sensationalism or inadequate reporting.

In the third part of each chapter, called "Analyzing the news," a more in-depth analysis of a larger pattern is developed. For example, in the chapter on the misrepresentation of AIDS in the media, newspaper stories are used to show how, in the early 1980s, AIDS was often linked to deviant groups . Such coverage reflected and still contributes to homophobia and the misrepresentation of AIDS as a disease. This section is meant to challenge the reader to develop a more analytical view of the news by looking at a specific topic, such as how the fear of crime is exaggerated by newspaper reporting, and a deeper theme, such as how the fear of crime causes the law to become tougher in response. The analyses come from my own research and are meant to be used in an everyday reading of the news. Understanding how crime is presented in the media allows us to have more control over our lives.

Thinking about the news

Crime, deviance, delinquency and other social problems have always been a staple of newspaper accounts, television news shows and crime dramas (Stephens 1988). Knowledge of these events is secondhand, filtered through the media graphically and textually, but it appears immediate, shocking, entertaining and informative (Hailey 1990). In this society the media has replaced firsthand experience as our source of information, opinion and news about the world (McKibben 1992). The pervasiveness and assumed facticity of the news is rarely questioned, and sometimes it's a jolt to realize that memories of events can be created, which is the joke in this Doonesbury cartoon (Trudeau 1994).

— Remember that perfect wave, Cornell? Back in '73?
— Do I? It was a defining wave! We came of age on that wave!
— It doesn't feel like 25 years have gone by since Woodstock, does it, Cornell?
— Sure don't, bro.
— We were such children, weren't we? Sitting out in that soggy cow pasture, half naked, fully stoned, groovin' on the vibes of an era . . . I'll never forget it, man!
— Zonker, what are you talking about? You were never at Woodstock.
— I wasn't?
— No. You only saw the movie, remember?
— Oh, my goodness—you're right! How embarrassing. . .
— Media can mess with your mind like that, Z.
— Whoa! Do you suppose I wasn't at the moon landing either?
— Well, I always thought you were a little fuzzy on detail, man . . .

The media can make it seem as if you are at the scene of a crime down the street or seeing events half a world away in the Persian Gulf. The media can make it seem possible to pass judgement on complicated issues arising in the O.J. Simpson trial, or make it seem as if the divorce of the Trumps is actually important (Kurtz 1994). The media can help create opinions on events never to be experienced firsthand on the basis of evidence presented by people one will never meet. Viewers and readers accept the secondhand nature of the news. Only when a source is misquoted or an issue receives inadequate coverage is the media questioned or criticized on how they do their job (Lee and Solomon 1990). But what exactly is that job, and is it usually done "well enough"? When crime news is criticized as biased, is a deeper motivation behind how the media reports it being missed?

The media does not merely report the news; first it has to construct and assemble it—the perceptions of crime "created" by the news media are organized (Ericson, Baranek and Chan 1987, 1989 and 1991). When reading or watching the news, you are getting reports about events in the world, built from the work of reporters in the field and influenced by the perspective of editors who are anticipating the reactions of consumers. Consumers are getting more than passively relayed social facts because the news actively creates impressions and opinions about the world. News of violent crime in the media trades upon and creates certain subtexts—law and order, discipline, danger, fear, authority. These underlying themes implicitly define the boundaries of society and have an effect on how people think and live their lives.

The power of the media is evident in how it affects a whole range of attitudes about public and personal safety (Leyton, O'Grady and Overton 1992). Crime on television can influence the way people think about violence, leading them to a "mean world view," to thinking the world is a dangerous and violent place (Surette 1990 and 1992). The media can also play a reactive role, trivializing violent crimes such as sexual assault so people become desensitized, misconstruing violence and blaming the victim (Benedict 1992), or the media can be proactive in dispelling those same myths (Fairstein 1993). The media can sensationalize crimes, exacerbated by interest groups who have something to gain by creating moral panic around issues such as child abuse and Satanism; thereby inflating, if not actually creating, public anxiety (Best 1990; Jenkins 1992). The media can influence perceptions about everything from break and enter to terrorism (Herman and O'Sullivan 1989; Herman and Chomsky 1988). Media images of deviance and criminality can fuel the fear of crime and result in a tough law and order approach and calls for tougher penalties against criminals and people already in prison (Hall et al. 1978).

The media has an incredible power to set agendas and reflect political points of view, a fact recognized and often exploited by politicians (Clow and Machum 1993; Sabato 1991). It has the power to rock the foundations of a community when it reports crimes that appear to threaten the very fabric of social life (Jessome 1994). It has the power to create a fear of crime that is not necessarily based in real experience (Benett 1988; Berger 1988). Postman and Powers (1992: 23) note:

> The early-twentieth-century journalist Lincoln Steffens proved that he could create a "crime wave" anytime he wanted by simply writing about all the crimes that normally occur in a large city during the course of a month. He could also end the crime wave by not writing about them. If crime waves can be "manufactured" by journalists, then how accurate are news shows in depicting the condition of a society?

Crime waves are social constructions, accounts created by journalists, fed by competition and coherence of opinion among newspapers and reliance on a restricted pool of experts for opinions (Fishman 1978; Davis 1973). Consumers are not often in a good position to judge the veracity of the news because they do not know the background of the stories reported,

4

their editorship or the priorities assigned in their production. The production of news is not open to view, even though the news is relied upon increasingly as a source of "facts" about the world. The world is experienced through the lens of the media, and our understanding of the world is mediated through the abstraction of the news which stands in for experientially based knowledge. As knowledge is produced through the news, opinions, attitudes, fears and desires are produced in its consumers.

Comprehending how knowledge is produced (and distorted) enables citizens to be more critical in an increasingly complicated, alienating and technologically dominated society, amid all the noise, babble and chaos of the "information age." Yet even confusion is important because people's perceptions are consequential in their lives. For example, if the media reports that most sexual assaults are committed by strangers jumping out from behind bushes in parks, then that stereotype is more likely to be believed, reported to the police and taken seriously by the public. If the media portrays drug crime as narcotics handled in washrooms, then people will not worry about medicines their doctor prescribes them. If a crime wave is constructed around kids who swarm or muggers in dark alleys with knives, then people will not worry about bid-rigging, insider trading or environmental pollution. A steady diet of sensationalistic crimes hides more mundane and harder-to-detect crimes. The depiction of crime in the news affects people's perception of safety and danger in society with subsequent consequences (Gebotys, Roberts and DasGupta 1988).

The news is an endless torrent of babble, chatter and gossip about ephemera, issues that capture one's attention momentarily but are gone tomorrow. The babble and chatter might contain lies, distortions or half-truths but they nonetheless constitute the "facts" society lives by. But while people are drawn together through consuming the same news, they are also fractured. The media brings us together in a "global village" yet alienates us from control in the world (McLuhan 1964; McLuhan and Fiore 1967; Fawcett 1986).

> Our news media, especially television, fill our days with information from everywhere, about everything, we have increasing difficulty in deciding what any of it means. We do not have time to reflect on any piece of news, and we are rarely helped, least of all by television itself, to know what weight or value to assign to any of it. We have become information junkies, addicted to news, demanding (even requiring) more and more of it but without any notion of what to do with it. This development is usually called "the communications revolution," sometimes "the information explosion." Marshall McLuhan, the first "media guru" of our age, claimed that the

5

electronic world in which we now live has created a "global village," in which everything has become everyone's business. McLuhan probably never lived in a village; if he had, he might have used a different metaphor for our present situation. In a village, information is apt to be a precious commodity. Villagers seek information that directly affects their lives, and they usually know what to do with it when they get it. Villagers may like gossip, as it adds a certain zest to life, but they usually can distinguish between what is gossip and what materially affects their lives. Our relation to information is quite different. For us, information is a commodity. It is bought and sold. Most of it has little to do with our lives. And most of the time, we don't know what to do with it. (Postman and Powers 1992: 153-54)

It is estimated that 95 million American viewers watched O.J. Simpson "flee" from police down the freeway on June 17, 1994, and subsequently a grand jury probing possible murder charges in the case had to be dissolved on the grounds that it had been tainted by pretrial publicity.[1] Watching that chase, it seemed there was little doubt he was guilty; after only two hours, viewers had heard about the suicide note, the wife abuse, the divorce, the stalking and jealousy, and the bloody glove—even though this was for most an event hundreds and thousands of miles away, of which they had no direct knowledge.

To watch such spectacles is to rely less on direct experience of the world and more on an extralocally produced textual and graphic version. Subsequent gossip about crime is based on information brought by others via these texts and pictures. And because they are technologically produced, we tend not to give them a second thought. As Smith says (1990: 214):

Discourse creates forms of social consciousness that are extra-local and externalized *vis-à-vis* the local subject. As Foucault has pointed out, the subject in the texts of discourse "is a particular, vacant place that may in fact be filled by different individuals." . . . Television advertisements that show the housewife, her gleaming floors, and the floor wax provide an ideological coordination of the social relations of consumers and producers. Whether or not a given housewife "identifies" with the housewife in the commercial, the textual housewife's floors become a visual standard for her own in terms of which she may be appraised and found wanting.

In watching, listening to or reading the media, a person becomes a news subject, receiving a constructed knowledge of the world bounded in a discourse which has a beginning, middle and end. This standard, uniform knowledge does not always have a context or history, and it is not always apparent who wrote the news or from what perspective they wrote it. However, these atemporal events without context and author structure one's understanding of the world. In some ways, authorless information has the most authority because it cannot easily be dismissed as idiosyncratic. News, as opposed to personal experience, is "objective" information because it does not have the taint of subjectivity. Even seeing bias in the news presumes knowing what unbiased news supposedly looks like, and ironically this tends to be news that is authorized, broadcast and copyrighted by the news organization which produced it.

The consequence of learning about crime from a media which constructs stories extralocally, textually and institutionally is that misunderstanding and fear of crime may be increased. The world portrayed in the media can be disembodied, sensationalistic and stereotypical. When a crime is portrayed as an isolated event, nothing is learned about its underlying causes and the context which surrounds it, the decisions which motivated it, the actions which resulted in its detection and the search for suspects, or the actions of the police; moreover, crime is not seen as mediated by the news and the justice system (Ericson 1991). When crimes are not seen realistically, people become increasingly afraid to walk in their own neighbourhoods, they paradoxically become more desensitized to crime and they think the criminal justice system treats offenders too leniently. As Giles Gherson began a guest editorial in the *Globe and Mail*:

> In the tabloid media age of TV programs such as *Hard Copy, A Current Affair* and a host of "true story" police-beat shows, the sensationalization of violent crime has become a mega-business. The trend toward hyping crime stories in pseudo-newscast and documentary formats is making the already blurred line between entertainment and reality even fainter. One result is an uneasy, insecure public readily convinced that there's a crime-storm brewing— that the social order is crumbling under relentless siege from knife-wielding or gun-toting punks, some as young as 10 or 11. There is no shortage of anecdotes about brutal, senseless murders in every Canadian city, and they're being cited to back the call for a ruthless crackdown on criminals.[2]

Even though there is evidence that crime is *not* on the increase, major western countries have all recently introduced measures to "get tough on crime." Where do these ideas come from? In the study of sociology and criminology, examining the media is a way to analyze how crime, deviance and social problems are constructed as social facts; and not only does the media distort and sensationalize certain crimes, it tends to underplay others. Although researchers and academics have turned to the media as an important site of analysis, this area is still relatively underdeveloped and much remains to be done.

Studying the news

Canadian and international newspaper articles are used to illustrate certain points in this book. In many cases these articles are taken from clippings files I have developed for teaching and research purposes. In some cases these are supplemented with news articles from various sources: the *Canadian News Index* (CNI), public archives and newspapers on CD-ROM. This last source can be used to search hundreds of articles at a time, and one can also download articles from international news agencies from the Internet.

The *Canadian News Index* lists stories since 1977 by subject from seven major Canadian dailies: the *Halifax Chronicle-Herald, Montreal Gazette, Toronto Star, Winnipeg Free Press, Edmonton Journal, Calgary Herald* and *Vancouver Sun*. The CNI provides enough information to get the article from microfilm or interlibrary loan. Since 1993 the CNI has been called the "*Canadian Index*" and newspaper citations have been amalgamated with those for magazines and other periodicals. The *Index* does not list all stories on crime that have been published because only items of major interest are selected and compiled.

Historical research can be done with primary documents found in libraries and archives. A provincial depository such as the Public Archives of Nova Scotia has local community and provincial newspapers on microfilm from the 1800s and can be used to research how the Oka incident in Quebec of 1990 or the 1991 Halifax "riot" were reported in Nova Scotia, or the debate on the Juvenile Delinquent's Act of 1908, Winnipeg General Strike or Riel Rebellion, or why in Nova Scotia during the 1930s labour organizers were jailed as communists under the federal War Measures Act.

Daily newspapers are a good source of information on events that were not always important enough to be included in history books or academic journals. In Halifax, two local newspapers are available: the *Chronicle-Herald* (with its evening edition, the *Mail-Star*)[3] and the *Daily News*; plus there is a national newspaper, the *Globe and Mail*, and various other national and international newspapers are available as well. University and public libraries receive the daily, national and international newspapers and sometimes create vertical clippings files on specific issues. Reading international newspapers can take less time if one is looking for specific topics and it is also a good way to search for topics seldom covered, such as police deviance and political corruption.

Researching the news is something anyone can do, it's inexpensive but requires some time and organization. Once samples are collected, one can begin to see patterns that wouldn't have been immediately apparent in the length, placement or discourse of the articles. For example, why are there so few stories about wife abuse in the news, yet so many stories about youth crime? Why do community papers have a court report section, but national papers do not? Why are corporate crimes reported in the *Globe and Mail* often found only in the business section? What crime stories make the front page?

The theoretical basis for the analysis in this book is that news constitutes a textual (mis)representation of crime, and that analyzing the media involves examining discursive themes and patterns found in news reports. For example, in articles on youth violence, what might be of interest is whether the problem is characterized as widespread, how new it is said to be and the degree of violence reported. This characterization of youth violence can then be compared with official statistics on youth crime to see if there is any consistency between what is reported in the news and the crime rate. Comparing the patterns found in the news with the official incidence of crime is a way of obtaining a standpoint on the news. The textual characterizations in the news can also be examined internally to reconstruct the claims made about youth crime, to see which point of view is represented and thus analyze why the public has become more concerned with youth crime as an issue even though it does not appear that it has actually increased.

Specific devices are used in each chapter, such as analysis of metaphors, tropes, elisions and misrepresentations. An example of a *metaphor* (from the Greek: to bear or carry) is the use of a descriptive term in a way which is not intended literally, as in "crazed serial killer," where it is not really known whether the killer has a mental illness or not. Such metaphors easily lead to sensationalism and contribute to social panics. A *trope* (from the Greek: a turn) is a figure of speech, or figurative language, as in speaking of prostitutes as "ladies of the night," which is metaphorical and ironic, another sense of the word. Tropes can contribute to misperceptions and distortions of crime. An *elision* (from the Latin: to leave out) is an absence, a failing to include something essential in the account, as in omitting that most sexual assault is violent exploitation within a relationship or between acquaintances rather than a crime between strangers. An elision can contribute to ideological misunderstandings about crime that can actually increase their likelihood. There are clearly some overlaps in these textual devices, but they provide a connecting thread that links the topics of the chapters with a deeper underlying theme of social (mis)construction. Various ordinary misrepresentations, stereotypes and distortions are identified as well. To see how these textual devices work will require an especially close reading in some cases.

The analysis in this book draws from various sociological and criminological perspectives but is based generally on a social constructionist approach: the idea that our news about the world does not necessarily reflect reality and that crime topics are as much constructed as reported. This approach comprises a variety of research and is best known for its ability to deflate "social panics" (Best and Horiuchi 1985; Lippert 1990; Pfohl 1977). For example, crime news is often sensationalized and largely reflects the perspectives of the police and the criminal justice system. Crime waves can occur like fads, reflecting the fear of the day.

This analysis is not based on how people are affected by what they read in the news. Although that is important, this book is primarily concerned with an analysis of how reading is ideological, how the news takes possible interpretations of events in the world and constructs a dominant point of view. Crime news is ideological; through the media we acquire systematic misperceptions about the world, for example, that youth gangs are rampant. But news is not simply exaggerated or unreal, it has real consequences. Thus the pertinent question is not simply "how well" the news represents a crime but "how" the crime is represented. News is part of the ideological relations in our society. It supports the status quo and represents the point of view of the powerful. The distortion in the news might convince readers that the world is a violent place but this is not an analysis of how people read, it is an analysis of how the news could "possibly" be read to (re)create social order.

Various sources of official information are used throughout this book: crime statistics collected by police departments across the country and published by Statistics Canada; special statistical reports published by the Canadian Centre for Justice Statistics and analyses of victimization data obtained through the General Social Survey.[4] These and other secondary sources of information are used in part to compare what is officially known about crime with how crime is presented in the news, but there is no assumption that these official sources of information are perfect or that news accounts should necessarily match them.

Overview of the book

The research this book represents is organized by topics: sexual assault, prostitution, domestic violence, the Mount Cashel orphanage scandal, AIDS, crime fear, Crime Stoppers, serial homicide and the Westray tragedy. Each chapter also has an underlying theme, such as sensationalism, invisibility, orthodoxy or community.

The first part of the book discusses issues of gender and crime. In

Chapter 1, Sharon Fraser, a journalist and broadcaster, introduces the idea that the media is male-centred and issues which affect women are not presented from a woman's point of view. Focusing on a string of sexual assault reports from the summer of 1993 in Halifax, the analysis looks at how the police dominate as the authority on crime, providing readers with an "orthodox" version of events that can actually misinform women, and men, about sexual assault.

In Chapter 2, Anne Derrick, a noted criminal attorney, focuses on women who work as prostitutes and how they are very narrowly stereotyped as "hookers" in the media. This label becomes their main identity and much less attention is paid to the organization of the sex trade or their poverty and abuse. Examples of how the media labels such women are reproduced, and the characterization of prostitutes is shown to be part of the crime itself— by focusing too little on the role of men as johns or pimps, the media and the criminal justice system end up revictimizing these women.

In Chapter 3, Debi Forsyth-Smith, a civil servant and politician, introduces the topic of violence against women in relationships. In analyzing news accounts of violence against women, certain features are important, such as article size, whether the violence is portrayed as unusual or normal and whether the article points to the larger context within which individual incidents of violence have taken place. The ability of the news media to provide information on this topic is analyzed and compared to statistics on femicide in Canada.

The second part of the text, called "Distortion in the Media," deals with specific ways crime is misrepresented in the news. In Chapter 4, Gary Kinsman, a university professor and activist, looks at the Hughes Commission of Inquiry into child abuse at Mount Cashel in St. John's, Newfoundland. He describes how the media "inscribes" deviant categories, for example, how the Hughes Commission recreated the link between homosexuality and child sexual abuse, and how the media took up this idea, exaggerating and strengthening it in the process. Using examples of media coverage, inscription is seen to occur in larger patterns of child sexual abuse reporting.

In Chapter 5, Eric Smith, a former teacher and AIDS activist, talks about how AIDS is (mis)represented in the news media. Having AIDS is not a crime; however, it is distorted in the media and associated with drug users, prostitutes and other "deviant" groups. Similar to the process of inscription, "signification" is important in how AIDS comes to be depicted in the popular press. Authorities have called for quarantining people "infected" with the disease and people have been charged with criminal offences for infecting other people. Articles that exhibit this alarmist characterization of AIDS have an obvious tendency to scapegoat the problem, blame it on marginalized social groups and associate it only with them. The consequence of this misrepresentation is that many people still do not feel themselves to be at risk.

In Chapter 6, Joy Mannette, an academic, takes up the issue of ethnocentrism in the news, showing how "race relations" issues are portrayed in ways that reinforce ethnic bias. She briefly recounts three cases of lack of ethnic sensitivity in the news. The theme of extralocality, or distance from events, is discussed, using the example of the 1991 Halifax "race riot" where blacks "rampaged" through the streets committing "random violence," finally leading to a confrontation with the police. This analysis illustrates how the interpretation of crime in the news comes to stand in for direct experience.

The third part of the book looks at the relationship between the news media and the criminal justice system. In Chapter 7, a Halifax constable and former police media relations officer, Paul MacDonald, discusses how the media often fails to do a good job in reporting on crime and the workings of the criminal justice system and how this can lead to problems in policing. In this chapter the issue of exaggeration is developed by looking at fear of crime and how it is exacerbated by bad crime reporting and has led to a backlash against crime.

In Chapter 8, Tony Thomson, another university professor, looks at the relationship between the media and the police historically, discussing and criticizing how public relations has come to be an important part of policing. Using the example of Crime Stoppers, the analysis looks at how soliciting the help of the public through the media extends the influence of the police further into the community than would have been possible otherwise and is itself an exercise in public relations.

In Chapter 9, Darrel Pink, a lawyer, discusses sensationalism in the news and how difficult it is to work with reporters when they often do not have an adequate understanding of the criminal justice system and how it works. Pink's discussion is informed by his role as executive director of the Nova Scotia Barrister's Society where one of his responsibilities is preparing news releases for the media. The concept of sensationalism is developed through the example of the Homolka—Teale case in Ontario. Specific laws in Canada prohibit the media from reporting certain information so, while reporting on the Homolka case was banned in Canada, tabloid speculation in the United States and Britain was rampant.

In Chapter 10, Deborah Woolway, a radio producer, discusses "pack journalism" in the context of the inquiry into why Donald Marshall, a Nova Scotia Mi'kmaq, spent eleven years in prison for a murder he didn't commit. This theme is then taken up in a look at the media coverage of the Westray mine disaster and the subsequent criminal and legal issues that surrounded its inquiry. Pack jounalism is shown to contribute to uniformity in news reporting and to cater to a sense of personal tragedy instead of illuminating the underlying causes of such a disaster.

In the conclusion, some of the key issues presented in the book are brought together along with recommendations for change. There can be no magic solutions, but this text is designed to promote literacy in how the media (mis)constructs and (mis)represents the world. This is a text that can be read along with the news. It is not a textbook simply reporting facts and it is also not a how-to manual that breaks down the study of the news into easy-to-assimilate exercises. The book is neither overly theoretical nor abstract, and examples are used throughout to ground the concepts used in the analysis. In each chapter the specific techniques used to analyze the news are explained and shown and are not simply presented as a set of conclusions. The topics and themes explored in the various chapters all fit together and references are supplied for further reading. The important task is to learn all over again how to read the news for ourselves, not just to echo the conclusions other people have come to. If we stand on hills, we can see farther.

Notes

1. "Live from L.A.," *Globe and Mail* editorial, June 23, 1994: A20; "Judge dissolves Simpson grand jury. Case to go to preliminary hearing after inquiry tainted by pretrial publicity," *Globe and Mail*, June 25, 1994: A8.
2. "Rock's recipe for crime prevention: Give people a sense they have a future," *Globe and Mail*, June 8, 1994: A24, guest editorial by Giles Gherson.
3. I refer to these two papers as the *Halifax Herald* elsewhere in this book, especially in my notes, although no publication by that name exists as such. Both papers are owned by Halifax Herald Ltd.
4. See, for example, *Crime in Canada*, a Statistics Canada catalogue, various years; Roberts (1994); and Gartner and Doob (1994).

GENDER AND THE MEDIA

"British judge under attack for comments on date rape."
(*Toronto Star*, August 12, 1993: A15)

"Campbell to review remarks by judge in sex assault case."
(*Halifax Herald*, April 26, 1991: A8)

"Going home with man invites rape, judge says."
(*Montreal Gazette*, March 16, 1983: A1)

"B.C. judge's comments termed 'not acceptable.'"
(*Halifax Herald*, November 27, 1991: A8)

"Judge's alleged remarks on threats spur investigation."
(*Halifax Herald*, December 9, 1993: A29)

"Domestic violence costs taxpayers millions."
(*Halifax Herald*, April 11, 1991: A1)

"Former judge censured for slap."
(*Halifax Herald*, April 16, 1990: A1)

"Judge says woman responsible for her stormy marital situation."
(*Globe and Mail*, February 28, 1989: A1)

"Burmese child prostitution."
(*Daily News*, July 30, 1991: 9)

"Few Canadians think prostitution a problem—poll."
(*Halifax Herald*, March 9, 1992: C14)

"Working women are root of evil—university prof."
(*Halifax Herald*, April 4, 1992: A12)

"Body of woman may be missing Oakville nanny."
(*Toronto Star*, September 1, 1993: A4)

1

A String of Stranger Sexual Assaults:
The Construction of an
Orthodox Account of Rape

Distortion can mean many things: an issue may be exaggerated, downplayed or slanted. Essentially, the truth is not being accurately portrayed. Although it is difficult to know the full truth about the extent of sexual assault in our society, some distortions are obvious.

This chapter begins with a brief talk by Sharon Fraser, a journalist and broadcaster, who points out how issues are usually presented from a male-centred point of view in the media. Women's issues are often absent or distorted. The media likes to believe in its own myth that the news is objective and doesn't reflect any one point of view, but Fraser believes the news implicitly reflects a male perspective.

The next section underscores the issues Fraser raises, using the example of how sexual assault is reported in the newspapers. Various news accounts will reveal how the media communicates explicit and implicit messages about sexual assault; the selection focuses on a series of reports from the summer of 1993 in Halifax that were intended to warn women of the danger of sexual assault by strangers. It is appropriate to focus on these particular articles, because perhaps of all crimes, sexual assault affects women most pervasively.

In the third part of the chapter, distortion in crime news is examined more thoroughly. The idea that the news gives readers an orthodox or standard version of sexual assault is linked with the misinformation the public receives about it. While maintaining relative silence about sexual assault in general, the media makes it appear that the real danger is from strangers in public places, thereby constructing a rape myth. By making the police the authority on crime, underrepresenting women's experience and reproducing rape myths, the media can actually work against women.

The talk—Sharon Fraser

I was going to say stop me if you've heard this before, but I don't think I'll ask you to do that because I was accused rather harshly a few weeks ago in *Frank* magazine of being repetitive and I said well of course I'm repetitive. You know these issues won't go away, so someone has to keep harping on them and I guess it's me. And besides I guess it's women's role to nag, nag, nag, so listen again. I'm going to talk just in general about women's coverage in the media, being a woman, working in the media and also how the stories are covered.

I once asked a radio producer friend to put me on his radio show once a week and I'd do a five minute newscast on how that week's news would be interpreted by a feminist woman. He was aghast that I would even ask that. "He couldn't do that," he said. "If we had you on we'd have to have all the other groups on too." "But who in the world are these other groups," I said, "the Kinsmen, the Rotary Club?" I was talking about half of all humanity. I don't think of women as a group. I also don't think of all the people outside the straight, white, male, able-bodied power structure as being special interest groups. Indeed, the people who use the expression "special interest" tend to be the ones who have a very special interest indeed. And it's very well massaged by our mainstream media.

Not very long ago, I was interviewed on this subject by an interviewer who took exception to my views. He said, "How can you say this, I feel that we're constantly doing women's stories, native issues stories, stories about the disabled." "But," I asked, "who is defining the issues?" I used the example of a newspaper called *Atlantic Fisherman*, where I used to be the editor. I made a conscious decision when I was there that I was going to cover the fishing industry from the point of view of the people who catch the fish and the people who work in the plants. I went to them and asked them what was important, what were their concerns, define the issues, please. Then I would go back to my office and phone the cabinet ministers, the bureaucrats and the company presidents. They weren't used to this and they didn't like it—(they don't have all those PR people working in their offices for nothing) just as my interviewer didn't like my suggestion that a group of white males were sitting around in a newsroom tossing ideas back and forth defining issues, then going out and asking a list of already formulated questions.

Years ago when I was still a student, I didn't really like the study of history and I wasn't very good at it. I used to tell the teacher I was frustrated because I wanted to know about the people. I wanted to know how they lived, what their houses were like, what toys the children played with, what food did they eat, who cooked it, where did they get it, what did they wear. I would have been fascinated if I could have found this information, but I could never work up much enthusiasm for strings of dates that chronicled all manner of manly pursuits. It was many years later when I realized what I was missing was the history of women and children. And now when I read or listen to those outlets that are responsible for recording our day to day history, I see the same thing happening all over again. In general, what makes the news and how it's reported has very little to do with the reality of most women's lives.

I will tell you briefly about one of the story meetings I lived through when I was working as a writer-broadcaster in the current affairs department of CBC Radio. The three people in the meeting who spoke before me brought up story ideas about a new potash mine, about rising mortgage rates and about changes in the downtown traffic patterns. They were all feeling pretty good about themselves and all had big male plans to talk to the minister of natural resources, the president of a financial institution and the mayor. When it was my turn, I reported that the tellers in my bank had all been told when they came in that morning that they were being cut from full time to half time. Their wages were being halved accordingly, and they were losing all their benefits. They were given no notice; they were not even afforded the courtesy of an explanation; they were simply told. Before I was even part way through this short presentation, I was aware of six eyes glazing over with indifference and I could sense the barely stifled yawns. When I finished the producers said, "So, what's the story?" I thought I had given enough for a story proposal, but I went a little further and said I think it happened this way because the tellers are women and whoever is responsible for such decisions would simply assume the women were working for supplementary family income, and that's when the yawns became audible. "Oh no, not that women's stuff again." (I've started to spell "women'sstuff" as one word because I hear it so much.) Somebody else said, "We've already done women's stuff this week." Finally the producer said, "If you can prove it, if you can get the manager of that bank to tell you by three o'clock this afternoon that the tellers' hours were cut because they're women, you've got a story, otherwise forget it."

During the recent war, I began to use the expression "peacestuff" the very same way because I did ask a reporter why he wasn't covering the women's vigil down at the library every day. I said, "You know those women are handing out really excellent releases that have all kinds of information on them that's not going into the mainstream media," and he said, "Well, we can't put in peacestuff everyday." And I said, "Why not, you do warstuff every day."

Around the same time as my CBC story meeting, I was a judge in a competition to choose the best community newspaper in Atlantic Canada. Many of those newspapers are doing some good journalism on certain subjects, but that year I came away from them with the certain impression that the women who made it into their pages were winners of beauty contests, victims of rape or domestic violence, or graduating from a heavy equipment course, as if the emulation of men and the learning of men's work is in itself newsworthy.

The reason for all this is that we still live in a society where what is seen to be important and significant is determined according to a male agenda. Our institutions, the educational system, the governments and certainly the media have never acknowledged the realities of women's lives and therefore have covered women's issues as afterthoughts and fillers at best, with tongue in cheek and journalistic contempt at worst. Just as women and children are the first to fall through the safety net of our inequitable economic system, so too are stories that deal with women's issues the first to be cut when editors and producers lack space and time.

The chic notion that there are no women's issues, but only people's issues, is one that keeps being raised along with the mainstream media's continued use of the words "post-feminism," the implication, in fact the malicious intent, being that with the cooperation of all the sensitive and helpful men we know, everything's been taken care of. We've now reached an equitable society and now could things get back to normal? But there are women's issues; they're women's because they've been there forever and men haven't done anything about them. If women don't keep them in the forefront, those issues will become invisible again. Some of those issues are child care, reproductive rights, pay equity, women's health, sexual harassment, sexual assault, domestic violence and incest, pornography, stereotyping in the media, all those issues that are responsible for so many glazed eyes and stifled yawns in so many newsrooms.

There are people's issues but even they are not covered in a way that's meaningful to a majority of women. The coverage is geared toward straight, white, middle-to-upper class, able-bodied males, men with jobs, mortgages, car payments, stocks and bonds, credit cards, insurance policies, all those trappings which our media assumes to be common to everyone.

Women who are in the news business, women who work in the media, are something like women who play roles in male politics. I would like to see as many women as possible get into both, but the truth is, unless the male agenda is changed in some very fundamental ways, and unless the women in question have a strong sense of women's politics, it often doesn't matter too much whether the person filling the seat is a man or a woman. Women too have been socialized to believe our concerns are not very important and we shouldn't whine so much about wife battering and rape when there are more important things to cover, like wars and strikes and uprisings.

I've had this conversation many times about covering stories from a different perspective and with a rewritten agenda. Every time I've been greeted with a shocked response that news is news, and you can't cover it with a point of view. The last time it happened it was with a radio producer. I said to him, "Well, whose point of view do you cover the news from now?" He said, "No one's, the news is objective."

The final point is that wanting media coverage of issues is not simply egotism. In this day and age the media is a conduit to government, it influences public opinion. People outside the power structure require, in fact demand, that their voices also be heard."

Reading the news

Sharon Fraser's talk raises important criticisms, in particular that the media reports issues from a male-centred point of view and the news reflects male interests and a male perspective on the world. This bias places women into very particular roles, such as victim, and ignores the issues important to all people (Craft 1988; Mills 1990; Faith 1987; Adelberg and Currie 1987). In the reporting of sexual assault, the result can be distortion. Not representing sexual assault from the perspective of women can recreate a false understanding of sexual assault as a crime (Fairstein 1993; Soothill and Walby 1991; Voumvakis and Ericson 1984).

Sexual assault provides a good example because it is predominantly a gendered crime: most sexual assaults are committed against women by men. A survey published in 1993 found that one-half of all Canadian women have experienced at least one incident of violence since the age of 16, and one-quarter of all women have experienced violence at the hands of a current or past marital partner (Statistics Canada 1993). A 1994 study estimated that although an alarming 39 percent of all Canadian women have experienced at least one incident of sexual assault since the age of 16, only six percent of these incidents have been reported to the police (Roberts 1994). Given that sexual violence is so widespread, does the media cover the crime in a way that reflects one gender's perspective more than another?

The typical sexual assault news article is small and descriptive and excludes the female victim's perspective of events. In Article 1.1, "Cadet officer abused cadets," the assault was committed by a male in a position of authority against female victims. The article is 1.5 inches long, contains only reported facts and was located in a section called News Briefs, which provides a brief synopsis of various local items, not all of which are criminal in nature. The News Briefs format leaves little room for detail or to create a context that would help the readers to understand why the assault occurred.

Article 1.1
Cadet officer abused cadets
(*Daily News*, January 27, 1994: 11, News Brief)

1   St. John's (CP) —A former air cadet officer was found guilty yesterday of sexually
2   assaulting two female cadets. Gerald Joseph Wadden, 23, will be back in court for a
3   sentencing hearing today for the crimes, which took place between March 1990 and
4   October 1991. Wadden shook and sobbed uncontrollably after he was found guilty of
5   four sex-related charges. During the trial, one cadet said Wadden kissed her and
6   fondled her breasts after band practices. The second said Wadden made her masturbate
7   him.

The account summarizes a trial where the defendant was found guilty
of sexual assault. Aside from the conviction (line 1), we are not provided
with any information from the court proceedings of the case. We are told the
perpetrator is scheduled to appear at a later date for sentencing (lines 2–3),
but we aren't told what the grounds for the sentence will be. The portrayal
of the legal proceedings leaves it unclear whether the article is quoting or
paraphrasing the victim's testimony.

We are told the defendant "kissed" and "fondled" one victim, and made
another "masturbate" him (lines 5–7). These words make the acts seem
sexual rather than violent. A kiss implies consent and mutual attraction, and
fondling implies sensuality, not violence or coercion. This article reproduces
a common rape myth, that rape is sex. Such a myth might justify and excuse
rape from a certain male point of view, but certainly not from a woman's
(Kelly 1988).

This kind of article is typical sexual assault reporting: a brief account
of a court sentence or a police investigation. Because these articles are short
and few compared to actual rates of sexual assault, the impression conveyed
is that sexual assault is infrequent and isolated, leading readers to misunderstand
the extent and severity of the crime. Readers also end up being poorly
informed about investigative and court processes.

Although most sexual assault articles are brief accounts (of a widespread
crime), during one period in July and August of 1993, the Halifax news
media reported what they called a "string" of sexual assaults committed by
strangers. Fifty-eight news articles were published over six weeks, an
increase of coverage made all the more prominent by their link to a series
of assaults. The articles were lengthy and unusually located, near the front
of the newspapers. Thirty-five were accounts of the crimes, and twenty-
three were secondary articles, such as columns or opinion pieces.

The news clipping referring to the cadet officer illustrates the typical
brevity of many news accounts of sexual assault, but examining the reporting
trends during the "string" of sexual assaults brings out other issues. In the

"string," the media did not focus on lurid details with the traditional voyeurism of sexual assault reporting. The increased reporting of these assaults was problematic because all were committed by strangers, therefore reinforcing a second rape myth, that sexual assault is predominantly committed by strangers. In fact, sexual assault is usually committed by acquaintances; only 10–30 percent of sexual assaults are committed by strangers (DeKeseredy and Hinch 1991).

The topicalization of the "string" of stranger-related sexual assaults was constructed by bracketing out assaults committed by acquaintances. Assaults committed during the same period against women by men they knew in friendships, relationships and families were not seen as part of the pattern. Sexual assault is generally given low priority in the news and acquaintance-related assaults continue to receive very little attention in the local newspapers. Against the backdrop of relative silence concerning sexual assault, the spotlight had been turned up full.

The first of what would become the "string" articles were innocuous and occupied little space in the newspapers. If these assaults had not become part of a "string" (which can only be constructed in hindsight), it is doubtful they would have received much attention at all. Article 1.2, "Woman attacked in own apartment," was the first in the series of attack reports in the newspapers.

Article 1.2
Woman attacked in own apartment
(*Daily News*, July 5, 1993: 4, News Brief)

1 A woman was taken by ambulance to hospital after she was sexually and physically
2 assaulted in her St. Margaret's Bay Road apartment last night.
3   A man knocked on the woman's door at about 7 p.m., then forced his way in when
4 she answered, said Halifax police Sgt. Ron O'Neil.
5   "She thought it might be someone she knew," he said.
6   The 35-year-old woman, whose name has not been released, was taken to hospital
7 with injuries that were not life-threatening. O'Neil said police did not think a
8 weapon was used in the attack, which left the woman badly bruised.
9   She was traumatized and unable to give police many details after the attack, he said.
10   An RCMP dog master was called in to help search for her attacker, who ran away.
11 Police were still looking for the man late last night. The woman was still in hospital.

This article is relatively short and appeared in the News Briefs. Perhaps because of its brevity, it is also concise, stating at the beginning that a woman was sexually and physically assaulted (lines 1–2). The "factual" character of the account is maintained throughout: we are told the circumstances of the attack (lines 3–4), the condition of the victim (lines 8–9 and 11) and the efforts of the police (line 10). Even with such scant detail, or perhaps because of it, the account reconstructs a stereotypical idea of what sexual assault looks like: a woman was attacked by a male stranger who then escaped, and the police became involved. This is a false stereotype because most women victims are sexually assaulted by men they know (Boyle 1991). The account is organized from an official point of view; the only person who comments on the incident is a police officer, which promotes the seeming objectivity of the report.

The version of events found in the media during this period was homogeneous: these assaults against women were perpetrated by strangers, they were unrelated (but related as a "string") and the police were urging all women to be cautious. Similar messages can be found in other sexual assault news articles as evidenced in Article 1.3, "Women warned of attacker."

Article 1.3
Women warned of attacker
(*Ottawa Citizen*, January 18, 1992: A18. Police)

1   **Donald Street**. Gloucester police are warning women who live in two apartment
2   buildings on Donald Street to exercise caution after a second teenage girl in as many
3   days was assaulted by the same man.
4   The most recent assault occurred Thursday about 4 p.m., said Sgt. Andy Zmijewski.
5   A 15-year-old girl was grabbed by the arm as she stepped off the elevator on an upper
6   floor of 1240 Donald St. She screamed as her attacker tried to drag her into a nearby
7   doorway. Her screaming eventually drove him off. The girl was not hurt.
8   In the first attack Wednesday, another 15-year-old girl was walking into a
9   neighbouring highrise at 1244 Donald St. about 4 p.m. when she was grabbed by a young
10 male and dragged into the underground parking garage.
11   The girl screamed and fought with her attacker as he tore at her clothes. He finally
12 abandoned the assault and fled the parking garage.
13   Zmijewski said women who live in the buildings should take precautions such as
14 avoiding walking alone in poorly lit areas.
15   Police are looking for a 17 to 20-year-old male who is five-feet-three to five-feet-
16 five-inches tall with brown eyes and greasy brown hair. In the attack Wednesday, he
17 was wearing a green jacket and blue pants and had a knapsack on his back.

The account follows a recipe used in similar reports. It describes the crime concisely, characterizes the victims and the offender, reflects a police viewpoint and urges women to be cautious of strangers, poorly lit areas and so on. The reporting creates a "typical" sexual assault article, in which women are attacked in public places by men they do not know, and women are warned to take steps to prevent the violence, putting the responsibility for safety on them rather than on men.

Two days after the initial incident cited in Article 1.2, ("Woman attacked in own apartment" another report of the same event, reproduced in Article 1.4, went into far more detail.

Article 1.4
Child asleep in home during woman's rape, say sources
(*Halifax-Herald*, July 7, 1993: A1)

1   The woman who was brutally raped and beaten in her home Sunday night had a young
2   child asleep in an adjacent room during the ordeal, sources said Tuesday.
3   The toddler apparently slept through it and did not witness the attack, the sources
4   said.
5   Meanwhile, Halifax police confirmed a report Tuesday the woman was choked into
6   unconsciousness. The 35-year-old St. Margaret's Bay Road resident was barely
7   conscious when police arrived on the scene.
8   Police spokesman Const. Paul MacDonald would not say how she was choked.
9   The woman's face was also bruised and cut after being punched by her attacker. The
10   man forced his way into her apartment when she partially opened her door to answer
11   his knock at the door.
12   After losing consciousness, the woman awoke and phoned her boyfriend, who alerted
13   police.
14   It's likely the attacker approached the house earlier, while "casing the area for a
15   victim who was alone and could be attacked" Const. MacDonald said. "It definitely
16   appears premeditated."
17   Neighbors reported seeing a man in the community Saturday and earlier Sunday
18   knocking on doors and asking for a person. Police believe it was a ruse to choose a
19   victim, because robbery was not a motive.
20   Police interviewed a suspect for several hours Monday night, but released him
21   without laying charges. Police will only identify him as a metro man.
22   They released a more detailed description Tuesday of the man they are seeking,
23   including an unusual characteristic that he talks out of the corner of his mouth.
24   He stands five feet 10 inches to six feet tall, weighs between 180 and 200 pounds
25   and has blue eyes and wavy, dark brown collar-length hair. His mustache is lighter in
26   color than his hair and he was sporting a few day's growth of beard.
27   The man was wearing a jean jacket, a blue T-shirt with a blue shirt over it, jeans and
28   white, high-top sneakers.
29   Meanwhile, the executive director of the Service for Sexual Assault Victims echoed
30   police warnings for women to be careful in their homes. Ann Keith said Sunday's attack
31   was "particularly unnerving" because most sex assault victims know their attackers.
32   "We don't want to make people prisoners in their own homes, but until this guy is
33   caught they should be cautious." said Ms. Keith. "I can appreciate the reaction of
34   the residents. It's very frightening."
35   Anyone with information on the attack is asked to call Halifax police at 421-6869 or
36   Crime Stoppers at 422-8477.

This second article contains the typical elements of sex crime reporting: a crime occurred, a woman was the victim of an unknown male attacker, the police are involved and there is a warning for women to be careful. This article is longer, 451 words compared to the initial article's 159 words, and is detailed in a way to sensationalize and convey the horror of the event. This report also emphasizes the idea that people "should be cautious"; however, in general it is not "people" who are at risk of sexual assault, but specifically women. This failure to specify the gendered nature of sexual assault mystifies the crime.

Various textual elements construct the story. The crime is named in line 1: a woman "was brutally raped and beaten," and a more detailed description is provided (lines 5–6 and 9–12) than in the previous article: "the woman was choked into unconsciousness . . . the woman's face was also bruised and cut after being punched by her attacker . . . the man forced his way into her apartment . . . [and] after losing consciousness, the woman awoke and phoned her boyfriend." The assailant is described in lines 14–28: "the attacker approached the house earlier . . . police will only identify him as a metro man . . . he stands five feet 10 inches . . . the man was wearing a jean jacket." And at the end of the article (lines 29–34) women are cautioned: "police warnings for women to be careful in their homes . . . they should be cautious . . . it's very frightening." The image of women readers get in this type of report is: that they are victims of sexual assault, that their attackers are strangers, that they are not safe in their own homes, that they have to be careful to avoid being victimized and that the police are the experts on how women experience such crimes. The length of this longer article conveys a more serious tone but does not necessarily examine the issue in a better way than the briefer report.

What is not seen in such accounts is any analysis of men as perpetrators of sexual assault, of sexual assault as a crime in general, of why women are blamed for not keeping themselves safe, or criticism of how the criminal justice system deals with this kind of crime. However, during this series of sexual assaults, public forums on safety were organized, and the police were criticized for not doing enough to prevent these crimes from happening and for not adequately responding to community concerns.

Analyzing the news

The question posed at the beginning of this chapter was whether media issues are presented from a biased point of view. It can be seen from the examples examined above that in sexual assault cases women appear as silent victims, that there is a tendency to reproduce rape myths and that the police are made the authoritative voice on crime.

One method for the analysis of crime news is the "social panics" model which incorporates the idea that crime is exaggerated in the news and can create an unreasonable and distorted fear among the public (Cohen 1972). An analysis of social panics is important when looking at how news accounts are constructed and how certain stereotypes can be reinforced by reporting. For example, a social panic could be based on exaggerating the level of stranger-related crime in relation to sexual assaults committed by acquaintances. Given the amount of media coverage and the associated public concern, it could be argued that the "string" of sexual assaults reported in Halifax during the summer of 1993 created a social panic.

However, some problems with using a social panic model are the tendencies to focus on exaggeration and distortion while forgetting that a crime has been committed, and to neglect to analyze the consequences of distorted news. In focusing on news as true or false, we can lose sight of the reason distortion exists. Ideology serves a very real purpose in the world: distortion distracts us from the truth. The crime and its possibility fades into the background as we focus our interest on the transparency of the accounts themselves. The temptation is to say, "Well, it just shows that you can't trust everything you read," when the important thing is that the public trusts such accounts in general. Distortion of sexual assault draws attention away from the very real nature of the crime and from the responsibility of the media to report stories in an unbiased way.

Biased accounts of sexual assault are ideological—part of the problem and part of the crime. The distorted cultural messages our society receives about sexual assault are part of the reason the crime can occur; people buy into myths such as the victim was responsible, it only happens to bad women and only strangers commit the crime (Warshaw 1988). The various rape myths that circulate in our society—rape is sex, the offender is perverted, women provoke or somehow deserve rape, women fabricate rape stories or cry rape for revenge—are perpetuated in news accounts of the crime (Benedict 1992). These myths exist for a reason: to displace men's responsibility onto women. The discourse about sexual assault is anchored in cultural myths and consists of "rhetorical tropes" that carry meaning and come to mediate practical social relations (Valverde 1991). Our attention is drawn away from the experiences of women as victims of sexual assault. Saying that women are not cautious enough, were walking in the wrong place or put their trust in the wrong man shifts the blame onto the victim as if they are somehow responsible for the attack they suffered at the hands of another. This journalistic pattern of "victim-blaming" is part of the "normal" cultural construction of sexual assault where the woman is made responsible for the violent and "uncontrollable" sexuality of men. To find this idea reproduced in the news is not surprising, nor is it acceptable, but it is common.

The various misrepresentations evident in crime reporting, such as sensationalism, exaggeration of law and order issues and over- emphasis of atypical assaults can distort crime or even make it invisible. Against the background of a relative silence about sex crimes, any coverage would seem extraordinary, especially if it is flagged as unusual. Sexual assaults seldom appear in the news in numbers that reflect their true incidence, and those that do appear are often not reflective of reality, as in the case of sexual crimes committed by acquaintances. Tropes and dominant themes become part of the crime. If the typical sexual assault article dramatizes stranger-related assault, then jurors, lawyers, judges and the police formulate sexual assault in a similar way (Soothill and Soothill 1993). This, in turn, is a recursive relationship: court decisions can affect public perception of sexual assault as well, as in the case where a judge credited a man for having "spared" his daughter's virginity despite having molested her for more than two years.[1]

To appreciate the "silence" on sexual assault in the news, it is necessary to establish just how widespread sexual assault really is. In 1992, 34,352 cases of sexual assault were reported to the police in Canada (Roberts 1994). Even though this sounds like a lot, it is estimated that the vast majority of actual incidents are not reported to the police—the author cited estimates a report rate of only six percent! The police then screen out reports they believe are unfounded (where they believe the sexual assaults have not been committed), which in 1992 was 14 percent. How sexual assault is perceived, of course, determines the number of unfounded cases. After screening out the unfounded cases, the official incidence was 29,543 sexual assaults. However, if only six percent of total cases were reported to the police, the real number of sexual assaults in Canadian society in 1992 was more realistically about 500,000. Also in 1992, only 59 percent of sexual assaults the police deemed founded were cleared by charge (that is, resulted in a charge, or the file was otherwise closed). In another study, 34 percent of the original cases reported to the police went to court, with 12 percent of perpetrators eventually pleading guilty or found guilty (Gunn and Linden 1993). This erosion in the numbers is a process of attrition. Few of these cases would ever make it to the news.

These numbers, as we most accurately know them, form the objective baseline from which to measure how well the media reports sexual assault. When we go to the *Canadian News Index* and see how many sexual assault stories are reported in major newspapers every year, we do not find numbers to reflect either the official incidence or the estimated one. Thus more attrition occurs before sexual assault is reported by the media.

Figure 1.1 compares the difference between the incidence of sexual assault reported by Statistics Canada and those recorded in the *Canadian News Index* between 1986 and 1990, demonstrating the relative invisibility of sexual assault in the news. In 1990, for example, about 28,000 sexual assaults were officially reported in Canada, but the seven major dailies polled by the *Index* carried only slightly more than two hundred stories— only one news story for about every 140 reported cases, or less than one percent of the total reported sexual assault cases. If we consider sexual assaults thay may be estimated to have occurred but were not been reported, there was only one news article per 2,333 assaults, which means that only about 0.04 percent of assaults were reported in newspaper articles. This underreporting makes sexual assault seem far less common than it really is.

Figure 1.1
Sexual assault incidence and news coverage in Canada, 1986–90

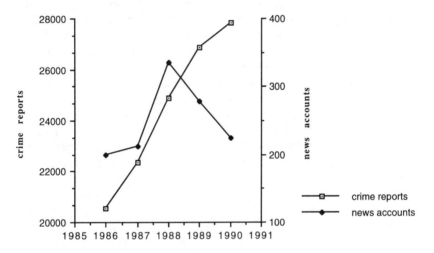

Source: Canadian News Index; Crime in Canada,
Statistics Canada Catalogue 85-205

We see that sexual assault is not overplayed in the media but is in fact made virtually invisible in comparison to its official and actual incidence. Unlike the social panic that has been generated around youth crime, sexual assault suffers a media silence. Understanding this general background of underreporting, the articles on sexual assault that do get printed in the newspapers can be analyzed: Do they present crimes committed by strangers; are they high profile assaults; are they cases where the accused is acquitted; what does the language look like; do we hear from the victims?

Figure 1.1 shows that the number of sexual assaults reported to the police has steadily increased since 1986, but the news has actually decreased its coverage since 1988. Though the former can be attributed to a general change in society's attitudes about sexual assault reporting patterns and perhaps to its better treatment in the criminal justice system, the decrease in media coverage is much more difficult to explain.

Public knowledge about the crime of sexual assault has several layers. For example, we now know that 100 percent of sexual assaults are known to the people they happen to, six percent are known to the police and less than one percent is communicated to the public through the news. This process of attrition introduces a subtle distortion as well. The media cannot represent the complete picture, in part because of a lack of information but also because of the priorities and agenda set by the media itself. Victims of crime are more likely to report those incidents committed by strangers, which are more likely to be believed by the police and in turn are more likely to be picked up by the media.

At the end of this chain of attrition, the public sees only a select few of the stories culled from the huge number of assaults committed, and these stories are slanted towards sensational crimes committed by strangers. The public receives information which implies that interpersonal violent crime committed by strangers is rampant and that the world is becoming an increasingly dangerous place to live. The image of fear is constructed in a distorted way which nonetheless has consequences for how people live their lives.

The media, then, is part of the system that makes sex crimes invisible. If a crime is seldom reported, then silence becomes the norm; if a crime is often distorted, then this is the message being presented to readers. Instead of a "social panic" model, this is the "orthodox version of events" model.

In looking at how accounts are constructed, we can see how our attention is directed to a preferred reading of events. This "directing," or "deixis," occurs in the creation of the "typical" account (Smith 1990). When an account directs our attention to one interpretation, it elides, or misses, other versions that are possible. An orthodox version of events is constructed in the course of the reporting on sexual assaults when attention is drawn to certain features that consistently appear. News accounts are doubly constructed: they are often truncated versions of police definitions of crimes and they fit social stereotypes of what the crime should look like. In these constructions, aspects of the initial event which are features of a "crime" must be "intended," or collected together, by the news account. Through the inclusion of selected features and exclusion of others, the accounts retroactively "accomplish," or transform, the event into a crime.

Various features of the account (the assault, a victim, an attacker, the police) become prescriptive aspects of the crime. These textual features are intended to be read as a reworked description of a sexual assault; thus the event becomes the textual reconstruction of the event. The account conveys information to extralocal readers who are far from the event (as observers, not participants) in a number of ways: by transmitting official information from the police (who are the authorities), by creating in readers (the public) a sense of passivity in response to the one-way flow of information and by substituting categories such as "attacker" and "victim" for people in the actual event. An event first experienced by the victim is reworked, translated and shown through a series of filters to become a crime experienced by the reader.

Thus, coupled with the relative absence of reporting on sexual assault is the slanted construction of crime that is reported in the news. Newspapers typically rely on the police or on trials for information, thus reflecting a law and order perspective, and an institutional perspective rather than those of victims, social organizations and other professionals. The overwhelmingly institutional focus in reporting means that the definition of crime is often constructed by the police, and the police emerge as authorities in the news accounts. In the "string" of sexual assault news accounts mentioned earlier, eighty-three sources were quoted in fifty-eight articles, and forty-nine of these sources were the police (59 percent); and because the police were only counted as a source once per news article, the percentage of times they appeared does not reflect the dominance of their point of view in the articles. The police were named in the headlines, and their opinions tended to be cited first and to be given the most space. The importance of the police and the criminal justice system as information sources is made especially evident by the comparison of primary and secondary news articles of the summer of 1993 found in Figure 1.2.

Within the thirty-five primary articles on the summer of 1993 sexual assaults and their investigations, the police are cited thirty-two times (65 percent) among a total of forty-nine sources. In comparison, participants are cited 14 percent of the time, experts and organizational representatives 16 percent and citizens four percent. In the secondary news articles, however, which reflect a more commentative approach, the dominance of police sources shifts. The police were quoted only 14 percent of the time, while experts and organizational representatives predominated (29 percent) in a much more divided field; citizens were cited 14 percent of the time and journalists 12 percent. An important difference, of course, between primary and secondary news accounts is that the former report the "facts of the case." In general the Halifax police media "spokesman" was usually the officer quoted, but other officers were sometimes cited as well. The Halifax police chief was the prominent subject of a column at the beginning of the third week of the "string" after his interview on the local CBC Radio. He was accused of not understanding the issues; women were said to feel afraid and angry that the only advice they were being given was to stay inside and lock their doors.[2]

Figure 1.2
Sources cited in news articles on sexual assault, summer 1993

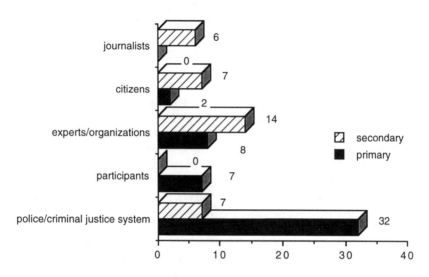

Source: Personal collection

Police not only supplied information and interpretation of the cases but were influential in a more subtle way. The "facts of the case" are owned by the police and the very way the cases are described is derived from a police perspective. It is only in the secondary news articles (columns, opinion pieces) that an alternate point of view not necessarily dominated by the police interpretation of events emerges. In this process, news organizations create a privileged interpretation of sexual assault by excluding women's point of view and replacing it with a more "authoritative" perspective. This might not be a problem if not for the fact that the dominant perspective tends to recreate mystification around sexual assault.

Police provided the descriptive information from an organizational point of view: they provided a report that an assault had occurred, a description of what happened and an opinion on whether they thought it was connected to earlier assaults. This was the general structure of the "events" during the "string" of stranger sexual assaults in Halifax, and it defined the character of the crime and the role of the victim; attention was not directed towards the police or towards the offenders. The textual ordering of the event constructs the social reality of the crime. The very words used by the police and reported in the media construct the character of what happened: "alleged assault," "assault," "misleading police," "false report."

The police version of events that dominated the news during the "string" was problematic because the facts became difficult to separate from interpretation. For example, in Article 1.4, "Child asleep in woman's home during rape, say sources," lines 5 and 6, the police spokesman "confirmed a report . . . the woman was choked into unconsciousness." He then went on to say in lines 14 and 15 that "it's likely the attacker approached the house earlier, while 'casing the area for a victim who was alone and could be attacked.'" The evidence given to support that interpretation was cited as statements by neighbours who reported having seen someone knocking on doors on the weekend. This interpretation probably contributed to whatever fear of strangers that did arise. That interpretation could also have been used to support a more general theory that a man known to the woman was stalking her. This theory was not addressed by the police and was only later mentioned during a criticism of the police and the media by a woman at a public meeting.[3] The topicalization of stranger-related sexual assault dominated the news and was never successfully resisted. Given police domination of the news accounts in their role as authorities, this comes as no surprise.

The police proffered various explanations of the crimes that become another important part of the orthodox version of events: victims were said to have left windows open, media reports might bring people out of the "woodwork" to copycat, and it was blamed on the warm weather.[4] After the fifth assault, police described an attack on a woman as occurring after she was struck in the face and forced to a secluded area.[5] The police interpretation was that the assault started after the abduction, not when the woman was hit in the face. The same police sergeant, commenting on the fourth and fifth assaults, said "assault victims normally know the person who attacked them, 'but these just seem to be unprovoked.'" The official explanations seemed to buy into rape myths.

Police were in the forefront in the media, urging women to be cautious, which included not to let people into their homes they didn't know, to "use common sense" and not take shortcuts, to resist, to scream and not to use pepper spray.[6] When the police were criticized for putting all the responsibility for safety on women, the police said the cautions were for everyone, both men and women. These tips tended to be supported by the Service for Sexual Assault Victims which appeared at a series of public workshops with the police.

The dominant discourse reflected an orthodox version of events that emphasized how not to become a victim and stressed the danger of public places. This orthodoxy focused on a series of stranger-related sexual assaults while disingenuously admitting their relative rarity, and played on the authority of the police. Thus news accounts focused on the details of the crimes, the stranger trope and the police version of events. A final aspect of the construction of orthodoxy was the suppression of alternate voices. Only in secondary news accounts were conflicting points of view on such topics as the ineffectiveness of the police even barely developed. The crime, and the fear of crime in particular, as experienced by *women* was absent from this orthodox version.

The police were also key in making the assaults appear largely made up. On the fourth of August the police laid four charges against the first complainant for misleading police and spreading false news.[7] Because only a small proportion of sexual assaults are committed by strangers, and a point was made of mentioning this in the news articles, this turnabout made it seem as if the other cases were suspect as well. In a news release, the Dartmouth police also announced the first woman was facing six counts of fraud against the Metro Food Bank and the provincial Community Services Department, further maligning her character. In another of the sexual assault cases the complainant decided not to proceed with the investigation, while in a third the victim was said to have provided incorrect information to the police.[8] In being unable to provide an explanation for these so-called "strange twists," the police contributed to the impression that the cases were false. The "string" of sexual assault reports came to a close and many rape myths survived intact.

Despite the importance of the social panics model, because it focuses more on distortion than on distraction, it fails to analyze deeper ideological constructions in the media and how these constructions reflect gender distortions which work to the detriment of women and society as a whole. Gendered violence in society needs to be reanalyzed, and the ways in which the media reports sexual assault need to be reformed. Tackling commonly held rape myths is a good place to start. It is easy to reproduce the status quo. It is much harder to challenge it.

Summary

This chapter began with the idea that women's issues are not represented in the news. I have taken the issue of sexual assault in order to show that news accounts are constructed in a very orthodox way to create a particular version of events. My argument is that a series of silences and distortions work to misrepresent crime in the news. However, it is not enough to show that the media gives us distorted knowledge; this knowledge, however distorted, exists for a reason. Ideological knowledge is "normal" knowledge. The focus on stranger rape, for example, is a way newspaper accounts structure knowledge of the world in ways that actually work to the detriment of women and to the advantage of men by not focusing on acquaintance-related sexual assault.

The emphasis in this analysis has been on a particularly sensational string of sexual assaults. However, most reporting of sexual assault is mundane, and this "news as usual" discourse reveals little information that is useful to women as they live in this world. Reporting of sexual assault that does contain greater detail also conveys little information and often serves to exacerbate public fear.

The textual construction of crime is circular: as the news constructs a "panic" about gender and danger, it draws upon the warrantability of that claim as a condition of its production. The media can play up fear of strangers because that is a pre-existing cultural idea. Because news is constructed extralocally, discourse that reflects dominant ideas reproduces the unequal relations of the genders. The in-depth reporting of sexual assault which occasionally is done relies on "normal" notions of gender and danger which give its text reasonability and which are in turn reaffirmed.

Notes

1. Stepdad gets 2 years for assault, Judge credits him for 'sparing' 9-year-old girl's virginity," *Montreal Gazette*, January 14, 1994: A1; "Crown appeals sodomy sentence, Quebec judge's comments causes uproar," *Globe and Mail*, January 15, 1994: A5; "Judge's competence queried by Quebec bar association, Promotion called deplorable after controversial sentence," *Globe and Mail*, January 20, 1994: A3; "Judge Verreault and the Quebec bar," *Montreal Gazette*, January 21, 1994: B2, editorial; "Quebec judge cleared of wrongdoing in incest case," *Halifax Herald*, June 30, 1994: A20.
2. "'He just doesn't get it,'" *Daily News*, July 22, 1993: 19.
3. "Sexual assaults keep police phone lines busy," *Daily News*, July 27, 1993: 6.
4. "Woman escapes naked assailant," *Daily News*, July 10, 1993: 3; "Tenants worry about security," *Chronicle-Herald*, July 10, 1993: A2; "Third sex assault perplexes police," *Chronicle-Herald*, July 12, 1993: A1.
5. "Latest sexual assaults by strangers perplex police," *Daily News*, July 19, 1993: 3.
6. "Suspect cleared in sex assault," *Chronicle-Herald*, July 9, 1993: A4; "Sexual assault by strangers rare—police," *Chronicle-Herald*, July 13, 1993: A4.
7. "Mischief charge laid against woman claiming stranger raped her," *Chronicle-Herald*, August 4, 1993: A1; "Woman charged as assault case takes 'weird' twist," *Daily News*, August 4, 1993: 3; "Alleged rape liar accused of fraud against food bank," *Daily News*, August 5, 1993: 3; "Woman in rape controversy faces new charges of fraud," *Chronicle-Herald*, August 5, 1993: A3; "Woman to plead guilty to misleading

34

police," *Chronicle-Herald*, August 6, 1993: A1; "Dartmouth police undermine themselves with press release," *Daily News*, August 8, 1993: 2, column.

8. "Doubts growing on two more sex assaults," *Daily News*, August 14, 1993: 3; "High-profile rape investigations hit snags," *Chronicle-Herald*, August 14, 1993: A1.

2

Women who Work as Prostitutes:
The Sex Trade and Trading in Labels

Women who work as prostitutes are often negatively and stereotypically labelled by the media. In sociology, "labelling" refers to how groups become stigmatized in society, such as "the mentally ill," for example. The labels come to represent the group and provide others with an easy way to categorize and discredit people.

Anne Derrick focuses her talk on prostitutes and how they are very narrowly stereotyped in the media. In her work as a lawyer she has had occasion to legally represent these women and their concerns and has observed the type of labelling women in the sex trade receive in the media. For women who work in the sex trade, "prostitute" or "hooker" becomes their main identity through the media. The media often shows little concern about the organization of the trade, how poverty might be a motivation to work as a prostitute or how prostitution can be very violent.

In the "Reading the news" section, some examples are provided of how the media labels women who work as prostitutes. Often, the media's representation of them is very shallow, further stigmatizing and reinforcing the negative image of the profession. Media coverage often uses the word "hooker" and focuses on individuals, failing to address the wider aspects of violence and exploitation.

The analysis section suggests that the characterization of the crime of prostitution in the media is part of the crime itself. It is easy to blame "hookers" for prostitution when that is the predominant image in the media. Furthermore, the definition of prostitution found in the Criminal Code of Canada is not represented in the news accounts, enabling further misrepresentation of the crime. By stereotyping women who work in the sex trade as "hookers" and by misrepresenting the character of the crime, the media fails to provide an understanding of prostitution that addresses the violence and exploitation in these women's lives.

The talk—Anne Derrick

I do not come with any particular expertise about what I am going to discuss but merely opinions that I have developed after some exposure to representing clients who are themselves subjects of controversy. In my experience, I have had some clients who welcome that controversy or at least welcome their role in it, and then I have had clients who have not welcomed their role at all.

One of the obvious examples of clients who do not welcome the controversy that they attract is the case of women who work as prostitutes. I try to use that term deliberately—"women who work as prostitutes"— because part of what I am going to say relates to the fact that I think one of the great weaknesses in our media is the tendency to label.

My own personal experience made me acutely aware of this danger of labelling or carelessness with language when I became involved with representing women who work as prostitutes. This was in relation to an action that the government took against a group of women who were plying their trade in the downtown area of the city. The government decided to try to get an injunction against them. This was back in 1984, and having become involved as one of the legal counsel to them, I became very interested in what I experienced as a result.

Part of what I did is that I tried to make some connections with other prostitute rights activists in other parts of the world, notably England, and also other parts of Canada. I had occasion when I was in Toronto once to get together with a woman named Amber Cook who worked for a very long time as a stripper and also did work as an activist for prostitutes' rights. I met with her to talk about her work. I was talking to her and all of a sudden she bursts out, "Why do you keep calling them "prostitutes"? They are women who work as prostitutes." She was a very big, striking, tall woman and she completely intimidated me. I felt like a stupid, white, middle-class, rude person who had been very careless and insensitive with my language. I hear Amber's voice in my head whenever I speak about prostitution.

What I really was exposed to in terms of the relationship with the media when I represented the women back in 1984–85, is a number of things and I will present them in no particular order. First of all, I thought that the media was generally sympathetic to the reality of these women's lives, sympathetic to learning more about what the women were experiencing or certainly how being under siege by a very unsympathetic and hostile government and ruling class was affecting them.

Along with that sympathetic disposition, I also found the media to be very lazy: lazy about their analysis and lazy about how they would access information. The easiest thing to do was to ring me. I became a sort of spokesperson on the issue of women on the street. They called me up and they would ask me my views and want to do an interview with me and it was easy to do that. They had my phone number and they knew where to find me and it saved all the trouble of maybe having to do some reading or speak to some other people, or think harder about the issues, or try to present them in a more challenging or provocative way.

One of the other things that they did in addition to the easy route of contacting me was that they wanted to talk to a woman: "Could you put us in touch with a prostitute?" "Would you be able to find us a prostitute?" I do not completely castigate that. I think it's very important to recognize that what women as prostitutes experience must be learned and understood from their perspective. It must be obtained through their eyes and through their voices, and middle-class lawyers are not to be relied upon to talk authoritatively about the issues.

Unfortunately I think it also reveals a tendency to put all the burden on the women to talk about the issue of prostitution. For a vulnerable and largely invisible population who don't invite controversy or media attention, I think that is a very difficult burden to bear. Therefore I think that if the media have a tendency to be lazy about some of these issues, then they do not properly occupy their role as critiquing the viewpoints of others. They need to challenge these viewpoints such that the onus is removed from the women and placed more squarely where it belongs, on the shoulders of the media and of other members of society. You have the viewpoint of one group so you get the viewpoint of the opposing group. That is very much true when you are dealing with the issue of prostitution.

The gentrified middle class talk about "what a terrible problem prostitution is and how inconvenient it is in our neighbourhoods and how we must get rid of it and our children are going to see used condoms." That is all reported and then you go to find the token prostitute and you ask her what she thinks, or you cannot find the token prostitute so you speak to the token prostitute's lawyer and you ask her. I guess I have had a very mixed view of my own role in speaking out in the issue of prostitution when I have been invited to do so and have chosen to do so, but chose to do so certainly at the time because there wasn't anyone else to say anything.

What you have is the legitimation that goes along with being heard in the media. All of that legitimation is placed in the hands of the middle classes who were protesting against women working the streets and therefore causing the government to act in this draconian fashion. And yet, no one to speak on the other side of the whole issue to say, "Why is it that prostitution is the problem? Why is it not that poverty is the problem. Why is it not that the way our society is structured is the problem?"

Without this more critical analysis on the part of the media, the issue is very much presented, you know, "What do we do about this problem of prostitution?" The middle class or the ruling class then say, "Well, we stamp it out, we get an injunction, we quarantine the women if they happen to be HIV carriers." That is an issue which was certainly discussed, I believe during the fall of 1987 or '88.

There are some real difficulties around the vulnerability of unpopular, unattractive populations being victims of easy reporting where there is not enough critique, there is not enough analysis and there is not enough willingness to go beyond simply presenting the two sides of the story. I think that relates to how the news media tries to be objective. It presents this, it presents that, and that's that. You have both sides of it, then you go off and formulate your own opinion.

The other important thing I think that I learned, and I hope that all the vulnerable populations can learn this as well, is that the media is very important in terms not only of influencing public opinion, but also in relation to the idea that if you are heard, if you are speaking out, if you are being reported, then you must have something that is worth saying or something that is worth listening to. I think that this is a tool that can be very useful in the hands of populations like women who work as prostitutes in being able to speak about what they know best—better than anybody else—and being able to be heard speaking about that and therefore acquire some credibility, which seems to be required in the way things are.

Unfortunately that hasn't happened with as great effect in Nova Scotia as it has in other jurisdictions where there have been prostitute unions developed and where women have very much grabbed media attention. For example, I think about the occupation of churches in England and France in the 1970s where that was a very effective, strategic move for capturing public attention and focusing the public mind on what is really going on for women on the street and what responsibility society has in relation to that.

The issue of how the media deals with women who work as prostitutes is very much an issue of dealing with "people that are acceptable and people who are not acceptable." The result is this terrible labelling that occurs, and I am made most aware of this whenever a woman who works as a prostitute is murdered. It is always "the prostitute is found murdered," a "woman who is a prostitute is found in a dumpster behind an apartment building," or whatever. I feel confident if someone murders me it is not going to be a "lawyer was found murdered." Maybe that will be somewhere in the story, but I will have a name, some other identity, but these women, this is their identification, they are a prostitute, that is it. It is not that it is their livelihood or that is their occupation, that is their identity, that is who they are. That is hard for me to fathom other than it is part of this "Are you an acceptable person or not?"

If you are an acceptable person you have a more developed identity than if you are not an acceptable person; then you have your label and you wear that like a yellow star or a pink triangle. I think women who work as prostitutes share this experience, they are not alone in experiencing this, but they share this experience with people who are HIV positive.

It is the same with people who are accused people or criminals. I was struck the other day in the newspaper by a report that the Dartmouth courthouse is going to be renovated and that judges will no longer have to share common elevators or staircases with criminals in leg irons. Yes, it is quite true that some people who are convicted and therefore could be labelled as criminals are placed in leg irons, but some people who are on remand and are innocent until proven guilty are also placed in leg irons.

There is very much this sense of carving up who you are in society and applying the label and leaving it at that without any further analysis. I think the media has been somewhat conscious of this—although they are guilty of it, they are also conscious of it being done by others, which is an important realization I hope will be reflected on so that the labelling and these divisions between acceptable and unacceptable people are critiqued more effectively by the media themselves.

As an example, I think of the Sutcliffe, Yorkshire Ripper case in England, where the judge made comments about how women were being found murdered and there was general societal consternation and outrage when "decent women were found dead" and that was when the whole police concern with the issue really took off.

I think that the media are guilty of buying into those kinds of divisions which once again reinforces the acceptance that there are some people who are disposable in society and there are some people who are not. That has a dramatic and definite impact on people's lives in the struggle against AIDS and certainly against the struggle that women in the street experience in terms of being very vulnerable to violence, being murdered and having those murders effectively investigated, because of the way they get reported on and they get labelled and the way public opinion is informed about them.

There is the example on the west coast of the Green River murders, where well over one hundred women have been murdered over the last number of years. There has been ongoing concerns about the way those murders are being investigated and concerns about how the press has been dealing with that phenomenon, which makes one very confident that if these were white, middle-class college coeds, there is no way that it would have gone to the extent of over one hundred women who happened to be prostitutes being murdered and there seeming not to be an effective investigation accompanying that. I think there is a lot that can be done to improve what I perceive to be the basic sympathy at least in the media, trying to better understand the experience of women in the phenomenon of prostitution in our society. I think many of the habits—which are easy habits and which result in the media not being sufficiently critical and not being sufficiently self-critical—continue.

Reading the news

Let us look at how women who work as prostitutes are stereotyped in the media. These stereotypes involve derogatory language and typifications about the profession. For women who work in the sex trade, being a "prostitute" or "hooker" becomes their primary identity, a stigmatized reputation provided to them by others (Goffman 1963; Becker 1973; Kitsuse 1962). Ironically, this stigmatized reputation is typically seen as a deviant variation on women's ordinary sexual "work" (Naffine 1987). Stereotypes about women who work as prostitutes are significant because the way prostitution is presented in popular culture inevitably becomes part of the crime and how it is treated in the criminal justice system, a theme that will be taken up in the next section.

Article 2.1, "Slain woman local hooker," illustrates how labelling and stereotyping can become the theme of a newspaper report. This is a news account of the violent death of a woman who worked as a prostitute which appeared on the front page with a banner headline. The slain woman was described primarily in terms of her purported occupation.

Article 2.1
Slain woman local hooker
(*Halifax Herald*, February 19, 1993: A1)

1   A young woman found shot to death Tuesday in North Preston has been identified as
2   a Halifax prostitute who was expected to testify against a man accused of beating her
3   with a stick.
4   Cole Harbour RCMP officers, who have set up a special tip line to aid their
5   investigation into the slaying of 17-year-old Kelly Lynn Wilneff, would not comment on
6   any link between the two cases.
7   They also said they don't have any "specific" suspects.
8   Kevin Whynder, 19, of Brunswick Street, Halifax, had been charged with assault
9   causing bodily harm in connection with an attack on Kelly on June 16, 1992.
10   The charge was dismissed Thursday in Halifax provincial court without a
11   complainant and without a case. Mr. Whynder appeared for trial accompanied by his
12   Legal Aid lawyer Bill Digby.
13   The trial has already been delayed twice—once on Nov. 19 when the accused
14   failed to appear and again two weeks later when Kelly did not show up.
15   The trial was rescheduled for her arrest, just as a warrant had been issued for Mr.
16   Whynder's arrest when he didn't appear.
17   RCMP were having trouble identifying Kelly after finding her body Tuesday, but got
18   a break Wednesday when they received a tip. Family members of the northend Halifax

19 girl were called in late that day to identify the body.
20   Police are releasing few details about her death and won't comment on reports that
21 she had been shot in the head about eight times and was badly beaten.
22   Sources have said the teenager was convicted twice last year for communicating
23 for the purposes of prostitution and was given a year's probation.
24   Cole Harbour RCMP Const. David Pike said Kelly hadn't approached metro's
25 police task force on prostitution.
26   A spokesman for the task force said he hopes other young girls will be spurred to
27 leave the prostitution trade by the news of Kelly's death. Sgt. Bill Price said he does not
28 see the killing as a message from pimps who have been the target of the force.
29   Although the killing might have been prevented even if Kelly had been under the
30 task force's wing, it does illustrate the importance of the operation and a safe house to
31 protect young women who want to escape the trade, Sgt. Price said.
32   Police have taken down the tent set up Tuesday to protect the body and the site
33 of its discovery from heavy winds and rains.
34   The body was found about six metres off a woods road near Stillwater Lake.
35   Investigators don't believe any evidence was lost due to the bad weather, Const.
36 Pike said.
37   The body was found fully clothed and was not covered by snow or brush. Police
38 believe it wasn't at the site more than 36 hours before it was found.
39   Anyone with information that could help solve the murder is asked to call the
40 RCMP's special line at 435-9644. Tips can also be made to Crime Stoppers' anonymous
41 line at 1-422-8477.

The account is deceptively simple in its descriptive detail. A woman was found murdered (lines 1 and 34–38) and was only identified after an anonymous tip (lines 17–19); she was a prostitute (lines 2 and 22–23), she had previously been assaulted by a man (lines 2–3, 8–9), but the police did not indicate there is any connection or that they have any "specific" suspect in mind (lines 4–7). The police do indicate they are in charge of the investigation (lines 17–21 and 32–33), the task force on prostitution is hoping the death will send a message to other young women (lines 24–31), and they are still looking for information (lines 39–41). So, we have a crime of murder, a victim who was a prostitute, the police are involved and there is a warning to other young women "like that."

The reported facts of the case are simply described. The article accomplishes its matter-of-factness through the descriptive character of the writing, which minimizes speculation or theory. There is an interpretation but it is not overt. For example, this article does not question our media-generated version of reality but confirms it by inferring that some women live deviant lives and there are dangers associated with that lifestyle. Some articles focus on the familiar theme of a serial killer at work—a favourite explanation for unexplained slain or missing women. Through these tropes, the facticity of the article is not simply anchored in the writing style but also in the fact that it trades upon an easy version of reality. The report does not challenge a stereotypical version of prostitution but confirms it, in the process confirming sexist assumptions.

On the following twenty-sixth of February, the newspaper's ombud wrote an article commenting on the number of calls made to the paper objecting to the use of the word "hooker."[1] In fact, that article was the only one to use "hooker" in the headline.[2] In various articles the victim was described as "a Halifax prostitute," "a 17-year-old prostitute," and "a part-time Halifax prostitute who worked the streets to support a crack cocaine habit." The ombud does not state what is insensitive about the use of the word, simply that it was—perhaps it was a mistake in this one particular case. However, this word is commonly used by the media in their portrayals of women who work as prostitutes, as any a sampling of headlines shows.[3]

"Hooker" appears quite often in news articles on prostitution. It is not simply a descriptive word, but is used in a negative and derogatory sense. The use of the term in the news reflects a sexism in society. There are 220 words in English for a sexually "promiscuous" woman (and only 22 for such a man), and these words are predominantly negative (Maggio 1988; Kramarae and Treichler 1985; Bell 1987). Even the word "john" is problematic, because it does not carry the derogatory connotation that "hooker" does. "John" is just faceless.

In 1994 another woman who worked as a prostitute was found dead. The headlines used the words "slain prostitute," "prostitute's body found" and "hooker." The accounts were much like the one above, simple in their description: a woman was found murdered, was identified as a prostitute, has a history of drug abuse, is reported to have had men looking for her, the police are in charge of the investigation and won't say there is any "specific" suspect in mind and so on.[4] Most of the news articles on this particular femicide were limited to the aspects of this case alone.

However, two articles in the first few days of coverage put the violence into the larger context of violence against women who work as prostitutes, moving away from the sensationalized and isolated treatment found in the other news stories. The two articles were published in the same paper, one day after the other, and the more specific one is reproduced in Article 2.2. Such coverage is both unusual and important, for most media accounts of crime report incidents as if they are isolated, failing to see how they are part of a larger pattern of criminal activity.

Article 2.2
Halifax streets growing meaner for dozens of prostitute victims
(*Daily News*, November 26, 1994: 5)

1 Halifax streets have been particularly violent for prostitutes recently, with dozens of
2 violent incidents ranging from beatings to murder.
3 This week's death of Kimber Lucas, 25, adds another name to the growing list of
4 prostitutes victimized.
5 Lucas, 25, was a prostitute and drug abuser. She was also seven months pregnant.
6 On Wednesday, her body turned up behind a north-end apartment building.
7 Just two days earlier, Kevin Whynder, 21, was sentenced to life imprisonment for
8 murdering Kelly Wilneff, a 17-year-old prostitute and crack addict. Wilneff's body
9 was found in North Preston woods last winter.
10 Other prostitution-related violence in metro:
11 •March 3, 1994—Dartmouth's Douglas Wade Brown, 34, is charged with pointing a .22
12 calibre pistol at a prostitute, pimping, and aggravated assault in incidents between
13 Aug. 31 and Nov. 15, 1993. Several charges are dropped when a Crown witness
14 disappears.
15 •Feb. 25, 1994—Dartmouth's Carl Fraser (alias Timothy Glasgow) is charged with
16 attempted murder, extortion, pimping, and exercising control over a prostitute. Fraser,
17 33, was accused with cutting the wrists of a 39-year-old woman, but the charges were
18 dropped when she fled to the Dominican Republic. Crown attorney Frank Hoskins said
19 the woman received a phone call, got scared and left the country.
20 •Dec. 27, 1992—Halifax's Michael Daniel Beals, 35, is sentenced to seven years in jail
21 for aggravated assault on a 17-year-old prostitute. Beals was also convicted of several
22 pimping charges. He held the girl's head underwater in a bathtub and choked her
23 unconscious.
24 •Dec. 17, 1992—Anna Marie Mason, 23, a part-time hooker and mother of three, is
25 beaten to death in the hallway outside her Windmill Road apartment by two men.
26 Ivan Bo Simmonds, 25, and Robert Williams Beals, 23, are charged with manslaughter.
27 •Dec. 9, 1991—Janet Ellen Davis, a 37-year-old prostitute, is sentenced to eight years
28 in prison for manslaughter. Davis stabbed Jack Moriarty, 36, six or seven times. A judge
29 said Moriarty was a "mean-spirited drunk ... who seemed to get some pleasure out of
30 physical violence." Moriarty had so much alcohol in his system he was in a stupor or
31 unconscious when he was killed. Davis had a history of drug abuse.
32 •Feb. 26, 1991—Kelly Lynn Whynot, a 17-year-old prostitute, is bludgeoned and
33 strangled to death in Dartmouth. Stephen McMaster, 25, and his wife Nina, 37, were
34 convicted of killing Whynot in their Rose Street apartment. They stuffed the body in a
35 garbage can outside their apartment.
36 •April 5, 1990—Jean Hilda Myra, 31, is found dead at the base of the grain elevators
37 on South Bland Street. Myra, a mother of three and part-time prostitute, was found face-
38 down and partly clad. She had been asphyxiated. She was seen the previous night
39 leaving the Lighthouse Tavern with a man. The case remains unsolved.

Article 2.2 states that dozens of violent incidents have occurred recently (lines 1–2). Going back only to 1990, it documents five femicides (lines 3–

4, 7–9, 24–26, 32–35 and 36–39), two incidents of aggravated assault (lines 11–14 and 20–23) and one case of attempted murder (lines 15–19). There is no mention of the other incidents of violence referred to, or of evidence that the streets are really growing meaner, despite the headline of the article. However, the account creates a context for prostitution-related violence in a way that few articles do. It documents a pattern of violence rather than focusing on the "seamier" side of the sex trade, avoiding the voyeurism of most news accounts on prostitution.

Besides labelling, crime news recreates a second distortion by focusing on prostitution as deviant women's work. The use of the word "hooker" is common, and when it isn't used the word "prostitute" is used instead. Both words are used derogatorily and unidimensionally and ignore the role men play in the sex trade industry. Men pay for sex with women and men, men organize the trade as pimps, and predominantly it is men who police it. However, men are seldom the subject of enforcement, as the following article shows.

Article 2.3 from the *Globe and Mail* appears in capsule form. This style is a popular one for newspapers because it enables a quick summation of stories that come across the newswire, giving the appearance of covering national and international news while also leaving room for more in-depth local stories. The interesting thing about this article is how prostitution, as a crime, is identified as a problem related to the presence of prostitutes providing the service, rather than to johns, pimps or other less obvious aspects of the sex trade. The article neglects work of the police in enforcing the law, and the social conditions which give rise to prostitution in the first place. The enforcement of prostitution law in Canada has historically been isolated and sporadic, influenced by moral entrepreneurs, and often simply results in the police moving the business from one area to another, a pattern that has not been without criticism (Lowman 1988; Shaver 1985; Lowman et al. 1986).

Article 2.3
Wants sex trade moved
(*Globe and Mail*, July 22, 1991: A4, Canada in Brief)

1   **REGINA (CP)** — A downtown Regina community group wants the city to get rid of the
2   sex trade that goes on right outside its front doors. The core community association will
3   approach city council at its July 29 meeting with a petition to move the prostitutes who
4   populate residential streets.

Newspaper reports represent a normalized point of view, a version of reality that locates the problem solely with the prostitutes and in so doing authorizes and reproduces that definition of the crime. This point of view has typically been the approach in the policing of prostitution as well: to focus on the women who work the street, not on the other aspects of the organization that maintain it. In this way, the topicalization of prostitution in the media mirrors the criminalization of prostitution by society. However, there are occasionally important fractures in the ideology around prostitution. Not everyone agrees with the dominant perspective that prostitutes alone are the problem. Article 2.4 displays some of this lack of consensus. Usually such attempts to control prostitution are informal, sponsored by business or property-owner associations, and not under the control of the police. They usually arise out of frustration and the perceived inability of the police to do anything about the problem.

Article 2.4
Billboard advises prostitutes to stay away
(*Halifax Herald*, April 22, 1991: C17, Canadian Press)

1   **EDMONTON** —The inner city neighbourhood of Norwood isn't one of Edmonton's hot
2   nightspots, and a group of area residents hopes a portable billboard will keep it that
3   way.
4   The double-sided sign reads Prostitutes Get Lost, You're Not Welcome in Norwood.
5   Sylvie Patoniec, president of the Norwood Neighbourhood Association, said the
6   group is also concerned about the hookers' male customers coming into the
7   neighbourhood.
8   "We just want them to know we're watching," Patoniec said Saturday.
9   The group holds monthly crime advisory meetings, and area residents have
10 recently noticed more prostitutes in their area and more slow-moving cars cruising up
11 and down neighbourhood streets and back alleys.
12   "We've had people in the back alleys frightening them away," Patoniec said. "We
13 take the license plate number and pass it on to the neighbourhood foot patrol officer."
14   At least one area resident thinks the plan may backfire. Albert Smith said the sign
15 attracts men looking for illicit sex by telling them where hookers hang out.
16   "I think they're just drawing some weirdoes in to the area," Smith said.
17   In fact one side of the signs had already been changed to read Prostitutes Welcome
18 in Norwood, an indication there may be more trouble ahead, he said.

In this article the "hookers" are identified as the obvious problem, but the role of the customers is referred to as well. The action the Neighbourhood Association has chosen, putting up a sign, does not tell johns to stay away, but the group says they have been taking license numbers and passing them on to police. This article, and this way of policing the problem, still gives the impression that prostitutes are the main problem, but it does show that opinion is divided on the cause of the problem.

Against this general background of selectively topicalizing the work of prostitutes, it's remarkable that in 1993 articles started to appear on a police crackdown against pimps in Halifax. In 1992 it had been announced that a prostitution task force would receive money from the Department of the Solicitor General.[5] A flurry of articles were published about pimps being arrested, charged and tried, and about prostitution rings, abductions and women fleeing the street.[6] Even though this slant focuses more on the exploitative side of the business, rather than the moral, it still leaves the role of the johns virtually invisible. The policing of prostitution and the reporting on prostitution parallel one another; both focus disproportionately on the women who work in the sex trade rather than on those who use and maintain it.

Deviance is not simply behaviour that violates the dominant rules of a society; "deviance" is also the result of the labelling of behaviour that is felt to violate cultural norms. A labeller is as necessary as a behaviour to label. We have explored the idea that "prostitution" is a label based on a negative stereotype which focuses on the sex trade as deviant women's work. In this process of topicalizing women as offenders and victims in the business of prostitution, attention is directed away from the activity of men. Now I want to focus on the link between media stereotyping and policing criminality, and the larger relationships in the reporting on prostitution.

Analyzing the news

Prostitution does not receive a lot of attention in the news, but what it does get is distorted. The coverage fails to make the connection to larger issues of violence against women in society; it portrays prostitution in a way that is derogatory to women and it makes men invisible. This distorted and incomplete picture plays a role in the social (mis)construction of prostitution in our society. The predominant image of prostitution we get is one of women standing on the street in fishnet stockings and a miniskirt, but in actuality there are more men than women engaged in the buying and selling of sex. There are the pimps who organize the trade and exploit the women; there are the johns who demand the trade and exploit the women; and there are, of course, men who work as prostitutes themselves. However, much of the men's participation is hidden and official statistics only tell part of the story. There is little research on the customers, but a call-person may have thirty to forty regular customers, and a streetwalker seven to ten a night (Gomme 1993).

Despite the preponderance of men in the trade, women are much more likely to be arrested on prostitution-related offences, although statistics show this is slowly changing. For example, by 1991 the proportion of men charged had risen to 48 percent; in 1989 the proportion of men in official reports had been 45 percent; and the proportion of men charged in 1985 only 40 percent. The near parity of these numbers does not suggest equality of treatment, because there is such an imbalance between the number of women who work as prostitutes and the men who engage their services. Moreover, the Canadian average disguises provincial differences in charge rates: in 1991, British Columbia charged 42 percent more women than men for prostitution-related offences other than bawdy house or procuring, Saskatchewan 99 percent more and Nova Scotia 188 percent more.[7]

In 1992, a Halifax woman charged with prostitution argued that the enforcement of Section 213 of the Canadian Criminal Code (communication for the purposes of prostitution) was discriminatory because more women are charged under that statute than men, even though "it takes two to tangle."[8] The lawyers argued that between June 1, 1990, and November 30, 1991, 84 percent of those charged under this statute were women, and that this was discriminatory under the Charter of Rights and Freedoms because the law was being unfairly applied to an identifiable group.

Several months later a provincial court judge ruled that the difference in charge rates was not sexist and did not violate the Charter. No explanation was given, but it was made to seem that the issue was one of policing, that it was easier to catch women than men. Halifax was said to have the highest ratio of charges against women in the country, but again no explanation was given as to why. In November, three years after the initial charge, the Nova Scotia Court of Appeal upheld the lower court ruling.

A traditional rationale for gender asymmetry in prostitution-related charging has been that there are not enough female police officers to go undercover to arrest johns, while there are more male officers available to pose as johns to arrest women streetwalkers. This answer begs the question of why police personnel is gendered itself, and points to an implicit gender bias in the law that mirrors the social stereotyping of prostitution as women's work.

Shortly after the provincial court case, the defendant was found guilty of communicating for the purposes of engaging in prostitution. Her "lenient" sentence of one day, however, was said to be given because this was her first offence.

The statute under which she was charged is one of several that define the offence of prostitution: keeping a common bawdy-house (section 210), procuring (section 212) and offence in relation to prostitution (section 213). The last section of the Canadian Criminal Code is the one most often applied (for example, it accounted for 92 percent of the reported offences in 1989).

Offence in relation to prostitution—Definition of 'public place'
213. (1) *Every person* who in a public place or in any place open to public view
(a) stops or attempts to stop any motor vehicle,

(b) impedes the free flow of pedestrian or vehicular traffic or ingress to or egress from premises adjacent to that place, or

(c) stops or attempts to stop any person or in any manner communicates or attempts to communicate with any person for the purpose of engaging in prostitution *or of obtaining the sexual services of a prostitute* is guilty of an offence punishable on summary conviction.

(2) In this section, public place includes any place to which the public have access as of right or by invitation, express or implied, and any motor vehicle located in a public place or in any place open to public view (emphasis added).

When we read this statute, we see that it says that *"every person* who . . . in any manner communicates . . . for the purpose of engaging in prostitution *or of obtaining the sexual services of a prostitute"* is guilty of an offence. The term "prostitute" is not defined as female, although prior to 1972 the law only criminalized women and did not apply to males.

Section 213 points to the behaviour of both parties in the transaction as criminal. It is illegal to ask for and to offer sex for money in Canada. The media finds it difficult to focus on the customers (men), however, just as do the police and members of the public. Men are virtually never portrayed in the media as the beneficiaries or organizers of prostitution.

Occasionally, attempts are made to publicize and criminalize the activity of men who are johns, pimps and sex workers, but these attempts are few and far between. In Toronto in the early 1980s an effort was made to curb the demand for prostitution by publicizing the names of customers in the newspapers. The effort was soon discontinued simply because of a lack of interest on the part of the newspapers. Various other cities have tried publication as a solution to the problem of prostitution, but have typically discontinued it after a short time.[9] In 1993, Halifax Herald Ltd. decided to publish the names of johns in a rather short-lived experiment. An article in *The Coast*, an alternative newspaper in Halifax, pointed out that this strategy does little to deter johns, who sometimes simply remove or distort their license plates.

The idea of publishing johns' names is an interesting one, for it shifts the media from crime reporting to crime control. While editors might simply be trying to be fair or balanced, publishing names is quite often seen by law and order advocates as deterring crime. This action moves the media from a reactive position to a proactive one, accepting without question, it would seem, that prostitution is deviant and the law is above question.

The media can sometimes find itself criminalized for its involvement in the sex trade. For example, on August 31, 1990, Toronto Metropolitan police charged *NOW* magazine and four of its directors with communicating for the purposes of prostitution. The basis for the action had been classified personals ads placed in the paper. However, three weeks later all charges were dropped. The police had taken their action independently, and the crown attorney and attorney general found there was no basis for the charges under Canadian law.[10]

Looking at media coverage from a longer perspective, there has been considerable variation in the amount of newspaper coverage, as shown in Figure 2.1. The quantity of newspaper articles over time is important for what it says about prostitution as an issue in the media and as a crime issue for the public, and for what it reflects about how society deals with prostitution as a problem.

Figure 2.1
Prostitution coverage, 1977–91

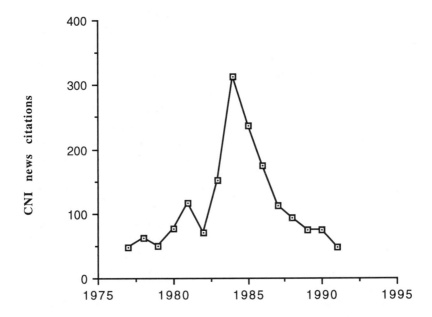

Source: Canadian News Index

Figure 2.1 shows that the coverage of prostitution issues as compiled from the *Canadian News Index* was not balanced between 1977 and 1991. In 1977 there were forty-eight stories on prostitution. This figure began generally to rise in the early 1980s, with 117 stories in 1981 and 312 stories by 1984. However, then the number slowly dropped off and by 1991 had returned to the level of the late 1970s. These numbers reflect the importance of prostitution as an issue in the media and in society. The sharp rise in the mid-1980s corresponds to drastic changes then occurring in the law which produced a sharp spike in coverage which stands out in comparison to the usual number of articles.

In 1978 the prostitution law (Section 195.1) was based on the new notion that "Every person who solicits any person in a public place" was guilty of prostitution. This idea was successfully challenged in the same year by an appeals court on the grounds that soliciting meant being pressing or persistent, which made the law very difficult to enforce. In response to this, various municipalities in Canada enacted by-laws to curtail street prostitution in the early 1980s. The Supreme Court of Canada ruled in 1983, however, that these by-laws infringed on the federal government's sole ability to make criminal law. Given that soliciting was difficult to enforce, and municipalities could not act on their own to control prostitution in the absence of federal action, this situation created a criminal law vacuum. It was not until 1985 that the soliciting provision was replaced by the section prohibiting communication for the purposes of prostitution. This new law was overturned by the Nova Scotia Court of Appeals as contrary to the Charter of Rights and Freedoms in 1987. The Halifax police then changed their method of policing to a more passive one, reflecting what was probably a widespread uncertainty about the enforceability of the new law. In 1990, however, the Supreme Court of Canada ruled that communications between a prostitute and a customer were not protected under the Charter and constituted a warrantable infringement.[11]

This legal chronology of prostitution law parallels the change in media coverage found in Figure 2.1. In the late 1970s the law was changed to make it more gender-inclusive and to redefine the terms of the offence. The enforcement of the solicitation clause soon proved unworkable in the early 1980s and media coverage started to rise. At the peak of newspaper stories in the mid-1980s, the law was changed again. Interest started to decline but still remained relatively high through the late 1980s as the law was clarified through the court system. By 1991 the crisis in law enforcement was over and media coverage returned to normal.

There is not necessarily any causal connection between the two trends; for example, it is not necessarily true that changes in the law caused the changes in media coverage. It is an interesting parallel, a puzzle searching for an answer; if there is a relationship, it is probably a more complex one. The media reflects social issues of the day, quite often without a critical perspective or from a longer, historical point of view. In this way, as prostitution law became an issue in Parliament and in communities, it would receive more coverage.

But the media does not simply take up social issues and report them like a mirror, for it is in a position to create and distort them as well. We have already looked at stereotyping and labelling of prostitution in the media, for example. With this in mind, increased coverage around prostitution in the 1980s could have crystallized and formed public opinion as well. The question is, what did that coverage look like and how was the problem characterized? With this recursive interchange between prostitution law and the media, the newspapers take up pre-existing issues in society and focus them as in a prism, perhaps distorting them, sometimes criticizing them but always transforming them in the process of reporting.

Summary

It would seem that the media is part of the crime in many ways. The media labels and stereotypes women who work as prostitutes, presenting them as "hookers" engaged in deviant women's work. The media not only ignores the role of men, but it can also gloss over the violence and exploitation of the trade, focusing on deviance as the critical issue. Furthermore, the media can influence crime prevention strategies by highlighting prostitution as a problem and can become a strategy itself when it chooses to do such things as publicize the names of johns. By not questioning the deeper causes of prostitution, the media can uphold the legitimacy of the law, how it is policed and why a moralistic law remains on the books. Finally, the press can be used against prostitution but can also become criminalized itself, as when it publishes personals ads which seem to solicit prostitution.

There are historical trends in how prostitution has been characterized as a problem in Canadian society, and understanding the relationship of the media and the crime means understanding their intertwined nature. It is not a linear relationship but a reciprocal one, based in a normalized and continually maintained system of sexism.

Notes

1. "Journalists daily grapple with 'sensitivity' issue, *Halifax Herald*, February 26, 1993: 12.
2. "Slain woman local hooker," *Halifax Herald*, February 19, 1993: A1; "Slain teen was to testify at trial, Puzzling cases remain on books," *Daily News*, February 19, 1993: 4; "Murder defendant acquitted of resisting arrest by police," *Daily News*, February 22, 1994: 8; "Preston set up by girl's killer, resident suggests," *Halifax Herald*, February 27, 1993: A4; "Murder probe setback denied, Six arrested in raid released," *Halifax Herald*, March 11, 1993: A1; "Unsolved murders still under investigation—RCMP," *Halifax Herald*, July 19, 1993: A3; "Two men charged in Wilneff killing, Teen shot to death seven months ago," *Daily*

News, September 27, 1993: 3; "Two metro men charged in death of Kelly Wilneff," *Halifax Herald*, September 27, 1993: A3, Metro in Brief; "Pair arraigned in Wilneff slaying," *Halifax Herald*, September 28, 1993: A1; "Pair held in teen's slaying, Arrest of murder suspect led to tussle, police report," *Daily News*, September 28, 1993: 3; "Witness 'will be there' for Wilneff murder trial," *Daily News*, November 8, 1994: 5; "Wilneff shot 10 times in head, jury hears," *Halifax Herald*, November 9, 1994: A3.

3. For example, "Hooker traffic near school angers community parents," *Edmonton Journal*, January 12, 1992: B1; "Female hookers caught, while johns often walk, court told," *Halifax Herald*, January 16, 1992: A5; "Dartmouth police target hookers," *Halifax Herald*, August 15, 1992: A6; "Hookers must charge pimps—youth worker," *Halifax Herald*, September 19, 1992: A4; "Hooker outreach program in jeopardy even after boost," *Halifax Herald*, March 27, 1993: A7; "Teen hookers tell of fear-filled days, nights," *Toronto Star*, May 16 1993: B8; "Parents rescue teenage hooker," *Halifax Herald*, November 4, 1993: D13; "Ruling won't alter MUC cops' anti-hooker work," *Montreal Gazette*, November 17, 1993: A3; "Judge doesn't buy $5 hooker story," *Halifax Herald*, November 20, 1993: A5; "Hooker cried wolf once too often, say police," *Halifax Herald*, December 2, 1993: C19; "Assault defendant denies hooker link, admits sex with girl," *Daily News*, December 8, 1993: 9; "Man found guilty of crimes against hooker," *Halifax Herald*, December 9, 1993: A4; "Hooker won't testify in upcoming trial." *Halifax Herald*, March 5, 1994: A5; "Hooker's memory failure foils Crown's case, Alleged pimp acquitted of five counts," *Halifax Herald*, May 14, 1994: A4; "Woman distraught as brother jailed for beating hooker," *Halifax Herald*, June 4, 1994: A4; "Dartmouth dogged over hooker issue," *Halifax Herald*, June 8, 1994: A9; "Hookers, Ottawa's proposed crackdown is madness and hypocrisy," *Montreal Gazette*, September 24, 1994: B5.

4. "Slain prostitute was pregnant, Slashed, naked body left in alley," *Halifax Herald*, November 24, 1994: A1; "Victim was an addict, hookers say," *Halifax Herald*, November 24, 1994: A1; "Body lay in yard for day, men say," *Halifax Herald*, November 24, 1994: A2; "Grim discovery. Prostitute's body found behind apartment building," *Daily News*, November 24, 1994: A1, cover headline; "Woman found dead, Prostitute's body found at north-end apartment building," *Daily News*, November 24, 1994: A3; "Fetus could turn case into double homicide," *Halifax Herald*, November 25, 1994: A1; "Police silent on how prostitute, 25, murdered," *Daily News*, November 25, 1994: 9; "Street dangers brought home by death," *Daily News*, November 25, 1994: 9; "Trio

sought dead woman, Gunmen said they would 'do her good' days before murder," *Daily News*, November 26, 1994: 5; "Halifax streets growing meaner for dozens of prostitute victims," *Daily News*, November 26, 1994: 5; "Callousness of hooker's demise hit nerve," *Halifax Herald*, November 26, 1994: A5, column; "Murdered woman eager to have baby, hoped for better life," *Halifax Herald*, November 26, 1994: A1; "More than 200 mourn murder victim," *Halifax Herald*, November 28, 1994: A3; "Halifax police follow leads in murder," *Halifax Herald*, November 29, 1994: A4; "Trail cold in search for killer," *Daily News*, November 29, 1994: 4.

5. "Prostitution task force gets $100,000," *Halifax Herald*, October 8, 1992: A3.

6. "Pimps procured women through terror, police say, Toronto detective describes use of stun guns, whippings to keep prostitution ring in line," *Globe and Mail*, September 18, 1992: A7; "Task force pushing for safehouse in metro," *Daily News*, October 28, 1992: 4; "$500,000 a year set aside for prostitutes' safe house," *Halifax Herald*, December 9, 1992: A3; "Safe home will help jail pimps, Crown predicts," *Daily News*, December 29, 1992: 6; "Fifth pimp suspect charged with attempted murder," *Daily News*, January 15, 1993: 4; "Police charge more men in pimping crackdown," *Daily News*, January 19, 1993: 6; "Not just pimps deserve outrage," *Daily News*, January 20, 1993: 22, editorial; "Prostitute's safe house set to open next month," *Daily News*, January 21, 1993: 7; "Pimping charges stayed," *Halifax Herald*, February 5, 1993: A5; "Prostitution task force makes 12th arrest," *Halifax Herald*, February 10, 1993: A8; "Bail revoked for alleged pimp," *Halifax Herald*, February 11, 1993: A6; "Task force too heavy-handed in hunt for pimps, says group," *Halifax Herald*, February 17, 1993: A5; "Police 'picking on' black men, Anti-harassment group alleges scapegoating in pimping probe," *Daily News*, February 17, 1993: 4; "Teenage prostitute tells of beatings, rape," *Toronto Star*, May 5, 1993: A7; "Safe house site widely known, ex-hookers say," *Daily News*, July 18, 1993: 3; "Safe house provides haven despite fact location known, Hookers can't be protected on streets—police," *Halifax Herald*, August 6, 1993: A4; "Ex-prostitute praises metro task force, Fight against pimps never-ending," *Halifax Herald*, September 2, 1993: A4; "Halifax police break up suspected abduction by pimps," *Halifax Herald*, September 19, 1992: A4; "Police confirm cutbacks to anti-prostitution force," *Daily News*, September 29, 1993: 8; "Anti-pimp task force to stay, Gillis says," *Daily News*, September 30, 1993: 5; "Ottawa cops nab metro man for pimp charges," *Daily News*, November 7, 1993: 3; "Pimping charge dropped against Dartmouth woman," *Halifax Herald*, November 9, 1993: A5; "Warrants

issued for main witnesses in pimping trial of Dartmouth man," *Halifax Herald*, January 5, 1994: A4; "Prostitution task force loses oficer from Halifax," *Halifax Herald*, January 5, 1994: A4; "Former teen prostitute thanks task force," *Daily News*, June 24, 1994: 8; "Ex-hookers put in protection program," *Halifax Herald*, March 1, 1994: A3; "Hooker won't testify in upcoming trial," *Halifax Herald*, March 5, 1994: A5; "Courage helps sex-trade fight," *Daily News*, June 27, 1994: 12, editorial.

7. "Canadian Crime Statistics," Statistics Canada. The three main prostitution-related offences are operating a common bawdy-house, procuring and communicating for the purposes of prostitution. The first refers to owning or operating a house where prostitution regularly occurs, and the second refers to pimping. The largest category of offences laid was "Other," which includes communication.

8. "Female hookers caught, while johns often walk, court told," *Halifax Herald*, January 16, 1992: A5; "Woman challenges prostitution charge, Low ratio of male customers arrested violates Charter of Rights, court told," *Daily News*, January 16, 1992: 5; "Prostitute arrests not discriminatory—judge," *Daily News*, March 7, 1992: 9; "Charter fight against prostitution charge not over," *Daily News*, March 19, 1992: 4; "Halifax prostitutes lose fight," *Halifax Herald*, November 25, 1994: A15.

9. "Police to publicize names of prostitutes and clients," *Globe and Mail*, n.d.; "Mug shots, fingerprints urged to curb prostitutes," *Globe and Mail*, November 29, 1989: A3; "Alderman advocates publishing names of hookers' clients," *Halifax Herald*, October 5, 1990: B4; "Publishing johns' names," *The Coast*, June 7, 1993: np.

10. "NOW charges dropped. Alright!," *NOW*, September 27, 1990: 5, advertorial.

11. "Top court strengthens prostitution law by ruling that solicitation is not a right," *Globe and Mail*, June 1, 1990: A1.

3

Domestic Terrorism:
The News as an Incomplete Record
of Violence Against Women

Violence against women, and the ability of the media to represent it in the news, is the focus of this chapter. In her talk, Debi Forsyth-Smith places violence against women in the context of how the media covers women's issues in general. Included in her discussion are some recent trends and the need for further change.

The "Reading the news" section analyzes a select sample of articles dealing with violence against women in relationships to find out how well the newspapers deal with the issue. Various measures are used, such as the size of the article, whether it portrays the violence as unusual and whether it locates a specific crime in the context of violence against women in general.

The issue of violence against women is addressed more broadly in the "Analyzing the news" section. Other sources of information pertinent to the analysis of violence against women are considered, and statistics on femicide and wife battery in Canada are examined. This chapter highlights how the media has only recently taken up this issue and still provides an imperfect record of violence against women. Coverage tends to be isolated and sensationalistic, and consequently further mystifies the problem by contributing to its invisibility and pervasiveness.

The talk—Debi Forsyth-Smith
One of the things I want to get across is that the whole issue of how the media has focused attention on women's issues has been given a tremendous amount of attention over the last twenty years, beginning with certainly the task force on the images of women back in 1978, which first really identified sexual stereotyping and the fact that there were a significant lack of women working within the context of the broadcast media in particular.

As a result of that task force, research was done to identify specifically what areas were really lacking in terms of the representation of women. There was the research that was done in 1984 which identified news coverage, programming coverage and advertising as well. I think the biggest news of all in that respect is that the exact same research was repeated in 1988, the results came out in January, and there has been no significant change statistically speaking since 1984 despite legislation and despite increasing numbers of women working in the broadcast media.

There's also some research being done right now in the national media archive in Vancouver, which I think is quite significant in terms of what it says about the coverage of women's issues. How they define women's issues is significant in itself. Certainly the whole identification of women's issues has been put in a framework of a confrontational approach. For example, when you talk to the National Action Committee you always have to have an opposing group, when you talk about the abortion issue you always have to have the opposing viewpoint in the context of media coverage. In terms of the National Action Committee and the coverage that's been afforded to their work and their views on issues, there is usually an accompanying response from a group such as REAL Women.

We saw the same thing happen in Halifax in just the last six months when a new organization was formed, sort of a moral majority group or a right-wing group. The issue was over their name, when another women's group by the name of Voice of Women opposed the name, which I think was United Voice of Women. The whole coverage of that episode was about the name issue and not getting to the root of what really were their issues and what really were their positions. I think that's a very important context of the coverage of women's issues is that there's so much worry and attention paid to opposing sides of the issue that the substance of the issue is rarely, if ever, covered.

With specific respect to the issue of violence against women, an identifying point where that began to get greater volumes of coverage would be the Montreal massacre in 1989. Certainly from a national perspective, the coverage on the Montreal massacre comprised the majority of the coverage in broadcast media and television news in particular. It composed the largest percentage of their coverage on women's issues for the entire year at about 15 percent, and both national broadcast outlets gave it about the same amount of attention.

What was interesting about that experience is the framework. For example, the "Journal" did a broadcast on the massacre and it was introduced as a discussion of the increased level of violence against women and the fact that this was not an isolated incident any more, that it was happening more frequently in people's lives, in women's lives in particular. What ensued was really a discussion about the psychological makeup of mass serial killers. There was really very little discussion of violence in women's lives. But since then the coverage by all various mediums has seen, quantitatively speaking, a significant increase.

The difficulty is that once again we're focusing on the most sensational end of the spectrum. I had a call from a television reporter a couple of weeks ago who horrified me by asking if we kept any pictures of battered women in our resource centre so that they could be used as part of his story.

The whole range of violence has not really been given substantive coverage in terms of the degree and type of violence that women experience in their lives, and I think that's really what's missing. There's certainly lots of action if you want to talk about broken bones, and broken ribs, and black eyes and so on, and you can draw a parallel between our cultural understanding of the whole issue of violence against women and the way that it is presented to us for consumption by the media.

And that, I think, presents a lot of difficulties when it comes to putting the issue of violence against women in context. Again, the research has indicated that when we're talking about sexual violence against women and children, it really is the most extreme and sensational cases that get coverage in terms of what kind of cases are reported and how they're reported, and often the victimization of the woman becomes secondary to the context of the story. For example, the remarks of judges and the remarks of lawyers becomes the story, rather than the story of the victimization of the woman.

It is interesting that in this process of identifying what are women's issues, what gets us bogged down is what we see in the media. Identify what are issues that are of concern to women and you have the usual list: pay equity, poverty, violence, you have all of those things, but I think there's a wider issue here which is that these issues are people issues, and what's missing from the media coverage that we see is the feminization of those issues with the perspective of women and speaking from a women-centred viewpoint.

So I think that there are several things that should be noted. We do have federal legislation with respect to employment equity in our media and our broadcasting industry. We do have sexual stereotyping guidelines which are presently a condition of license under the CRTC but are in danger of being removed because the broadcasters have made a significant case to the CRTC that in fact everything's OK now, which every bit of research that has been done has indicated is simply not the case.

The broadcasters, however, have gotten together in a very significant way and developed some red herrings to distract us from what's really needed, which is some significant enforcement of those guidelines. The CRTC is delighted to accept the broadcasters' pitch for self-regulation because they don't have the resources or the people power to enforce guidelines any more. So the latest move by the CRTC was to call for submissions on the whole issue of sexual stereotyping, for which they supplied, I believe, three weeks notice. Through the efforts of the organization MediaWatch, that's been extended. It's doubtful, though, that even significant public representation on that issue will change the approach that CRTC has to this issue, which is to put the responsibility on the broadcasters and subsequently on the viewing public.

I think we have to redefine what we're referring to as women's issues. One of the very serious concerns that women themselves have is their dealings with the mainstream media, particularly women who are working on equality issues, and providing them with some support to deal with that. They obviously want their issues mainstreamed but at the same time they feel abandoned by the kind of coverage they receive from the mainstream media.

I think the other issue that's worth mentioning is the fact that even though the research numbers show very little difference between 1984 and 1988 in terms of the portrayals of women and the images of women, there has been even less of an increase in the numbers of women who are involved in the positions of power within the media. And that really hasn't changed at all. It is still male city desk editors and male news directors who are calling all the shots. And I think we've heard what that's like for a woman who is working inside the media in terms of selling stories.

I think, though, that the fundamental concern that women have I talked to have about dealing with the media is the one-dimensional approach to women's issues. In other words, getting back to the REAL Women versus feminists for example, getting down to the abortion versus the anti-abortion forces, that is the only dimension that is applied to many of these issues, is getting those two sides of the story but not allowing any sort of multifaceted dimensions in on the coverage.

The final thing that I want to mention is the critical need that we have when we're talking about an issue like violence against women, to pressure the media not to increase its quantity of reporting but to widen the dimensions of the kind of coverage that we have, and to lead the story of violence against women into the impact that it has on society as a whole and other levels of our society, the costs that are associated with it. And I don't mean in a very shallow way, I mean in a far more dimensional way, you know, the health care costs, the costs to generations of families who are victimized by violence in their lives, and tremendous more work needs to be done on the psychological and emotional violence that's being done to women not only in the context of the domestic relationship but in the context of women's lives in general in our society, and I think that's something that's really been missing from identifying what we call violence. And perhaps it's redefining violence against women altogether.

Reading the news

The news does not tell readers much about the reality of women who are battered in the home. The terms used in the media for battered women tend to misname the experience and thus become part of the problem. The term "spousal abuse" misnames the problem, making it seem as if either spouse is equally at risk or fault. "Wife-beating" is also problematic because it does not identify women who are assaulted in common-law relationships or battered by a boyfriend. "Domestic violence" has come to identify family violence in general but fails to specify the gendered and intimate character of the problem.

Violence against women is specifically related to their relationships with men. The Canadian Panel on Violence Against Women released a report called "The War Against Women" in 1993 that documented widespread abuse and recommended zero tolerance of violence against women.[1] The results of a survey by Statistics Canada, excerpted in an editorial in the *Toronto Star*, indicated that 51 percent of women have experienced physical or sexual violence at least once.[2] More than 78,000 women are admitted to shelters for battered women in Canada each year.[3] A report published in 1994 indicated that three in ten women currently or previously married to men in Canada had experienced at least one incident of physical or sexual violence at the hands of their partners (Rodgers 1994).[4] The risk was highest for young women and for those in partnerships that had begun less than two years previously. Violence against women in relationships is widespread.[5] However, the criminal justice system has often been accused of not taking the crime seriously enough.[6]

Violence against women in relationships is an underreported crime. And in spite of the pervasiveness of domestic violence that does come to light, it is underreported in the media as well. Only a few articles on the topic appear in the media; those that do comprise a small sample of the cases that occur in society, just the tip of the iceberg. The result is that domestic violence is portrayed as an isolated event and the systemic reality of violence against women in this society is denied.[7]

Article 3.1, "Calgary man sentenced for assault in intersection," displays some of the inadequacies in the media's treatment of violence against women. The article describes a man who assaulted his former wife in a busy intersection (line 1) after kidnapping her. The reader gets the end of the story, that he has been convicted of kidnapping, sexual assault causing bodily harm, and break and enter (lines 5–6) and that he is a manic depressive (line 3) and has been sentenced to a mental institution (line 2).

Article 3.1
Calgary man sentenced for assault in intersection
(*Globe and Mail*, April 9, 1990: 11, News Capsule)

1   **(CP)** — A man who assaulted his former wife in a busy Calgary intersection has been
2   sentenced to two years less a day in jail and three years in a mental institution. The
3   man, described as manic depressive, is "in urgent need of psychiatric help," Court of
4   Queen's Bench Justice Allen Sulatycky said Friday. The 32-year-old man, who cannot
5   be named to protect the woman's identity, pleaded guilty to kidnapping, sexual assault
6   causing bodily harm and break and enter. During the Feb. 5 attack, the near-naked
7   woman tried to escape from his car at an intersection. A public furor erupted when a
8   witness said passing motorists cheered the man and taunted the woman.

The way the incident is written up makes it appear unusual and bizarre. The report provides no explanation of how the crimes originated, the underlying nature of the man's emotional instability, how the assault may have been connected to former abuse in their relationship, the frequency of the abuse or the private terror that many women experience before they finally leave or seek help. The account is isolated and decontextualized. The main reason for publishing the story was probably that it had been reported that bystanders had "cheered" the man as the "near-naked woman" tried to escape (lines 6–8). The facts that the man was reported to need psychiatric help and that the assault happened in public further emphasize the unusualness of the event, unconnected except for its violence to the ordinary reality of many women's lives.

Article 3.2, "Man goes on rampage in Virginia," begins virtually the same way as the previous article. A man beat up his former girlfriend (line 1) and then acted in what seemed a totally bizarre way by going on a rampage (lines 2–3). These attacks are described in a concise, matter-of-fact way, which lead in the article to various charges for criminal offences (lines 7–8). Again, no background information is given to help readers put the crime in context. The report appears in the News Capsule section on page D16 of the paper, which indicates the relative unimportance of the story from the newspaper's perspective. If it hadn't been for the "rampage," it is doubtful the item would have been carried on the newswire and reprinted thousands of miles away.

Article 3.2
Man goes on rampage in Virginia
(*Halifax Herald*, April 28, 1993: D16, News Capsule)

1   **RICHMOND, Va (AP)** — A man beat up his former girlfriend, then went on a rampage
2   in which he drove from place to place, slashing one man's throat and stabbing four

3   other people, authorities said.
4   The attacks began Monday night in south Richmond, moved through neighbouring
5   Henrico County and ended with the man's arrest back in the city, Richmond police said.
6   They identified the suspect as Kenneth Hall, 21, of Chesterfield County. Hall is
7   charged with multiple counts of aggravated assault, simple assault, hit and run and
8   robbery, said police.

These examples show how violence against women tends to be portrayed as unusual and episodic. There is little or no analysis, the coverage focuses mainly on the individuals in the case and no context is provided to help the reader understand these incidents are anything other than unusual. The reader becomes an unchoosing voyeur, catching a glimpse of tragedy in someone else's life. This "individualism" can easily lead to blaming the victim, asking how she got herself into such a situation and why she hadn't left—being a victim of violence can discredit a woman's reputation (Loseke and Cahill 1984). In Article 3.3, the violence is framed in terms of the victim's occupation. This article portrays the violence without context or interpretation. The report discredits the reputations of both the offender and the victim, easily supporting the claim that "this is what can happen to bad girls." This discreditation is found not only in the text of the article but also in its headline which focuses on the word "stripper." In order for the reader to be able to deconstruct the layers of the story and interpret its meaning, articles need to focus more on the background of the cases and to critically analyze the legal system and its response. The reason background and contextual details are often missing is because more work is required to get them—a good organizational reason for bad behaviour—an explanation but not an excuse.

Article 3.3
Police hunt stripper's murderer
(*Toronto Star,* November 16, 1993: A10)

1   **SURREY, B.C. (CP)**—RCMP have launched a massive manhunt in the wake of the
2   dismemberment killing of a Surrey exotic dancer.
3   Police were seeking David Ernest Rhodes, 31, for questioning in the death of
4   Lalonnie Frances Thibert, 25.
5   Her nude, mutilated body was found Friday in a shallow grave in this Vancouver
6   suburb.
7   RCMP said that, on Thursday, a group of Thibert's male friends chased down
8   Rhodes on a Surrey Street, forced him into a motorhome and contacted an off-duty
9   Vancouver RCMP drug squad constable.
10   The men turned Rhodes over to the officer but, during the transfer, Rhodes escaped.
11   RCMP officials said that Rhodes is extremely dangerous and could be armed with a
12   handgun. They also said he is a heroin addict.

13   The body was so badly mutilated it took some time to identify her, said Hepburn.

14   Police believe Thibert was slain in a Surrey house in the past week or so.

Article 3.4 outlines the response of the legal system to criticisms that it is insensitive to women's needs. In this article more information is provided on the need for the legal system to respond more effectively to the issue of domestic violence and protect women who are its victims.

Article 3.4
Peace bond information to be given to police
(*Halifax Herald*, December 23, 1992: A3)

1   **By Janice Tibbets, Staff Reporter** — Nova Scotia women will no longer have to carry
2   copies of peace bonds in order to prove to police that the orders exist.
3   By Jan. 31, police dispatchers will have their own copies of peace bonds, provided
4   by court officials soon after they are issued, the Attorney General's Department said
5   Tuesday.
6   "It would be as close to instantaneous as we could get it," said department
7   spokesman Peter Spurway.
8   Eventually, the information will be available provincewide on a police computer
9   network, the department said. It is also taking steps to have police bond information
10   available on the computerized Canadian Police Information Centre.
11   In a policy statement issued Tuesday, the Attorney General's Department said it
12   is still looking at ways to speed up the process of obtaining a peace bond.
13   Mr. Spurway said the length of time women are waiting for peace hearing to obtain
14   the bonds is getting shorter. In some areas of the province they can be obtained in a
15   few days.
16   Earlier this year, Attorney General Joel Matheson promised to look into the speed
17   at which peace bonds are issued after critics charged it can take up to three weeks after
18   making an application to obtain the order.
19   Debi Forsyth-Smith, president of the Advisory Council on the Status of Women,
20   could not be reached Tuesday.
21   However she said earlier this year that police do not respond quickly enough to
22   complaints about peace-bond violations and women are forced to persuade judges to
23   renew an order by citing new instances of violence. A peace bond is a court order for
24   one person to stay away from another.

The article mentions the problem women have had in getting the police to acknowledge and enforce peace bonds against their husbands. The article makes it seem like a simple technical issue of getting the right information out and does not go into how criminal justice system officials often have misconceptions about wife abuse that get in the way of their doing anything about it (McLeod 1987; Denham 1990). The article also does not go into the difficulty of implementing change around gendered issues such as wife abuse. In contrast, Article 3.5, which follows, does get at some of the larger issues around the problem.

Article 3.5
Wife beating called epidemic in South Asian community
(Globe and Mail, November 19, 1990: A5, Nicola Pulling, special to *The Globe and Mail)*

1   **TORONTO** —Wife assault in Toronto's South Asian community has reached epidemic
2   proportions, but the victims often do not seek help because mainstream social-service
3   agencies do not meet different language or cultural needs, the Canadian Council of
4   Muslim Women was told on the weekend.
5   The 40 people attending the council's educational workshop, including 12 men,
6   heard the story of Aruna Papp, who came from India with her husband 14 years ago and
7   was an abused wife. She left her husband, put herself through university and graduate
8   school and became the founding director of South Asian Family Support Services,
9   which counsels immigrant women from India, Pakistan and Sri Lanka. She later
10   remarried.
11   "What we're facing is an epidemic of wife abuse in the South Asian community,"
12   Ms Papp said.
13   "Nothing is as degrading as lying on the floor in front of your children and being
14   kicked by your husband," she said.
15   In August, she produced the Report on Abused South Asian Women in Scarborough.
16   She interviewed 100 immigrant women who had been abused during their marriages.
17   Of these, 21 had to be admitted to hospital for stab wounds, broken ribs and noses,
18   slashed breasts and sexual attacks. Eleven were under psychiatric care and two were
19   later stabbed to death.
20   She found women would not report abuse because they were afraid of deportation
21   and divorce.
22   "The patriarchal structure makes women believe it's their duty to take the abuse.
23   Many are afraid to leave their husbands because it brings shame to the family," Ms
24   Papp said.
25   Many women are unaware of support services because they do not speak English.
26   Others who have tried such services have had bad experiences.

This article begins to show how the structure of the family can allow abuse to happen and prevent a woman from doing anything about it. It is a good report because it is informative, offers an overview of the situation of women who are battered, and points to how the social organization of women's lives can contribute to the violence. However, it does not get at the role of the criminal justice system in controlling the violence, a feature which tends to be absent in crime reporting in general.

The next section takes up the idea that violence against women in relationships is largely invisible. The news is a record of events, but it is an imperfect one that often misses or disguises the systematic character of violence against women. The news tends to represent violence against women as episodic, isolated and individualistic.

Analyzing the news

We have discussed some of the problems with newspaper articles on violence against women in relationships, such as silence, sensationalism and individualism. The limited number of articles on domestic violence that do appear tend to highlight outrageous crimes and ignore the scope and enormity of the problem. At another level, the problem in *researching* the news is getting enough information to see these kinds of patterns. Reading and researching the news are connected; "researching" means going back over the news to see what the patterns are, to see how well the media records violence against women, for example. In this section I want to discuss the use of a news index to research the news. Though most people are not likely to engage in this type of research, it can indicate how important specific issues are to the news media. And then I want to look at some recent statistics on patterns of violence against women in relationships that will put both reading and research in context.

As previously mentioned, the *Canadian News Index* (or CNI, now called the *Canadian Index*) is a topical index of articles that have been published in seven major Canadian daily newspapers. The CNI began in January 1977 and is published monthly with a cumulative year-end index. Its scope and history provide an important tool for an analysis of Canadian newspapers. If you pick a topic such as homicide, for example, the CNI lists the titles and page numbers of articles published on that topic among the papers it surveys. The articles can be retrieved from microfilm or through interlibrary loan, so the *Index* is a good source of information from which to construct patterns of topical news reporting.

However, this method has several limitations. For example, not all news articles are indexed. Items of significant reference value, synopses and feature articles are indexed, but routine news reports are not included and duplicate wire service articles are screened for content. With respect to crime stories, daily update reports are rejected in favour of summary articles. Most stories are indexed under the type of crime they report ("securities—fraud" for example) but some are found under more topical titles, such as the "BCCI scandal" (the collapse of the Bank of Credit and Commerce International in 1991). In general, then, it is difficult to know how much variation there may be in the rules of inclusion and exclusion. Sometimes it is difficult to determine the type of crime the indexers feel a story represents, but the CNI provides a good guide, short of actually doing a newspaper survey.

However, it is not always easy to find certain articles or topics: for example, infanticide is grouped under "homicide," and Mount Cashel can be listed under "Hughes Commission" or the "sexual abuse of children." Even though there are many substantive differences between manslaughter, first-degree and second-degree homicide, and infanticide, the categories used do not always correspond to those used in the Criminal Code. If one wishes to use the *CNI*, one needs to get used to its limitations as a socially constructed record.

So, overall, several problems emerge when using the *Index*. First, because not all articles are represented, it cannot be regarded as a uniform database upon which to do research. However, the *CNI* does contain a considerable number of citations spanning several years. The second, deeper problem with the *CNI* is that articles are organized by topic or subject, which provides a secondary filter. The *CNI* creates topics as they become socially relevant and thus reflects the topics the media is interested in reporting.

The very lack of information can be an important aspect of the topic. For example, as Figure 3.1 shows, "family violence" did not appear as a category until 1980; "battered women" appeared in 1985 and "violence against women" and "men who batter" became categories only in 1990. There were eleven citations under "family violence" in 1980, and this number had risen more than 350 percent to fifty items a decade later. "Battered women" had ninety-seven citations in 1985, and this figure actually dropped 42 percent to fifty-six by 1990. "Men who batter" had a mere six citations in 1990, and eleven a year later. The number of citations in each of these categories is hardly reflective of the pervasiveness of the crime, to say the least.

Figure 3.1
Dates *CNI* categories began and number of articles listed

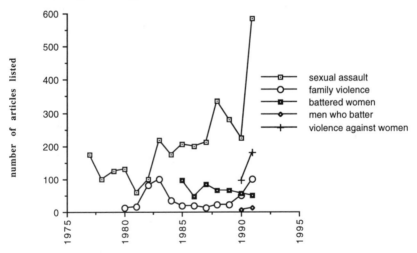

Source: Canadian News Index

Charting the chronological development of the topic of "family violence" shows that it has a relatively long history as an issue but very few citations. The more specific topic of "battered women" is newer and has had more citations but still a low absolute number. "Violence against women" is the newest category and starts to place violence against individual women in a larger context. Naming the source of the problem—"men who batter," however, does not seem to have a high priority.

Domestic violence existed long before it began to appear in the *Index* or in the news. However, the topicalization of the problem in the media occurs in a reflexive relationship to the construction and definition of the problem in society (Tierney 1982; Loseke 1987). The categories provided in the media reinforce and limit how we see the topic in society; at the same time, the media reflects changing social sensibilities. Topics can remain invisible or hidden in the world and in the media simultaneously. For example, gay-bashing is subsumed under "assaults" and is largely hidden in society, while "date rape" has recently surfaced from the "sexual assault" category just as it has recently been recognized as a prevalent social problem. It is also extremely difficult to sort out femicides, or homicides committed against women, because there is no category which labels it as such.

So, the *Index* is an imperfect but still important record of articles published in the news. There are limitations to the way the items are organized and, in order to do a proper analysis, a reader has to be aware of them. It is difficult to know how the recording is done, yet the CNI enters into the social construction of "matters of fact" by appearing to exist as a true record, a claim the media in general also makes.

Looking at another type of record, Figure 3.2 is a list of women killed in Nova Scotia between 1989 and 1993 compiled from information supplied by the Nova Scotia Advisory Council on the Status of Women and from local newspapers. A picture emerges of women who were killed by men they knew. In fact, of all known or solved cases, not one woman was killed by a stranger! There were twenty-two solved femicides, eight unsolved and two cases of missing women, for a total of thirty-two over this four-year period. The unsolved cases constitute 25 percent of the total, falling close to the national average of 23 percent for cases "not cleared" by a charge (Juristat 1991b). Almost 70 percent were solved, and the perpetrator in almost every case was known to or acquainted with the victim.

Figure 3.2 is a record of gendered violence that places the information in a pattern that is hard to retrieve from the media. The media tends to focus on individual cases, which isolates crimes, making it harder to see them as part of a larger pattern.

Figure 3.2
Femicide cases in Nova Scotia, 1989–93

Name	Date	Location	Perpetrator
•Suzanne Dube	Nov 17, 1988/ Mar 25, 1989*	Halifax	unknown
•Janice Faye Johnson	Died Feb 20, 1989	Lockeport	husband
•Catherine Lee Doyle	Died Aug 6, 1989	Eastern Passage	husband
•Gale Laura Naugler	Died Sept 18, 1989	Bridgewater	old boyfriend
•Jean Hilda Myra	Died April 5, 1990	Halifax	unknown
•Deborah Ann Neary	Died Aug13, 1990	Glace Bay	neighbour
•Barbara Baillie	Died Oct 19, 1990	Spryfield	husband
•Yvonne Margaret Donovan	Died Oct 24, 1990	Sydney Mines	old boyfriend
•Barbara Anne Parrish	Died Jan 4, 1991	Kentville	husband
•Theresa Maureen Carrick	Died Feb 12, 1991	Dartmouth	old boyfriend
•Kelly Whynot	Died Feb 27, 1991	Dartmouth	john
•Bernice Bridget Whiffen	Died March 6, 1991	Sydney	old boyfriend
•Carla Gail Strickland	June 3/June 5, 1991*	Dartmouth	unknown
•Kimberly McAndrew	Missing June 29, 1991	Halifax	unknown
•Leslie Anne Katnick	Missing Oct 31, 1991	Halifax	unknown
•Emma Anne Paul	Died Sep 26, 1991	Sydney	boyfriend
•Marilyn Rose Sabean	Died Jan 7, 1992	Halifax	husband
•Mary Anne Lamrock	Apr 6, 1990/Jan 29, 1992*	East Pubnico	unknown
•Marie Lorraine Dupe	Died March 22, 1992	Sydney	unknown
•Margaret Lorraine Halnuck	Died April 30, 1992	Sydney	husband
•Deborah June Harvey	Died May 17, 1992	Windsor	husband
•Unnamed woman	Died June 2/3, 1992	Belle Cote	male youth
•Daisy Jean Jefferson	Died Aug 30, 1992	Digby	husband
•Beatrice Marie Wright	Died Sept 30, 1992	Stellarton	husband
•Vanya Jean Dunn	Died Nov 16, 1992	Beaverbank	son
•Virginia Webster	Died Dec 9, 1992	Whites Lake	husband
•Anna Marie Mason	Died Dec 17, 1992	Dartmouth	old boyfriend
•Andrea Lynn King	Jan 1992/Dec 23, 1992*	Lr Sackville	unknown
•Shirley Irene Bain	Died Jan 16, 1993	Victoria Bch	husband
•Kelly Lynn Wilneff	Found Feb 16, 1993	North Preston	acquaintance
•Shelly Connors	Found June 1, 1993	Spryfield	unknown
•Gisele Pelzmann	Found Sept 9, 1993	Halifax	unknown

*Missing/Found

Source: Nova Scotia Advisory Council on the Status of Women, 1993; local newspapers.

This pattern of violence against women in relationships is important to topicalize, to identify and name. In case after case, the relationship of the perpetrator to the victim is named: husband, boyfriend, estranged partner, old boyfriend. The great majority of women murdered knew their killer. Unsolved femicides are a minority of the cases but could involve acquaintances as well. Acquaintance-related homicides are easier to solve than stranger-related ones, but in some cases the police know who the perpetrator is but do not have enough evidence to lay charges. In other cases it may be years before charges are laid. In 1991, of 753 homicides in Canada, 582 were "cleared" (Juristat 1991b). Eighty-seven percent of these involved family members or acquaintances and, of female victims, 92 percent were killed by family members or acquaintances. The percentage killed by a stranger was 13 percent in general: for women, it dropped to eight percent. A woman was four times more likely to be killed by a current or estranged intimate than was a man, 120 cases compared to 31. A woman is far more at risk at the hands of someone she knows than a stranger. In 44 percent of all cases of immediate familiar-related homicides, there was a previous history of domestic violence.

Recent changes in the law that have made stalking an offence highlight the growing sensitivity of lawmakers to the problem of violence against women in society.[8] These changes have perhaps been fuelled in part by highly publicized cases involving battered women, some of whom had to kill their abusive partners in order to save their own lives (Bembenek 1992; Walker 1989; Vallee 1986).

"Battered wife syndrome" has been recognized in Canada recently, but it is not an easily won defence, in part because it requires revision of the concept of what constitutes a reasonable defence in the face of "imminent danger" (section 34, 1995 Canadian Criminal Code). In early 1990 the Supreme Court of Canada reinstated the acquittal of a woman tried in Manitoba on a charge of second-degree murder after she had shot her abusive boyfriend. In their ruling, the justices wrote that "it is not enough to consider what a 'reasonable man' might do in certain circumstances, because 'the factor of gender can be germane to the assessment of what is reasonable.'"[9]

Various jurisdictions now have guidelines to reinforce the need for police to lay assault charges under section 266 of the Criminal Code when there are reasonable grounds to believe an offence has been committed, regardless of the wishes of the victim/complainant (Nova Scotia, Attorney General, 1992). This change in policing comes after years of criticism of the police for being part of the problem, for not charging men who batter and putting the responsibility on the woman to leave the abusive situation.

In Canada and the United States, prominent cases of women who killed their abusive male partners are being reviewed and the media is increasingly focusing on the topic.[10] And, as mentioned above, in June 1993 the government of Canada passed legislation on stalking that would make it illegal to harass someone by repeatedly following, watching or phoning them. This was part of a larger set of Criminal Code amendments. The subsequent law defines the offence of criminal harassment (section 264, 1995 Canadian Criminal Code) and sets a maximum penalty of five years imprisonment. This law follows legal measures already available in many U.S. states and adds more weight to pre-existing statutes related to intimidation and uttering threats. Hopefully, such amendments signal a new commitment on the part of the criminal justice system to take violence against women seriously.

Summary

The news is both a resource and a topic, a source of information and a reflection of social awareness. In looking at how well the topic of violence against women is represented in the news, Debi Forsyth-Smith suggests that although women's issues have been getting more attention in general, more improvements should be expected. The treatment of violence against women in relationships is incomplete and presented in a way that removes it from the context of the very structures of male power and violence that allow it to happen in the first place. The news imperfectly records the extent and character of violence against women.

As a true reflection of what goes on, the news is often flawed, consistently overlooking some issues and playing up others. Silence on violence against women becomes part of the social structure that perpetuates violence and thus has to be part of the story. Ignorance becomes an ideological tool; if we misunderstand the world, we are systemically unable to do anything about it. We need to record violence in a way that will help us to understand and change the world for the better.

Notes

1. "Violence to women is blamed on sexism," *Toronto Star*, July 29, 1993: A1; "Panel on women's abuse aghast at tales of terror," *Toronto Star*, July 30, 1993: A1; "Abuse of women at crisis level, panel says," *Toronto Star*, July 30, 1993: A22; "98% of Metro women suffer sexual violation, panel says," *Toronto Star*, July 30, 1993: A23.
2. "Violence to women a national shame," *Toronto Star*, November 22, 1993: A16, editorial.
3. "Battered women, children flock to shelters, study says," *Globe and Mail*, November 10, 1993: A4.
4. "Wife assault widespread—Statistics Canada," *Halifax Herald*, September 20, 1994: A14.

5. "Violence against women soars—national advisory council head," *Halifax Herald*, February 20, 1990:np; "Wife beating called epidemic in South Asian community," *Globe and Mail*, November 19, 1990: A5; "Rise in family violence concerns RCMP," *Halifax Herald*, March 1, 1991: C23; "Shelter director unsurprised by rising violence," *Halifax Herald*, March 4, 1991: C3; "Domestic violence costs taxpayers millions," *Halifax Herald*, April 11, 1991: A1; "Systemic violence decried," *Halifax Herald*, May 30, 1991: B13; "Spousal abuse no stranger to Winnipegers," *Winnipeg Free Press*, January 2, 1992: B15; "Quick action demanded on family violence in B.C.," *Globe and Mail*, March 11, 1992: A6; "Doctors are advised to screen women for abuse," *New York Times*, June 17, 1992: A26; "Beatings are common, Japanese wives report," *Toronto Star*, April 4, 1993: A2; "Muggings in the kitchen," *New York Times*, April 23, 1993: A34, editorial; "Collapse of Newfoundland fishery fuelling domestic violence: study," *Montreal Gazette*, November 8, 1993: A7; "Hospitals find abuse of women pervasive," *Toronto Star*, January 26, 1994: A24; "6% of women admit beatings while pregnant," *New York Times*, March 4, 1994: A23; "Military struggling to stem an increase in family violence," *New York Times*, May 23, 1994: A1.

6. "Judge says woman responsible for her stormy marital situation," *Globe and Mail*, February 28, 1989: A1; "Sexist attitudes revealed in N.B. study," *Globe and Mail*, December 6, 1989; "P.E.I. women decry sentence, Top court upholds absolute discharge in assault on wife," *Toronto Star*, July 6, 1990; "Woman abuse: low priority for N.B. police," *Pandora*, October 1990: 9; "C.B. police chief rapped for stance on abuse stats," *Halifax Herald*, April 5, 1991: A1; "Judges scorn abuse policy, Zero tolerance called waste of time," *Winnipeg Free Press*, June 27, 1992: A1; "Battered woman horrified when laughed at in court," *Daily News*, August 28, 1992: 32; "Judge's alleged remarks on threats spur investigation," *Halifax Herald*, December 9, 1993: A29; "Quebec judge's remarks keep courts in spotlight, Judicial council to probe comment that if woman killed by spouse, 'I won't lose any sleep over it,'" *Globe and Mail*, December 9, 1993: A3.

7. "Tenants ignore woman's screams," *Halifax Herald*, May 12, 1990: np; "Jilted lover uses truck to smash home of ex-girlfriend," *Halifax Herald*, July 30, 1991: A9; "Burnaby man, 26, denies he spent evening torturing wife," *Vancouver Sun*, December 14, 1991: A3; "Wedding-day wife-beater jailed 10 years," *Vancouver Sun*, December 21, 1991: A11; "Husband found guilty of setting wife on fire after she refused sex," *Vancouver Sun*, December 21, 1991: A1; "Woman evicted after standoff between police, boyfriend," *Edmonton Journal*, January 24,

1992: B3; "Man gets 16 months for keeping wife in chains," *Edmonton Journal*, February 23, 1992: B13; "Judge finds man guilty in strangling, beating," *Daily News*, September 16, 1992: 6; "Spouse beater with violent past gets two years," *Daily News*, December 15, 1992: 8; "Attacker's sentence too light—abused wife," *Halifax Herald*, December 15, 1992: A5; "Man is charged with using a pit bull as murder weapon," *New York Times*, April 25, 1993: 31; "Woman keeps 24-hour police protection," *Toronto Star*, May 4, 1993: A2; "Man beat wife with tire iron, court told," *Halifax Herald*, June 9, 1993: A17; "Plastic surgeon who beat his wife to be sentenced," *Toronto Star*, June 14, 1993: A22; "MD gets one year for beating up wife," *Toronto Star*, June 15, 1993: A6; "Man sentenced to month in jail after admitting assault on spouse," *Halifax Herald*, September 24, 1993: C10; "Wife-beater's 10-year term reduced," *Toronto Star*, September 28, 1993: A26; "Pregnant woman fled husband's beatings," *Montreal Gazette*, November 24, 1993: A3; "Wife says 'raving' husband tried to burn her," *Daily News*, January 7, 1994: 8; "Man, 28, arrested after girlfriend, 19, savagely beaten," *Toronto Star*, January 8, 1994: A4; "Man jailed 5 years for vicious sex assault on wife," *Toronto Star*, January 21, 1994: A13; "Father jailed for subjecting wife to rape, 'stark terror,'" *Toronto Star*, February 18, 1984: A24; "Victim's friend swears at lawyer as bat-wielding man sent to jail, *Daily News*, June 29, 1994: 8; "Mullah convicted of torturing wife," *Globe and Mail*, July 15, 1994: A7, News Briefing; "Woman stabbed in domestic dispute," *Halifax Herald*, September 23, 1994: A2, Capsule.

8. "Stalker law in the making, Legislation designed to help women hassled by men," *Halifax Herald*, April 27, 1993: A23; "A closer look at the stalker law," *Globe and Mail*, April 28, 1993: A20, editorial; "Stalking law targets predators, Tories tap into safety concerns," *Globe and Mail*, April 28, 1993: A1; "Tories propose anti-stalking law to free victims from life of fear," *Toronto Star*, April 28, 1993: A2; "Stalking the voter," *Halifax Herald*, April 30, 1993: C1, editorial; "Antistalker laws get mixed reaction, Proposed measures termed repressive," *Globe and Mail*, April 29, 1993: A6; "Bill seeks to make stalking a crime," *Daily News*, June 11, 1993: 10.

9. "Ms Lavallee's reasonable apprehension," *Globe and Mail*, May 7, 1990, editorial.

10. "Supreme court upholds acquittal of battered Winnipeg woman," *Halifax Herald*, May 4, 1990: np; "Court widens use of self-defence plea in battering cases," *Globe and Mail*, May 4, 1990: np; "A new meaning for self-defence," *Daily News*, May 6, 1990: 11, column; "Court ruling could lead to appeals—legal experts," *Halifax Herald*, May 8, 1990: np;

"Battered women battered justice," *Halifax Herald*, March 18, 1991: A7, editorial; "Killed husband, woman freed, Judge ruled justice would not be served by jail sentence," *Globe and Mail*, August 12, 1991: A5; "British women's groups fight judicial bias in assault cases," *Toronto Star*, January 7, 1992: B1; "Battered wife cleared in B.C. manslaughter," *Winnipeg Free Press*, January 31, 1992: A3; "Wife found not guilty in stabbing, Husband abused her," *Edmonton Journal*, June 3, 1992: A1; "Clemency given Jean Harris leaves 3 others wondering," *New York Times*, January 1, 1993: A1; "'Til death do us part, *Time*, January 18, 1993: 34-41, cover story; "Parole advised for woman who killed abusive partner," *New York Times*, January 21, 1993: A18; "State parole board gives Jean Harris her freedom 13 years after killing of Herman Tarnower," *New York Times*, January 21, 1993: B7; "Clemency pleas denied in 14 abuse-defense cases," *New York Times*, May 30, 1993: 21; "Free killers of abusive spouses, NAC urges," *Toronto Star*, September 1993: A15; "Female killers often abused," *Montreal Gazette*, September 27, 1993: C1; "Film depicts plight of battered women," *Halifax Herald*, February 22, 1994: B16.

Distortion in the Media

"Vampire psychic sex fiend faces rape charges."
(*Halifax Herald*, March 3, 1994: A8)

"2 convicted in 'Lesbian Vampire Trial.'"
(*Halifax Herald*, February 16, 1991: D21)

"Mount Cashel story told on Geraldo show."
(*Halifax Herald*, September 13, 1990: A12)

"Former Mount Cashel resident knew of homosexual activity."
(*Evening Telegram*, March 23, 1990: 1)

"Lawyer for defence argues boys consented to homosexual acts."
(*Evening Telegram*, March 17, 1990: 6)

"In Satan's circle. Bereaved parents relate horrors of devil worship."
(*Halifax Herald*, December 8, 1990: A1)

"Man believed Reagan was the Antichrist."
(*Halifax Herald*, December 4 1990: B18)

"Bizarre HIV-injection case winds toward conclusion."
(*Halifax Herald*, November 15, 1993: C16)

"Prisoner with AIDS bit jail guard."
(*Montreal Gazette*, November 2, 1991: A10)

"Magic Johnson retires after getting AIDS virus.
Basketball star to campaign for safe sex."
(*Globe and Mail*, November 8, 1991: A1)

"Race riot rocks downtown." (*Halifax Herald*, July 19, 1991: A1)

"Renewed violence feared in L.A."
(*Halifax Herald*, May 9, 1992: A13)

4

The Mount Cashel Orphanage Inquiry: The Inscription of Child Abuse

"Inscription" is a term that describes how the media takes up socially deviant categories and reproduces them. For example, an assumption already exists in society that homosexuality and child sexual abuse are linked. The media takes up this idea, exaggerates, strengthens and reifies it, making it seem an established fact. By placing the idea in print, a stereotype becomes a "fact."

Gary Kinsman talks about the Hughes Royal Commission of Inquiry into Mount Cashel, the so-called "sex scandal" at the Christian Brothers orphanage in St. John's, Newfoundland. He describes how the work of the commission recreated the link between homosexuality and child sexual abuse, especially because it focused on allegations of sexual violence against male children. The media then took up this imputed link, with consequences reaching far into the community.

In the "Reading the news" section, some examples are given of how inscription worked in the media treatment of Mount Cashel, how the violence was represented as "homosexual acts." In the next section some of the larger patterns of child sexual abuse reporting are developed, showing how skewed coverage actually disguises the reality of sexual violence against children.

The talk—Gary Kinsman
The Hughes Royal Commission of Inquiry in St. John's, Newfoundland, looked at coverups of sexual and physical assault on residents of Mount Cashel in the mid-1970s. I've not been a journalist covering the royal commission, and I've not been employed by it, so my research is a critical analysis of the workings of that commission and its relationship to media coverage.

When I first went to St. John's, I had some knowledge of the different controversies around sex-related matters involving priests and adolescent boys, what had gone on at the Mount Cashel orphanage and about the royal commission. I arrived in this context as a gay man who had done work on sexuality and the policing of sexuality in a number of different locations across the country.

One of the things that became clear to me was that the media was picking up, amplifying and selecting out certain aspects of the work process of the commission and were once again associating homosexuality with child sexual abuse. Given my own experience, I've been trying to understand the relationship between this royal commission and the mass media coverage, in how it was taking up the question of homosexuality, and how it was organizing an association that was unfounded and mythological between homosexuality and child sexual abuse.

Once again the media was using the framework that there was a relationship between homosexuals and child sexual abuse. I'll just read you an account of one of the outcomes of this media coverage and the whole climate that has been organized against homosexuals in Newfoundland since some of the royal commission charges have been laid. I'm not saying that the violence against gays is in any way caused by media coverage or by such things as the Hughes Royal Commission, but I think they shape the context in which violence has taken place.

This comes from a letter that was published on June 4, 1989, in a St. John's newspaper: "Being a homosexual in Newfoundland is a difficult lifestyle due to the ignorance of the majority regarding homosexuality. The social difficulties associated with my lifestyle I have learned to accept and have learned to cope with until a recent incident of gay-bashing. The incidents of gay-bashing seem to be on the increase since the media coverage regarding the church-related sexual assaults on young boys. I was a victim of gay-bashing as I was walking home from a gay club downtown— surrounded by three adult males who verbally and physically abused me because they saw me leave the gay club. They informed me they were doing society a justice by getting rid of "another faggot child abuser." The cuts, the bruises, the broken ribs will heal, but the anger, frustration and fear will be a part of me for a long time. The fear not only stems from being beaten because of my sexual preference but also because of the sarcastic attitude of the Royal Newfoundland Constabulary officer when I reported the incident, requesting surveillance in the area so as to help others avoid the horrible beating I had received.

Now this is not just an experience that this one man had, or that I've had; this is a fairly generalized experience that lesbians and gay men have in Newfoundland. It has certainly set back the struggle for lesbian and gay rights—the provincial government is saying that sexual orientation protection in human rights legislation for the province is a "no go," at least for the present. This is also having an impact in Nova Scotia, where in the spring of 1990 the government used what was going on in Mount Cashel, the evidence that was being produced in the Hughes Commission and the media coverage, as a justification for why sexual orientation protection should not be enacted in this province as well.

How was it that this royal commission and the media coverage were once again associating homosexuality with child sexual abuse? Some accounts have been put forward in the lesbian and gay community suggesting homophobia, that individual journalists or the commission counsel were prejudiced. However, I didn't think the individual attitudes and prejudices of some of the commission counsel or some of the journalists involved in covering the royal commission actually could account for what was going on. It was a much more systemic social process. The reassociation of homosexuality with child sexual abuse was also being put together in an extralocal way, outside of our everyday lives, in the work process of this royal commission and in the work that journalists were doing in selecting out the major stories for that day.

The social process of associating homosexuality with child sexual abuse involves the gender inversion of the problem of sexual assault and harassment towards young people in our society. The perception that has been created and disseminated through the Hughes Commission and the media is that young boys are the major targets of sexual assault and harassment in our society, and that is not accurate. Feminists' concerns over violence against women, and sexual violence and harassment towards young girls in particular, have been obscured through the way in which the Hughes Commission inquiry process has been taken up in the media coverage.

This is a quote from the Working Group on Child Sexual Abuse's submission to the Hughes Commission Inquiry. They say, "the commission, however, has presented a somewhat skewed vision of abuse because it is primarily a judicial inquiry into the events of one institution. We are learning much as a result of this inquiry, but the general public is starting to believe that abuse is a religious affliction, that young boys are the primary targets, that sexual abuse is primarily a homosexual issue, that abuse happens primarily in institutions or other state-sponsored systems. We also fear that the general public response becomes that this all happened a long time ago, that we have unmasked the issues and finally taken care of the problem."

The lesbian and gay studies group at Memorial University organized a forum to dispute the association of homosexuality with child sexual abuse. We managed to gather the media's attention to another way of looking at the stories; for about a week they gave us a fair amount of coverage. The media went to the commission counsel and asked them questions almost as if we had instructed them, and we learned from the responses how it was that homosexuality was being created as the problem.

Royal commissions do important work for state institutions and agencies. They are a response available to various levels of the state when a government faces a legitimation crisis, when the criminal justice system seems no longer to have worked properly in a particular case. A royal commission is a way in which the government can set up a supposedly independent body that is going to investigate these questions. There's a number of common features to these types of commissions of inquiry. They have terms of reference that are given to them by the government which organize their work, and they're allocated funding by various state agencies.

Key to analyzing the Hughes Royal Commission are the terms of reference set by the provincial government. These organize the work process of the commissions, structuring its work, limiting what it addresses. They provide boundaries for the work and mean that certain questions are not going to get raised. Analyzing those terms of reference begins to account for how the homosexualization of the problem could take place, and also how, by focusing only on a male institution, questions of what was going on with girls and women have been completely obscured in the commission process.

Royal commissions are supposed to be independent and autonomous from the everyday workings of the state and various institutions, but that is not actually the case. One of the ways in which the state comes back into these independent legal processes is through police evidence and through different legal documents that have already been produced in various state agencies. But there's an appearance of independence, of impartiality, of objectivity which commissions have to constantly construct. In the Hughes Commission, Judge Hughes never wanted to deal with media coverage but was forced every once and a while to address it whenever it challenged the impartiality of the commission. He would take time at the beginning of the day to challenge the way in which the media was reporting on what was going on at the royal commission.

On the other hand, the commission would get taken up by the mass media as an authoritative source of news. In the *Evening Telegram*, the only daily newspaper in St. John's, it was consistently a front-page story for the first couple of months. Journalists were assigned to cover the story, and it became a major news story not only in St. John's but also across the country. So there's a relationship between the way in which the royal commission was taking up what went on at Mount Cashel and the different accounts put forward to explain it, and how the media would then pick that up.

The commission takes up forms of knowledge that have already been defined in relationship to the dominant power relations in our society, forms of knowledge that are taken for granted and just assumed in terms of how the commission works. One aspect of this "inscription" is how the term "child sexual abuse" itself is mobilized by the commission and used in the terms of reference. The people who originally raised the question of violence against young people in our society in the early 1970s were feminists doing grassroots work, raising these questions in the political context of a critique of family relations, the power of adults in our society and the power of men over younger people. There is a gendered character to this violence.

But as this term has entered into the official bureaucratic procedures of social work, government agencies and institutions, particularly through the work of the Badgley Commission in the early 1980s, all of those earlier political concerns have dropped away. We now have an administrative category of child sexual abuse which no longer raises the same types of political connotations, no longer raises fundamental criticisms of patriarchal relations in our society and the way in which masculinity is constructed and associated with violence and aggression. That's one question that the Hughes Commission of Inquiry is not exploring, the social roots of where violence toward young people comes from.

The term "child sexual abuse" is now used in a more official way in the Newfoundland context. It was not available in 1975 in official agencies, who squelched the issue of abuse at Mount Cashel. They knew about it and they prevented it from becoming a public and visible issue in collaboration with the criminal justice system, the social work system and the Catholic Church itself. But now, many of those same institutions are trying to make this a crucial issue that must be addressed. Child sexual abuse has entered into the Newfoundland context as an official, administrative category.

The second process of inscription that the Hughes Commission and media coverage depends on is the homosexualization of the issue. In the 1950s and into the 1960s there was a consistent construction of sexual violence and harassment as being not within the private realm but within the public realm, and in particular associated with notions of sexual deviancy and homosexuality. There's a mythology that homosexuals or gay men are child molesters, child sexual abusers. It doesn't have any accuracy to it, but it's still an available interpretive framework to account for and explain the problem. That discourse has been remobilized in this context, having entered into some of the initial media coverage of the Mount Cashel incident. When Shane Earl went to the *Sunday Express*, the way in which those initial stories were framed up was that homosexuality at Mount Cashel was the problem. There's also a problem in *Unholy Orders* [Harris 1990b], where this is provided as an interpretive framework for reading what went on.

Police work also defines how homosexuality becomes a problem in the royal commission. The original Detective Hillier report in 1975 that was investigating the problems at Mount Cashel was entitled "Homosexual Acts and Child Abuse at Mount Cashel Orphanage." When he wrote those reports in 1975, he intended homosexuality to be seen as the problem at Mount Cashel. That report has now been recovered and is used as a central piece of evidence in the Hughes Royal Commission. It carries with it and recreates in the late 1980s and into the 1990s this association of child sexual abuse with homosexuality, which has been a consistent part of police activity for a long time—the criminalization of homosexuality.

So the Hughes Commission is producing homosexuality as a problem, making that available for the mass media, which has taken it up as a framework of interpretation, not because of the individual prejudices of the commission counsel or of some of the journalists, but as an intrinsic part of the work process of the inquiry itself. The documents, the knowledge upon which it depends, labels homosexuality as the problem. It takes up that knowledge, it does not challenge it, it takes it for granted. It is released into the work of the royal commission, which comes to take up the standpoint of seeing homosexuality as part of the problem, and the media coverage takes up that way of framing the issue.

Reading the news

Gary Kinsman points out that the media uncritically adopts the misconception that homosexuals engage in male child sexual abuse. The problem with this is that homosexuality and child sexual abuse are not linked. There is far more sexual abuse of female children than of male and most abuse is committed by heterosexual men. Child sexual abuse is probably more a matter of power and the desire to control than of sexual orientation. Writing up the crime in this way is called "inscription," which doesn't mean misrepresentation, but rather constructing stereotypes and reproducing "matters of fact." (Raffel 1979).

The inquiry into Mount Cashel dominated the news for some time. For 1989 the *Canadian News Index* lists 238 citations on the Hughes Commission. However, early articles on Mount Cashel appear relatively innocuous, as the news brief in Article 4.1 shows. It does not mention homosexuality or details of the abuse; if anything, it is quite technical in form.

Article 4.1
Sexual abuse inquiry considered
(*Globe and Mail*, March 1, 1989, Brief)

1   **St. John's (CP)**—Government officials are considering calls for a public inquiry into
2   sexual abuse in Newfoundland, Health Minister John Collins said yesterday. But no
3   decision will be made until a study of existing data on the problem is completed. "It's in
4   a fairly preliminary stage and there is a lot of information to go through before a
5   decision is made," Mr. Collins said in an interview. There have been several calls for
6   an inquiry in the wake of a series of charges against Newfoundland priests accused of
7   sexually assaulting young boys. Support for the idea has come from members of the
8   Roman Catholic Church, provincial NDP Leader Peter Fenwick and Fisheries Minister
9   Thomas Rideout, who is running for the leadership of the provincial Conservative
10   Party. Mr. Collins said officials in the departments of Health, Justice and Social
11   Services are looking into the calls.

In the article, the problem is defined as one of studying "existing data" (line 3) and going through "information" (line 4) in order to make a decision whether an inquiry should be called (lines 1, 5–6). The matter is an official one and does not include criminal charges against priests who allegedly committed sexual assaults against young boys (lines 6–7). Various politicians, organizations and bureaucratic officials are involved in deciding whether there will be an inquiry (lines 1, 2 and 8–11). The character of this article is influenced by the fact that it appeared in the national press and was consequently compressed to include just the "facts"; articles that appeared in the Newfoundland press at about the same time are lurid in comparison, detailing personal shame and tragedy.[1] In the "Brief" reproduced in Article 4.1, there is no sense of personal shame or ordeal, simply talk about a bureaucratic process.

Article 4.2, published one year later in a St. John's newspaper, testimony from the Hughes Inquiry which addresses the question of whether there was homosexuality and sexual abuse at Mount Cashel is cited. The article is interesting precisely because it does not offer unequivocal testimony of abuse by brothers at the orphanage. In fact, the witness does not recall any abuse at Mount Cashel, although he does remember some "homosexual" behaviour among some of the boys.

Article 4.2
Former Mount Cashel resident knew of homosexual activity
(*Evening Telegram*, March 23, 1990: 1)

1   **By Cathy Finn, Telegram Staff Writer**—For the first time in weeks, a former resident
2   of the Mount Cashel Orphanage took the stand at the Hughes inquiry Thursday.

3   But unlike other young men who have told the commission devastating tales of
4   abuse, Craig English did not talk about being molested or beaten by Christian Brothers.
5   At the orphanage from April, 1974 to late December, 1975, Mr. English testified that
6   he knew of sexual activity among a small group of eight-to-10-year-olds at one of the
7   Mount Cashel dormitories in 1975.
8   Now 23, Mr. English is a nephew of Br. Edward English, one of several Christian
9   Brothers charged with sexual abuse after police re-opened their aborted 1975
10   investigation of the orphanage.
11   The witness didn't discuss his experiences at Mount Cashel with police until last
12   week, when he was reached at his home in Toronto. He made no complaints to
13   investigators at the time.
14   Commission co-counsel David Day restricted his questioning to the witness's
15   knowledge of "problems" among former residents.
16   "What sort of problems, do you mean sexual activity between boys?"
17   Yes ... between small groups of boys, five or 10, all in one dorm, really ... probably
18   eight to 10 years old," Mr. English said.
19   He never reported the activity, he told Mr. Day.
20   Mr. English couldn't remember being interviewed by anyone at Mount Cashel 15
21   years ago concerning his care and education.
22   The inquiry also heard from Tom Mills, senior Crown attorney for eastern
23   Newfoundland. Involved in the prosecution of young offenders in 1985, he recalled one
24   case in which a youth had pleaded guilty to several criminal offences.
25   One of the youth court's options, Mr. Mills said, was to place the boy in an open
26   or secure custody setting.
27   The province has three secure custody youth facilities, the Whitbourne closed
28   custody youth facility, formerly the Whitbourne Boys' Home, the Torbay Youth Home and
29   the Remand Centre in Pleasantville.
30   While the young offender had alleged sometime before 1985 that he had been
31   sexually assaulted by another boy, the lawyer said he felt no obligation to report the
32   allegation because authorities were aware of the charge.
33   "'The allegation that (the boy) had been sexually assaulted by another boy was
34   already information in the hands of social workers representing the director of child
35   welfare," Mr. Mills said. "The indication that I received was that an investigation
36   had in fact gone on. The third factor to be considered was that neither (the boy) nor the
37   parents of (the boy) wanted any further action and, in fact, were quite adamant that no
38   references be made at all (to the allegation) either in the sentence hearing, nor indeed
39   in any other proceedings."
40   Such a request by parents is not unusual, he added.
41   Mr. Mills acknowledged the boy's parents had expressed concern that their son
42   might be sent to the Whitbourne home. While the lawyer said he was personally unaware
43   in 1985 of any problems with the safety or security of youths at the home, Mr. Mills
44   recalled that concerns were raised in the House of Assembly and in the media during
45   the period.
46   "I personally had no concerns with regards to the well-being of individuals placed
47   in Whitbourne," he said.
48   In April, 1985, the report of a judicial inquiry cited negligence in the death of Alonzo
49   Corcoran, 16, who froze to death in late January, 1984, after he and another youth

50 escaped from the Whitbourne facility.
51   In his report, provincial court judge G.J. Barnable stated that given the high ratio
52 of escapes from the home in the early- to mid-1980s, "not to have addressed this problem
53 amounts to negligence on the part of the public authority responsible for the care of
54 these boys."

In the article, the witness does not talk of being molested or beaten, unlike other young men who had told "devastating tales of abuse" (lines 3–4). He did know of any sexual activity, except among young boys (lines 5–7 and 16–18). The bulk of the article (lines 22–54) is taken up with hearsay testimony from a lawyer about a young boy who alleged sexual assault by another resident at a different institution, a secure custody youth facility, an event that was never reported. Note that the headline states there was homosexuality at Mount Cashel, but then in the article it is seen that it was only among young boys—and sexual experimentation among children is not the same as sexual orientation. This witness is unlike other witnesses who did allege sexual abuse and furthermore is a nephew of one of the charged Christian brothers. So, the article constructs homosexuality as having occurred while undermining the credibility of the witness.

Several months later at a Supreme Court trial, testimony was heard about sexual behaviour on the part of priests, which served to anchor the connection between the sexual abuse and exploitation of young boys and homosexuality. Article 4.3 is unequivocal about the nature of the acts and who they were done with. There is testimony that a priest gave a homeless boy a place to stay in return for unnamed sexual favours (lines 1–3), that they had sex (lines 6–7) and that there were sexual acts with other men (lines 8–10 and 11–13). It is unclear from the account whether the sex was coerced or abusive, but the article anchors the point that these are men who have sex with males, and that they are priests who were later charged with sex-related crimes (lines 4–5 and 11–13).

Article 4.3
Priest sheltered boy for sex, trial told
(*Halifax Herald*, May 11, 1990)

1   **ST. JOHN'S, Nfld (CP)**—A Roman Catholic priest picked up a homeless 16-year-old
2   boy one night in 1976 and for six weeks gave him a place to stay in return for sexual
3   favours, the Newfoundland Supreme Court heard Thursday.
4   The boy, now 30, was testifying against Father Gordon Walsh, 41, who is on trial
5   on two sexual abuse charges.
6   The complainant testified that over the course of his stay, he had sex with Walsh
7   three or four times a week.
8   The complainant, who cannot be identified, said he was also exposed to other men

9   during his stay with Walsh. He said he passed out during a Christmas party and woke
10 up to find one man performing oral sex on him while Walsh watched.
11   At another all-male Christmas party he said he was fondled by Father James Hickey
12 — who is currently serving a five-year sentence after pleading guilty to more than 20
13 sex-related charges.
14   The complainant said he'd been in and out of foster homes and orphanages his
15 whole life — including the infamous Mount Cashel orphanage.

Various media articles cumulatively fed into the perception that homosexuals were the problem.[2] During a 1990 Newfoundland Supreme Court trial on indecent assault and gross indecency, the actions in question were defined as "homosexual acts." In 1991, during another Newfoundland Supreme Court trial, the prosecution defined the defendant as a "homosexual," as if that proves his guilt. In another article on the same case the accused was said to be "an admitted homosexual."[3]

The consequence of these characterizations is that they link homosexuality to sexual abuse against children. The specific criminal charges arose out of the Hughes Inquiry which itself constructed the same linkages. The question to be asked, however, is why homosexuality is being linked to abuse and pedophilia in a way heterosexuality never is? In one case, the judge said, while sentencing a pedophile, "Mount Cashel was torn down today."[4] In contrast, two articles and a letter to the editor on the Mount Cashel inquiry in the *Globe and Mail* pointed out that homosexuality is not the same as pedophilia.[5]

Of parallel interest, on March 11, 1994, a Halifax newspaper ran the cover headline "Pedophilia & Homosexuality—A connection?"[6] The columnist wrote about the inquiry into abuse at the Kingsclear Youth Training Centre, and how the New Brunswick Coalition on Human Rights Reform disagreed with the imputed link between homosexuality and pedophilia at the inquiry. Citing questionable statistics, the article said "only 1.1 percent of men are exclusively homosexual," but that "homosexuals are, at minimum, five and a half times more likely to molest children than are heterosexuals." The fact that the human rights group had requested a clarification of the difference between homosexuality and pedophilia was described by the columnist as merely political correctness.

On the following day, the provincial paper reported that the Gay and Lesbian Association of Nova Scotia planned to launch a human rights complaint against it.[7] A clinical psychologist was quoted as disputing the initial column, saying that most pedophiles are heterosexual, particularly in cases of incest. From there the issue quickly faded from vitriol to accusations of censorship.[8]

These examples show how the link between homosexuality and pedophilia is very much alive for some people, and that the topic continually receives play in the news. The questions that need to be asked are why is the media so willing to take up that imputed link and reproduce a discredited stereotype; why does it not show as much interest in labelling heterosexual child abusers; and why is child abuse in the family hardly discussed in the media at all? Whose interests does it serve to construct the link between abuse and homosexuality and detach it from the context of its actual occurrence?

Analyzing the news

The particular way child sexual abuse was inscribed during the Hughes Inquiry detached it from its most common location, in the family, and homosexualized it in the process. Focusing on the abuse of boys by brothers in this inquiry, and on priests in others, overlooked the view that the abuse was made possible by an institutional structure of traditional, male authority. In topicalizing the violence this way, the usual pattern of the sexual abuse of children was disguised and the abuse in this particular instance was mystified. This kind of obfuscation can be found repeatedly in news coverage in general.

It is obvious, of course, that the Hughes Commission on Mount Cashel served as a lightning rod for issues of abuse and was probably a catalyst for reports of institutional abuse in general; certainly in the intervening years there have been inquiries in many other provinces. In 1990 the *Toronto Star* published details from a 1960 confidential report into male sexual abuse in Ontario at St. Joseph's Training School in Alfred, and St. John's in Uxbridge.[9] The consequent inquiry resulted in two hundred charges against twenty-nine men at these Roman Catholic reform schools. The investigation eventually widened to include five provincial reform schools.[10] There were also charges of widespread sexual abuse against adolescent girls at the Grandview School for Girls detention centre in Cambridge, Ontario, before it closed in 1976.[11] In 1992 the police investigated sexual abuse which allegedly occurred in the 1960s at the Kingsclear Youth Training Centre in New Brunswick, and at the East Saint John Boys' Industrial Home, the New Brunswick Protestant Orphans' Home and the Dr. William F. Roberts Hospital School.[12] The subsequent inquiry was also accused of blurring the very important distinction between homosexuality and pedophilia.[13] In 1994 the Nova Scotia attorney general announced an inquiry into violent sex abuse at the former Shelburne School for Boys, an inquiry which was subsequently widened to include the Nova Scotia School for Girls in Truro.[14]

In Figure 4.1, however, it can be seen that there are important differences in the amount and duration of news coverage of various issues related to the abuse of children. The Hughes Commission received heavy coverage, with 238 citations in 1989, dropping to 45 citations in 1990. As the *Index* only covers major Canadian papers, this number does not even begin to get at the local Newfoundland newspapers such as the *Evening Telegram*, where coverage was probably at saturation level. The sexual abuse of children became a category in 1989 and, at 469 stories, had the highest number of citations in 1992. There would appear to be a blossoming of child sexual abuse cases or, more likely, the media has suddenly discovered an interest in them.

Figure 4.1
Reports on abuse of children, 1978–92

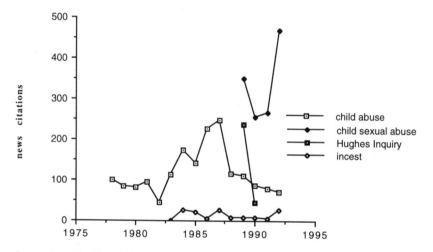

Source: Canadian News Index

Many of the citations listed under "child sexual abuse," in fact, were for trials of people named at the Hughes Inquiry. The total number of cases under this category, then, is inflated by articles that would have been listed under the Hughes Inquiry two years earlier. The interest in the sexual abuse of children is conceivably an interest in other well-publicized cases, as well, which again would inflate the citations. In 1991 the Hughes Report was published and the Mount Cashel trials started; in 1992 there were the Martensville trials in Saskatchewan, the investigation at the Grandview Reform School in Ontario, the case of the Duplessis orphans in Quebec, the ban on the film "The Boys of Saint Vincent" and the scandal at the Christian Brothers schools in Ontario. There is thus a lot of interest and publicity about the sexual abuse of children, especially if they are male.

The topic of "child abuse" has the longest continuous coverage. It climbed in the 1980s, with the highest number of citations in 1987, and then steadily fell thereafter. As the number of child abuse stories in general dropped (from 248 in 1987 to 115 in 1988, 110 in 1989, and 87 in 1990, an overall decrease of 65 percent), stories on the sexual abuse of children rose (from 256 in 1990 to 469 in 1992, an overall increase of 83 percent). The coverage of "child abuse," which includes cases of physical abuse, does not seem to have been affected by the sensational cases mentioned above. The topic of "incest" had the lowest number of citations overall, averaging slightly more than a dozen per year over the ten-year period from 1983 to 1992; most of these would be against female children by males in their family.

One way these figures and trends can be interpreted is to conclude that sexual abuse of boys by adult males in institutions is far more newsworthy than "child abuse" in general or "incest" against female children in families. The coverage is more extensive and more sensationalistic in cases where it is the least likely to occur.

More interest in extra-familial abuse of males becomes a problem if most abuse of children occurs in the home against females, for it means that sexual violence against female children has become invisible through lack of coverage. Furthermore, it means that while newspapers cover "homosexual pedophiles" they are actually missing the far greater pervasiveness of violence against children in the home by heterosexual male family members.

When we look at the statistics on child sexual abuse, gender is an important factor. In a 1991 report of a survey of police departments in Canada that analyzed almost 300,000 criminal incidents, 2,000 of which involved a violent crime against a child less than twelve years old, 56 percent of the victims were female (Juristat 1991a). Among child sexual assault victims, over two-thirds were girls. Intimacy was also a factor: in sexual assault cases, 41 percent of the accused were family members and the percentage was higher for girls (48 percent) than for boys (33 percent). Sexual assaults against children are more likely to happen in a home setting (girls 75 percent, males 63 percent) than in a public area. Type of assault was an issue too: sexual assaults comprised 50 percent of the total and physical assaults 28 percent. Boys tend to be more at risk of (non-sexual) physical assault and were more than 70 percent of its victims. For other sexual offences, such as invitation to sexual touching, two-thirds of the victims were girls.

The picture of "reality" we receive from the newspaper coverage presented above is one with a preponderance of sexual abuse, especially against boys. These cases seem to get the most media attention, as evidenced by the heavy coverage of Mount Cashel and the high number of child sexual abuse citations. The criminal statistics bear out the fact that child sexual abuse occurs more frequently than physical abuse and is largely against female children. The sexual abuse articles in the media are inflated by stories from inquiries into institutional abuse against boys. However, most child abuse (physical and sexual) is committed in the home by a family member or acquaintance. The media picture is skewed and misdirected and misnames the problem by ignoring the predominance of sexual abuse of female children, and of physical abuse of male children in the home.

A second issue, which may cast light on the first, is the role commissions of inquiry play in the maintenance of order in a modern society (Doern 1967; Sheriff 1983; Apple 1986). Royal commissions are a specific way the state can handle a legitimation crisis. If there's been a problem in the criminal justice system, for example, a commission of inquiry can be given a limited mandate to investigate and make administrative recommendations to the state on how to repair the problem without posing fundamental questions about how the problem may be rooted in deeper social relations. Their proposals may be good in certain cases but don't necessarily get at the social roots of problems. Given the way commissions function, they inevitably work in the interests of the state and, in establishing consensus, re-establish the legitimacy of the state.

A royal commission has a very authoritative air. The head of the Hughes Commission of Inquiry, for example, was a retired Ontario Supreme Court judge. With the Mount Cashel inquiry, the Hughes Commission had to deal with a very emotional and volatile issue. The Hughes Report noted that sexual abuse at the orphanage was known and hushed up in the 1970s. Other allegations were that it went back to the 1940s or 1950s. The deputy justice minister, a police chief and the Canadian head of the Christian Brothers were alleged to have arranged to send two abusers from the province in 1975. The original investigation lasted less than a week, no charges were laid and it took until 1989 to reopen the investigation. There were also allegations that reporters were told of the events in 1975 and 1976, but no stories were published about the issue.[15]

A former provincial government lawyer alleged that the former deputy minister of justice concealed from provincial child welfare officials a police report detailing physical and sexual abuse, and statements from a former member of the Royal Newfoundland Constabulary that the justice department was active in having the case dropped.[16] Moreover, there was evidence from the former director of public prosecutions that he had briefed the justice minister in 1979 about the suppression of child abuse charges in 1975. There was also evidence that social services workers knew of the abuse of one of the boys in 1976 and returned him to Mount Cashel because the abuse was considered an isolated incident.[17] Similar allegations of coverups and collusion to protect offenders at some of the institutions mentioned above were made as well.

There isn't enough space here to go into the history of allegations in the Hughes Inquiry, the recommendations published in the report, the outcome of the subsequent court trials, the media coverage in books and the like (Newfoundland and Labrador 1991; Harris 1990b). However, the point being made here is that the inquiry was needed so someone could be seen to be doing something about the abuse at Mount Cashel after the incidents had occurred and been known about for years.

The crisis of legitimation for Mount Cashel was also a crisis of confidence in the criminal justice system itself and its ability to protect children. The inquiry focused attention on a case which was potentially embarrassing to the criminal justice system, especially after the high level of collusion in silencing the victims and protecting the guilty had become apparent. By highlighting the homosexuality of the brothers, rather than the pedophilia, attention could be drawn to a small minority of an already stigmatized group and away from institutional culpability and abuse of power and authority.

This same legerdemain, or sleight of hand, is routinely accomplished as child abuse is topicalized in the media, when attention is drawn away from the family and the relationships of intimacy and gender where abuse routinely occurs. The treatment of the issue of child abuse in general fulfils the same implicit need to preserve the legitimacy of the status quo.

Government officials do not necessarily set up commissions of inquiry to protect themselves from scrutiny and put the blame on homosexuals, but the misplacement of blame is not simply a mistake. From a larger point of view, the news media misses the crime. First of all, there is a tendency to devote a lot of coverage to institutional abuse and neglect intrafamilial violence and, secondly, there is a tendency to focus on marginalizing and individualizing the problem instead of focusing on how structural relations of authority and power make it possible in the first place. Commissions of inquiry can fall into this trap just as well as the media; in so doing they create a mutually reaffirming myth of blame that leaves most everyone comfortable, thinking that justice has been served, when the very conditions which enabled the violence to occur have not been addressed.

In the final analysis, the Hughes Commission needed to rectify the imbalance and re-establish the status quo, to restore faith in the criminal justice system and identify dangerous offenders in the community. And the media performed its role of returning affairs to "normal" as well.

Summary

We see in the media coverage of Mount Cashel that the consequence of airing dirty laundry through the Hughes Inquiry was to focus attention on the physical and sexual abuse of male children by adult males in an institutional setting. Those crimes certainly did happen and deserve to be reported. However, in the process, *child abuse*, a term originally developed to describe the abuse of female children in families, became inscribed with new meaning, as abuse outside families. Through the second inscription of homosexuality and pedophilia, the danger was posed so as to focus blame on an already stigmatized group. Danger was marginalized and legitimation was restored.

The consequence of such inscriptions is to make the violence against female and male children in the home invisible and to miss the point that abuse of power and authority is not about sexual orientation. In these ways both the reporting on the inquiry and media coverage in general keep society safe from the dangerous questions and return us to the status quo, to confidence that things are as they should be.

As for Mount Cashel, in the end some brothers went to jail, several of the former residents went on the Geraldo show and the orphanage was torn down. A proposal was made to build a McDonald's on the site but was unsuccessful.

Notes

1. "Mount Cashel nightmare: the infancy of shame," *Sunday Express*, March 19, 1989: 1; "The ordeal of Shane Earle: return to Mount Cashel," *Sunday Express*, March 26, 1989: 1.

2. "Lawyer for defence argues boys consented to homosexual acts," *Evening Telegram*, May 17, 1990: 6; "Man accused of sexually assaulting boys at Mount Cashel is a homosexual, trial told," *Evening Telegram*, May 4, 1991: 2.

3. "Accused in sexual assault trial claims not knowing witnesses," *Evening Telegram*, May 7, 1991: 2.

4. "Court of Appeal cuts sentence for homosexual pedophile minister to six years," *Vancouver Sun*, January 19, 1994: B5; "'Monstrous' pedophile gets 6 years," *Toronto Star*, July 25, 1992: A3; "'Trusted man molested boys for 3 decades," *Toronto Star*, July 24, 1992: A1; "Serial pedophile fears he'll abuse boys again," *Toronto Star*, June 2, 1994: A4.

5. "Abuse not the same as homosexuality, gay man tells panel," *Globe and Mail*, July 8, 1989; "Not a homosexual scandal but a frightening abuse of power," *Globe and Mail*, November 3, 1989: A7; "Stop searching for scapegoats," *Sunday Express*, July 16, 1989: 7.

6. "If the shoe fits," *Metro Weekly*, March 11, 1994: 12, column.

7. "Anti-gay column prompts complaint," *Halifax Herald*, March 12, 1994: A4.

8. "If the shoe fits," *Metro Weekly*, March 11, 1994: 12; "Anti-gay column prompts complaint," *Halifax Herald*, March 12, 1994: A4; "Gays Move to Muzzle Media, Free speech, freedom of press should not be sacrificed

for convenience of special interests!" *Metro Weekly*, March 18, 1994: 5; "We must be able to express opinions," *Daily News*, March 20, 1994: 22.

9. "Reform school sex abuse case winding down," *Toronto Star*, May 1, 1993: A17.

10. "$23m fund established for male sex assault victims," *Halifax Herald*, June 9, 1993: A16; "MPP alleges sexual abuse 'cover-up,'" *Toronto Star*, May 29, 1993: A14.

11. "Ex-reform school inmates charge staff abused them," *Montreal Gazette*, January 3, 1992: B1; "Ontario cabinet minister quits over sex allegations," *Daily News*, February 14, 1992: 12; "Sex for smokes claimed rule at reform school," *Vancouver Sun*, January 3, 1992: A5; "Ontario attempting to decide abused girls' compensation," *Montreal Gazette*, February 1, 1993: A7; "Province still fighting release of abuse report," *Toronto Star*, May 3, 1993: A12; "Former Grandview guard released on bail," *Toronto Star*, March 17, 1994: A28; "MPP cleared of Grandview sex charges," *Toronto Star*, June 15, 1994: A1.

12. "Saint John abuse allegations being investigated," *Halifax Herald*, December 10, 1992: C11; "Inquiry postponed into sexual abuse at reform school," *Halifax Herald*, October 5, 1993: A8; "Toft fails lie-detector test about link with Hatfield," *Daily News*, August 23, 1994: 8; "N.B. sex abuse probe closed to public," *Toronto Star*, December 2, 1993: A16; "Boy tried to kill abuser with 'rat pie,' inquiry told," *Daily News*, December 8, 1993: 10; "From the mouths of abused children," *Globe and Mail*, December 20, 1993: A4; "Reformatory boys say cries for help were ignored," *Daily News*, December 14, 1993: 17; "Questions remain unanswered as Kingsclear probe adjourns," *Globe and Mail*, February 28, 1994: A8; "Lawyer wants to know why cops didn't charge Kingsclear guard," *Daily News*, June 10, 1994: 10; "Staff knew of abuse, inquiry told," *Toronto Star*, January 6, 1994: A10; "Bureaucrats axed over Toft affair," *Halifax Herald*, September 23, 1994: A15.

13. "Kingsclear testimony 'feeds homophobia,'" *Halifax Herald*, January 18, 1994: A6; "Homosexuals sullied by N.B. inquiry, gay-rights advocate says," *Globe and Mail*, January 18, 1994: A3.

14. "Sex-abuse probe OK'd," *Daily News*, November 3, 1994: 3; "No full-scale sex inquiry, Gillis decides," *Halifax Herald*, November 3, 1994: A1; "Betraying the children," *Halifax Herald*, November 4, 1994: B1, editorial; "Province widens mandate of investigation into abuse," *Halifax Herald*, November 8, 1994: A1; "Nova Scotia resists investigating girls' school," *Halifax Herald*, November 4, 1994: A1.

15. "Abuse was covered up, Cashel probe says," *Montreal Gazette*, April 25, 1992: A5; "Sex abuse investigation reopened in St. John's," *Globe and Mail*, February 17, 1989: np; "Lawyer says media dozing when

abuse claims arose," *Globe and Mail*, November 1, 1989: np.

16. "Former official concealed report of orphanage abuse, panel told," *Globe and Mail*, February 21, 1990: np; "Was unaware of problems at Mount Cashel Orphanage, former justice minister says," *Globe and Mail*, March 30, 1990: np.
17. "Minister was aware of allegations in 1979, Cashel inquiry told," *Halifax Herald*, January 24, 1990: np; "Boy returned to orphanage after beating, inquiry told," *Halifax Herald*, January 31, 1990: np.

5

AIDS Fiends and High-risk Groups: Misrepresenting and Signifying a Disease

Having AIDS is not a crime, but it is often distorted in the news and has been reported as associated with gay men, drug users, prostitutes and other "deviant" groups. Feeding into the hysteria, authorities have called for quarantine and segregation of people "infected" with the disease, as was done in Haiti and Cuba. Further heightening the fear, in Canada and the United States people have been charged with criminal offences for exposing other people to the human immuno-deficiency virus (HIV).

In his presentation, Eric Smith talks about how acquired immune deficiency syndrome (AIDS) is misrepresented in the media. For example, the stereotyping of "AIDS carriers" and the misidentification of who is at risk has created social panic over the disease.

In "Reading the news" we look at articles that contain alarmist characterizations of AIDS and portray it as being spread by deviant, marginal groups to the so-called "general population." Although many sensitive and thoughtful articles have been written about AIDS, the news examined here construct a sense of danger threatening to the broader community. Through the misrepresentation of AIDS in the news, there is a tendency to find scapegoats for the problem and to blame it on certain marginalized groups in society. Consequently, many "normal" people still do not perceive themselves to be at risk. The metaphor of demonization is also coupled with the metaphor of plague: it is implied that people who are contagious spread AIDS through casual contact.

The next section, "Analyzing the news," looks at the broader coverage of AIDS, focusing on how the threat of AIDS is topicalized as a "risk" in a way that creates a signification crisis, where the symbolic exaggeration of threat actually makes the problem worse (Hall et al. 1978; Becker 1973).

The Krever Inquiry into Canada's blood is uncovering new evidence of the prejudice and negligence which contributed to the spread of AIDS among hemophiliacs in Canada but does not address the wider symbolic misrepresentations that continue to contribute to the spread of the disease.

The talk—Eric Smith

I have two responses on how I think the media has dealt with AIDS issues. In my own case the media has been very good. If the media is dealing with a person who they see as an underdog, then you'll be treated fairly and they'll run stories that you like. However, if you look at AIDS issues in general, the news media tends not to do a very good job in covering them. Unfortunately the media is probably only a couple of steps ahead of the government in the way it deals with AIDS issues in general, and there are several problems that I want to mention that I think tie in a bit.

First of all, as nosey as media people can be, when it comes to AIDS issues they're very willing to simply accept and print the press releases the government hands out. They don't check to see if anything that the government is saying is right, they simply run it. There are a number of examples, and if you want to get an idea of the poor job the media's done there's a book called *And the Band Played On*, which details some of the problems with the media.

One of the first news stories on AIDS was done I guess in the fall of 1982, and at that particular time AIDS researchers were trying to get some money out of Ronald Reagan so they could increase their research. When the press decided to cover the story, the PR people put out press releases that indicated there wasn't a problem. For instance, at the time the articles were written in fact there were only twelve people in the federal government working on AIDS issues. However, the PR people issued statements saying that there was a seventy-five-member Centre for Disease Control task force working on the issue. Two weeks later, when *Time* magazine did an article on it, the press releases had increased that to 120 people. And instead of reporters checking to see if those numbers were right, they simply ran the story.

We find the same thing here in Nova Scotia. At the end of 1990 the press ran a story saying that the Department of Health declared there were only five AIDS deaths in Nova Scotia in all of 1990. Anybody working in any of the AIDS groups in Nova Scotia will tell you that that's very far off the mark. At our organization [People Living with AIDS Coalition] we keep a memorial book where we keep track of names of people who have died. We have 11 or 12 names in the book for 1990, plus there are 3 or 4 more others who died that we're aware of, but we don't know their names. But it's the same thing, the press is quite content to run what comes from the government.

Furthermore, when the government is attacked on issues like not doing enough on AIDS education, one of their typical responses is that all the education we need to be giving people is to tell them not to have sex with prostitutes. And unfortunately those are the stories that get printed, with headlines that prostitutes are a major problem as far as spreading AIDS in Nova Scotia. So it would be nice if reporters could do a bit of follow-up on the things that come from the government.

Although I think the press is improving, one of the other issues that was especially a problem in the early 1980s, before it was even called AIDS, was the fact that the press simply wouldn't write stories about it. No self-respecting newspaper wanted to print articles about "those kind of people." And in fact that's exactly what we saw. If you look back you find the stories did not really start until it was white heterosexual males who were becoming infected. Once those acceptable people were becoming infected, then it was okay to print the stories. By and large, that attitude is changing.

The press, certainly in Nova Scotia, has done a fair amount of coverage on AIDS issues in the last while. But compare the number of early press stories on AIDS to the way they handle certain other problems. For instance, in the fall of 1982 there was a big scare when several people died from taking Tylenol that someone had put cyanide in. The *New York Times* ran a story every day during the month of October, plus twenty-three stories in the two months following that. However, in the first two years of the AIDS epidemic they managed to write six stories. You can also compare that with the press coverage of the outbreak of Legionnaire's disease. That was in the press every day. But because of the group that was affected—veterans, who are acceptable people for most of society—it was all right to run stories on them.

Another issue the press seems to have a hard time dealing with is appropriate language to use, and we keep trying to train media people to use or not use certain words, but some of them just don't get it. It may not be fair to blame the reporters themselves, as I'm not sure who writes the headlines, for that may be the problem of people higher up. One of the words that we don't like is the word "victim." Personally, if someone calls me an "AIDS victim" it doesn't bother me. After several years at Cape Sable Island I've been called a lot worse, so the word "victim" doesn't bother me.

The problem is, though, with AIDS we're moving to a stage where it is seen as a long-term, manageable illness. We're trying to get people who are infected to stop seeing it as a death sentence. They keep seeing these words with negative overtones, and it makes it very hard to convince them, in fact, that they may have a long time ahead of them. In Halifax there was certainly a lot of upset at the headline several years ago, "AIDS Fiend Strikes Again." I think most people in the AIDS community found it inappropriate.

One phrase that does bother me is "admitted homosexuals." Every time I read my name in the paper, I'm "an admitted homosexual." If they have to discuss my orientation at all, can't they just say "homosexual?" The day

I read about "admitted heterosexual Premier Cameron," then fine, I'll accept "admitted."

There are also times when reporters are inaccurate in the language they use. When I had a press conference saying that I would not be returning to the classroom for the next year due to stress, I thought it had been made clear to all the reporters that it was stress related, it had nothing to do with progression of full-blown AIDS. However, most of the press I saw talked about deteriorating health. The impression that you get is that probably in a couple of years I won't be around. That's not my plan, I hope to be here in a couple of years so I can still torment certain people.

One thing I've complained to some reporters about is the lack of follow-up. They do a story and you wait for a few days to see what's going to happen, or what the next step is, and you don't hear any more. I'm thinking in particular of the Nova Scotia Task Force on AIDS, reported on in the fall of 1988. The government at the time said it was accepting thirty-nine of forty-seven recommendations. I don't know that anybody has ever gone back to check.

One of the task force recommendations in 1988 was that HIV infection, and other illnesses that are transmitted the same way, be protected in the Human Rights Act. Well, in 1988 the minister of health at the time, Joel Matheson, said the government wasn't going to accept that because they thought it was already protected under the disabilities section of the Human Rights Act. Several weeks ago [1991] Attorney General Joel Matheson was asked what would happen if I were to take my case to the Human Rights Commission. He said, well, I certainly had the right to do so, but he wasn't sure I would win because he didn't think disability included HIV. So you get rather bizarre messages from government and nobody seems to be there to pick up on them.

The last thing I think would be nice is if media outlets could use the same reporter to cover all these issues. For some issues, or at certain times, you get reporters who seem to know as much about AIDS as you do, and within the space of five minutes they've got their story all wrapped up. At other times you get reporters who don't know much more than how to spell the word. Obviously I certainly have my favourites in the press that I prefer to talk to. At the same time there are other press people who come in the door and I think, where can I hide?

We had the situation several months ago where one of the AIDS groups, ACT-UP, presented a cake to the advisory commission on AIDS just to let them know that they were going to be keeping an eye on what they were doing. For ACT-UP the issue they were concerned about was anonymous testing. The press happened to be there and asked a few questions, so one of the spokespeople for ACT-UP was talking about why they thought anonymous testing was really important, and just out of the blue the next question was, "Does this mean you're also going to be protesting against the Gulf War?" So, it's clear there are extremes in reporters.

I would like to see the media in general take a bigger role in doing education on AIDS issues. I know some press people don't think the media should be doing education, but if we have to wait for the government in this province to do it, they're going to be a hell of a lot of people who are dead.

I'll close with my favourite line from the media. When I'm doing interviews with the CBC I'm usually introduced as "Nova Scotia's most well-known homosexual and carrier of the AIDS virus." If it points out anything, it's certainly shown me that I chose the wrong way to become famous. There must be a better way.

Reading the news

Eric Smith identifies several issues associated with the reporting on AIDS in the news media: inappropriate language such as "victims," an inordinate focus on the sexual orientation of a person if they are not heterosexual, a disinterest in the disease when it was seen as simply the "gay plague," and inadequate education on the disease and its prevention. These problems can be grouped together as a mistake or as a problem of inadequate representation, but they can also be seen as the way AIDS is misrepresented—they are its metaphors (Sontag 1990).

From the very earliest days of AIDS reporting, it has been associated with gay men (Shilts 1987; Kinsella 1989; Watney 1989). Article 5.1 is an early news report. The term "gay plague" is used overtly (line 2), as if there actually is such a disease. Then, however, this label is referred to as a nickname (line 4) for a disease which is mysterious, deadly and rare (lines 1–3). The article reports that "groups" other than homosexuals are also at risk (lines 5–7), such as intravenous drug users. Furthermore, it is mentioned that AIDS was discovered five years earlier and, although researchers are uncertain of its origin or cause, there is speculation that it is contracted and transmitted sexually or through blood (lines 1214). It is important to note, however, that in 1994, in spite of this knowledge about transmission, there was still no large-scale screening of blood products or mass education campaigns on safer sex.

Article 5.1
15 Canadians reported killed by "gay plague"
(*Winnipeg Free Press*, February 19, 1983: 15)

1   **KITCHENER, Ont (CP)**—Acquired immune deficiency syndrome a mysterious,
2   often fatal disease known as the gay plague—has claimed the lives of at least 15

3   Canadians since it was first reported in this country one year ago.
4   Despite its nickname and a general belief the disease affects only male homosexuals,
5   other groups—including Haitians, intravenous drug users and their sexual partners and
6   hemophiliacs—have contracted the disease and are considered at risk. Some children
7   also have been identified as suffering from the syndrome.
8   A total of 26 Canadians have been diagnosed during the last year as having the
9   disease, which breaks down the body's natural defences, leaving victims susceptible to
10   infections such as pneumonia and cancer, the Kitchener-Waterloo Record says in a
11   copyright article.
12   It has no known cure and researchers are uncertain of the origin or cause. They
13   have speculated it might be transmitted by sexual contact or through the blood.
14   The mortality rate since the disease was discovered five years ago in the U.S. is
15   between 40 and 60 per cent.
16   One of the Canadian victims last year was a 36-year-old man from adjoining
17   Waterloo who died in October, The Record says.

The article is definitive and unequivocal in identifying the groups at risk—male homosexuals, Haitians, hemophiliacs, intravenous drug users and their sexual partners. This characterization makes the disease seem marginal, as not affecting most people, but only members of minority or deviant groups, groups that are small in number and not very important. In the early media discourse on AIDS, such characterizations structured the difference between what were considered to be "high-risk groups" and "the general population." Athough AIDS is identified in the article as no longer solely a gay disease, it is still consistently presented as marginal. Sexual activity and blood products could imply a threat to anybody, but that link is not constructed, as it would break the normalized ideology of how the virus is transmitted. Although the article expresses uncertainties about transmission, the danger is construed to be for "those people" who are at risk. Regardless of how true the article was in terms of the knowledge at the time, the consequence of characterizing AIDS as a marginal threat makes it seem like something that should be worried about.

Article 5.2 contains an attitude that was not uncommon in the early 1980s but should have been uncommon in 1988. The health minister of Nova Scotia is said to have advocated quarantining "AIDS carriers," conjuring up the image of a contagious plague.

Article 5.2
Politicians want AIDS carriers in quarantine
(*Calgary Herald,* January 13, 1988: B3)

1   **HALIFAX (CP)**—Two Nova Scotia politicians are suggesting that some AIDS
2   carriers be quarantined.
3   Health Minister Joel Matheson and Halifax Mayor Ron Wallace said it is in the best

4   interest of the public to separate from the rest of the community those AIDS carriers
5   who are sexually active and spreading the disease.
6   Matheson said his department and legal experts are investigating whether he has
7   the power to include AIDS carriers among those he can quarantine.
8   Wallace also called for the quarantine of some AIDS sufferers to help stop the
9   spread of the disease.
10   Halifax police are currently looking for a bisexual male who recently infected two
11   women with the AIDS antibody.
12   However, the director of Manitoba's communicable disease control office said
13   rubber gloves are not needed to safeguard health workers from AIDS when handling
14   bodily fluids other than blood or semen.
15   Dr. Margaret Fast said she has rejected advice from the federal government and
16   Centres for Disease Control in Atlanta that gloves be used by staff when handling any
17   bodily fluid, even tears or saliva.
18   "So often with public health ... some things would not hurt, but they don't help," Fast
19   said.
20   She said there is no proof anything except blood and semen can transmit the virus,
21   although the virus has been detected in small quantities in other bodily fluids.

This article construes the danger as from the outside, from sexually active AIDS carriers who are spreading the disease (lines 4–5). The "fear of plague" sentiment is buoyed by the report that Halifax police are looking for a bisexual male who infected two women (lines 10–11). It is now a police matter, a criminal matter and not just political grandstanding. The report does not say that there were two cases of human immunodeficiency virus (HIV) transmission during heterosexual sex, but that a "bisexual male" infected two women, reflecting earlier accounts.[1] The danger is constructed as one of "normal" women being contaminated by a sexually deviant man.

The rest of the article (lines 12–21) is written from the point of view of health management and appears a bit nonsensical because it is unrelated to specific incidents in Nova Scotia. The article quotes the director of Manitoba's communicable disease control office on how to prevent the spread of AIDS to health workers. It again raises the spectre of HIV being present in bodily fluids other than semen or blood. However, the disease control director offers no information on how to practice safer sex. The article explicitly deviantizes the transmission of disease, while the subtext anchors the perception that AIDS is a problem for the authorities: politicians, the police and health workers.

The tone of the article is alarmist and at the same time patronizing. The image is one of a bisexual man preying on innocent women, and that police and politicians are involved. However, there is no health or safety information, leaving the public to misconstrue the nature of AIDS transmission.

Eight months later there is a follow-up article (Article 5.3) to the previous news story. A front-page banner headline read: "AIDS Fiend

Strikes Again." The article says official concern over the "bisexual man" infecting women with AIDS has continued and escalated. The health minister, the police chief and the director of the Atlantic Health Unit say there is an AIDS carrier "knowingly" spreading the disease (lines 1–4). The man is once again identified as a "bisexual AIDS carrier" who has so far infected three women with the "virus" (lines 8–10). The "public" is being threatened and it is serious enough that the police are involved (lines 11–14). Certain key words are emphasized, establishing the metaphor of threat: "AIDS carrier" or "male carrier" is mentioned five times in the article, "disease" is mentioned once and "virus" five times.

Article 5.3
AIDS Fiend Strikes Again
(*Halifax Herald*, September 19, 1988: A1)

1   **By DALE MADILL, Staff Reporter**—Health Minister Joel Matheson and Halifax
2   Police Chief Blair Jackson knew up to 10 days ago that an AIDS carrier is knowingly
3   spreading the disease in the city, Atlantic Health Unit director Dr. David MacLean
4   said Sunday.
5   "The information the police are now acting on was furnished to them by our
6   department," said Dr. MacLean. "Probably within the last 10 days we first brought it
7   to their attention."
8   He confirmed that a bisexual AIDS carrier linked to two Halifax women who tested
9   positive for AIDS last spring has been linked once again in Halifax to a woman who is
10 six months pregnant and also tested positive for the virus.
11   "My concern of course is that the public is being exposed to a very serious health
12 hazard," Mr. Matheson said. "The police are the appropriate agency to handle the
13 situation and I cannot make any further comment due to the sensitivity of the matter
14 both in legal terms and otherwise."
15   While Mr. Matheson declined to categorically confirm the existence of the AIDS
16 carrier or comment on what police or Health Department response might be expected,
17 he did admit to "being fully aware of the situation" and said he would be following its
18 progress.
19   Dr. MacLean said he has previously met with the four individuals involved in the
20 case but does not know the immediate whereabouts of the male carrier, although the
21 man's recent presence in Halifax has been confirmed.
22   In addition to the three women, who tested positive for the virus, there is a 60
23 percent chance the pregnant woman's baby will also contract the virus.
24   Officials of the Halifax Police Department, Attorney General's Office, and the
25 Department of Health were consulted on appropriate action, Dr. MacLean said, adding
26 that the problem is now in the hands of the police and not the Health Department.
27   Halifax Police Chief Blair Jackson could not be contacted for comment.
28   AIDS-related charges in Canada and the United States have ranged from willfully
29 attempting to injure, to attempted murder.
30   A Toronto prostitute, whose identity was made public by police when she admitted

31 to being an AIDS carrier, threatened to sue the Toronto Police Department in January
32 1987 after she was tormented by public attention.
33   Dr. MacLean said efforts to curb the fear associated with AIDS through education
34 programs will suffer a "setback" because of the incident, although it drives home the
35 point that every individual must take responsibility for protecting themselves.
36   "I don't have any doubt that this will add fuel to the fire of those who feel that
37 people that carry the virus should be locked up ... but when you are dealing with
38 human behaviour it is not surprising that, at some point in time, you would find this."
39   The incubation period for the AIDS virus can be several years and the long-term
40 survival rate for those developing AIDS-related symptoms remains zero, he said.

The first part of the article details the facts of the "bisexual AIDS carrier," but the second part ranges more widely to similar situations in the United States where people have been charged with willfully attempting to injure and with attempted murder (lines 28–29), presumably for knowingly spreading the disease, although the article simply mentioned "AIDS-related charges." The tone of the article is alarmist, painting the picture of a deviant and dangerous bisexual man who has already infected three women and one unborn baby and could be subsequently charged with a criminal offence.

The facts, however, are not simply reported by the article as much as constructed by the words used to describe the case. The authenticity of the account is based on quotations from the health minister and the director of the Atlantic Health Unit. The danger of the bisexual AIDS carrier is linked to past cases in the spring and to a prostitute in Toronto. The director tacitly legitimates the opinion of those who argue for quarantine and expresses the opinion that it is human nature that (some) people will knowingly act irresponsibly (lines 36–38). The conclusion is alarmist, that the disease can remain hidden for several years and the survival rate is zero (lines 39–40). The article also gives an indication of risk to the general population. Typically, authorities have emphasized the notion of "who is at risk" rather than what activities can put a person at risk. Thus, they are responsible for the fact that most people don't think they themselves are at risk.

More and more cases have appeared in the news of people charged with various criminal offences for what could be described as acts of omission. These cases reinforce the criminal character of AIDS. The man identified in the above articles was subsequently found guilty of criminal negligence causing bodily harm and sentenced to three years in prison.[2] In another case in Vancouver, a woman was charged with aggravated sexual assault for not telling two men she had sex with that she was HIV positive.[3] In a civil case in Ontario, a woman sued her divorced husband because he was a "practising bisexual . . . [and knew] his sexual practices put him in a high-risk category for contracting AIDS," but did not tell her.[4]

In a long-standing case, a man was arrested in Vancouver in 1991 on charges laid in Ontario of aggravated assault, criminal negligence causing bodily harm, and common nuisance. He was alleged to have infected three unidentified women and of subsequently violating a celibacy order. In 1993 he was tried in Ontario, acquitted of the aggravated sexual assault charges in May and died in July before the judge could deliver a verdict on the remaining charges. In December the judge said he would not deliver a verdict posthumously.[5] A compensation board finally awarded each of three victims $15,000 but ruled that one victim's sexual behaviour had contributed to her acquiring HIV, suggesting that "a reasonable person wouldn't be so quick to hop into bed." Later, a *Toronto Star* editorial pointed out that the only question for the compensation board should have been whether the women were victims of a crime, not whether it approved of their relationships.

Some cases of AIDS transmission have been seen as acts of commission. An HIV-positive prisoner in the United States was convicted of attempted murder for biting a prison guard, and it was ruled that it did not matter whether the virus could be transmitted through a bite as long as he believed it could.[6] In a similar case, a prisoner at the Guelph Correctional Centre in Ontario was sentenced to three months for biting a guard.[7] A man with AIDS in New York was charged with attempted murder and jailed in a state psychiatric centre for biting an emergency services technician;[8] and a man committed robberies in Los Angeles by threatening people with a blood-filled syringe.[9]

In what was continually described as a "bizarre case," a man and a woman were charged with conspiracy to commit murder after injecting an Edmonton man with blood contaminated with the HIV virus. The murder conspiracy charges against the man were subsequently dropped for lack of evidence, but the woman remained charged with aggravated assault and threatening to cause death or serious bodily harm.[10] In another case, the Supreme Court of Canada in 1993 upheld the conviction of a man found guilty in 1989 of committing a common nuisance by endangering the lives or health of the public.[11]

By late 1992, more than twenty-five American states had laws that forbade passing or intentionally exposing others to the "AIDS virus."[12] In United States cases, victims of sexual assault have gone to court to compel their attackers to have HIV tests but have not always been successful.[13] In Canada there is no specific law regarding the same, but by 1994 one was under consideration.[14] In the meantime, ordinary provisions in the Criminal Code such as assault are used to charge people instead. However, there is no unanimity on how to deal with people who transmit HIV. In 1992 in British Columbia it was decided to use more caution in dealing with HIV-infected people who are having unprotected sex, in order not to scare off people from being tested for the virus. Deciding to treat the matter as a health issue rather than a criminal one, charges would be considered only in cases of so-called "sexual predators," whatever that might mean.[15]

The purpose of citing these cases is not to show that people with HIV or AIDS are dangerous, but rather that there is a tendency to treat HIV and AIDS as a plague, and people with the syndrome as a threat to society. However, certain *categories* of people are not dangerous—people are at risk from certain *behaviour* which might expose them to the virus. However, as these sensational cases demonstrate, it is easy to invoke the power of criminal law to protect "us from them." In a case in Oregon, a man was convicted of third-degree assault and reckless endangerment for not telling his girlfriend he was HIV positive.[16] In sentencing him to no sex for five years, the judge said, "How do you fashion a sentence for someone who has a fatal illness? . . . In one sense, he has already received the ultimate punishment." It seems the judge thought of AIDS not as a disease, but as a judgement against people who are already guilty, sinners who then assault innocent people. Such a characterization contributes to the demonization of AIDS.

Analyzing the news

In the previous section we looked at a dominant theme in AIDS coverage: the portrayal of a plague-like disease spread by sexual predators to an innocent public. In this section, we look at some larger patterns in AIDS reporting. The first striking thing about AIDS in the news is the simple enormity and intensity of coverage. AIDS has been the subject of extensive reporting in the press, especially since being seen as a disease that threatens "the general population." Figure 5.1 is a graphic representation of the explosion of articles on AIDS listed by the *Canadian News Index* since 1983, the first year articles on AIDS appeared there.

In 1983 and 1984, articles on AIDS are indexed under "diseases." There were 99 articles in 1983 and 112 the following year. By 1985, "AIDS" had its own category and 643 articles were indexed for the year. This 474 percent increase in news articles shows that HIV/AIDS has gone from being considered as a relatively rare disease to being seen as a major health threat. By 1987 there were 1,423 entries, the highest number during the 1980s. The number dropped but remained steady for 1988 and 1989, and then dropped to 578 in 1990 as interest in the new-found epidemic waned. However, interest in the topic did not disappear but became broader and more focused. Beginning in 1991 there was a new subcategory, "AIDS and women," which along with "AIDS and health care workers" received increasing attention. The numbers rose again overall in 1991 and 1992.

A more intensive analysis would be needed to document the type of coverage and how or whether it changed during the 1980s. However, the sheer increase in news articles on AIDS shows it is being seen as more and

Figure 5.1
AIDS stories, 1983–92

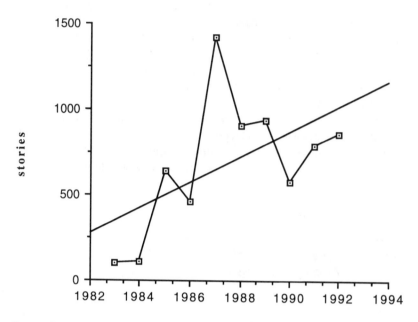

Source: Canadian News Index

more of a health threat, rather than simply as a rare disease which affects a small subgroup of society.

The growth of articles on AIDS reveals the extent to which this disease dominates the news. In a science column in the *Globe and Mail,* Stephen Strauss commented on how some diseases are reported more than others. Writing in 1993, he said that in the previous two years six hundred stories were published on AIDS, six on arthritis, eleven on prostate cancer, twenty-five on diabetes and forty-four on heart diseases. Cancers killed 50,749 Canadians in 1988 but were written about only 219 times, while only 1,097 people died of AIDS in 1991 but the disease received more extensive coverage. The Laboratory Centre for Disease Control is quoted as saying that less than two hundred women died of AIDS between 1990 and 1992, reported in twenty-five articles, but ten thousand women died of breast cancer, an issue written about thirty-nine times. The reasons given for the preponderance of coverage of AIDS are that it is incurable, strikes a prurient chord and is about "sex, death, and criminality."[17]

After establishing that AIDS coverage grew through the 1980s, the second pattern that is important to look at is how "being at risk from AIDS" is portrayed in the news media. Having AIDS is not a crime, but by being linked to "deviant" groups, it was certainly treated that way in the early 1980s. Initially it was linked to the "deviant lifestyle" of gay men, prostitution and the use of illegal drugs, and not until later was it seen as a threat to "other people" in society. The unfortunate consequence of the early typification of AIDS is that it created a way of "signifying" the disease that persisted long after it became patently untrue. The consequence of the early deviant signification of AIDS kept people from seeing their own risk, which increased the spread of the virus.

In 1983, the first year the CNI listed "AIDS" articles, there were ninety-nine citations, some of which were reproduced on microfilm in the CPNewsFile (or later in CNI Clips). The list in Figure 5.2 outlines how the "risk" was portrayed: who was at risk, what causes the disease and how it is spread:

Figure 5.2
Representing risk, AIDS in the news, 1983

"Specialist warns of AIDS epidemic"
> (*Winnipeg Free Press*, January 13, 1983: 18)

cause: "AIDS—a mysterious disease"

"15 Canadians reported killed by 'gay plague'"
> (*Winnipeg Free Press*, February 19, 1983: 15)

cause: "a mysterious, often fatal disease known as the gay plague" "researchers are uncertain of the origin or cause . . . might be transmitted by sexual contact or through the blood."

at risk: "male homosexuals . . . Haitians, intravenous drug users and their sexual partners and hemophiliacs"

"Man contracted AIDS through 'plain bad luck'"
> (*Halifax Herald*, July 2, 1983: 43)

cause: "It was just plain bad luck . . . Little is known about it"

at risk: "it is most prevalent among homosexuals, Haitians, intravenous drug users and hemophiliacs . . . AIDS is not believed to be a threat to the general public"

spread: "doctors . . . believe it is spread by bodily fluids such as semen, saliva and blood . . . homosexuals are being warned to limit their sexual partners and maintain a healthy lifestyle."

"AIDS strikes fear, baffles MDs" (*Winnipeg Free Press*, July 4, 1983: 15)

cause: "Its cause is a mystery . . . 'It's quite inexplicable.'"

at risk: "But researchers, while describing it as one of the most serious health threats in the history of modern medicine, stress that the general public has little to fear
. . . no health care workers—outside the high-risk groups—have ever contracted it . . . AIDS is most likely to be contracted by homosexual and bisexual men, Haitians, intravenous drug users and hemophiliacs."

spread: "There is no evidence it can be passed through the air or by mosquitoes"

"AIDS panic unfounded, experts say" (*Vancouver Sun*, July 7, 1983: A15)

cause: "An infectious diseases specialist has blamed 'sensational media coverage and poorly-informed doctors' for panic about AIDS . . . Researchers do not yet know what causes AIDS . . . News stories have been geared to the 'horror stories' about AIDS"

at risk: "homosexuals and . . . Haitians . . . are known to run high risks of contracting the disease . . . people who do not fit into these high risk groups can rest assured they will not contract AIDS . . . 'it is only a particular sub-group of a subculture that is at risk.'"

spread: "risk factors: using dirty needles to inject drugs, or leading an active gay life, including sexual contact with many partners. AIDS has also struck a number of Haitians, but again, researchers do not know why, and some hemophiliacs have contracted it, presumably through blood products . . . 'no reported cases of someone getting the disease other than through sexual contact, maternal-infant contact, primarily in the womb, and blood products.'"

"AIDS fears unfounded" (*Globe and Mail*, November 18, 1983: 5)

at risk: "fears of nurses about caring for patients with AIDS are unfounded"
"'no known cases of AIDS have appeared among hospital workers.'"

"AIDS cases doubling every 6 months: Official"
(*Toronto Star*, November 25, 1983: A14)

at risk: "Homosexuals, users of illicit intravenous drugs, hemophiliacs and Haitians are considered to have a higher risk of getting AIDS."

spread: "The condition seems to be spread through semen or blood."

"AIDS cases on increase" (*Halifax Herald*, November 25, 1983: 13)

cause: "statistics confirm earlier fears . . . AIDS . . . cripples the body's immune system and leaves it open to attack by rare and often deadly diseases" . . . experts are baffled by statistics"

at risk: "Homosexual men, users of illicit intravenous drugs and hemophiliacs are other groups considered to have a higher than normal risk of getting AIDS."

spread: "The condition seems to be spread through semen or blood."

In these early articles, AIDS is characterized as a mysterious disease whose cause is inexplicable and baffling for experts and one that is caught through plain bad luck (and has been sensationalized by the media, which just contributes to unfounded fears). The people most likely to contract AIDS are said to be male homosexuals, Haitians, intravenous illicit drug users and their sexual partners, and hemophiliacs, a characterization which has contributed to ongoing discrimination.[18] People who do not fit into these "high risk groups" are assured they will not contract AIDS. It is explicitly said that it is not perceived to be a threat to the "general public," that it is only a "particular sub-group of a subculture" that is at risk. AIDS is said to be spread through bodily fluids such as semen or blood, by dirty needles used to inject drugs or by leading an "active" gay life. While sexual contact with many partners is also mentioned, it is "homosexuals" who are being warned to limit their sexual partners.

The "risk" in early articles was uniformly portrayed as marginal, mysterious and terrifying.[19] Headlines used phrases like "terror," "killer disease," "deadly" and "mysterious illness." AIDS was explicitly said to be a threat to high-risk groups, not the "general" public. Because of this misrepresentation, recognition that it might be unsafe practices that put a person at risk was overshadowed by the identification of unsafe people.

In 1984, news articles continued to represent AIDS as caused by unsafe people. This "mysterious and deadly syndrome" was said to be primarily found among homosexuals, drug users and hemophiliacs.[20] A Gallup poll on AIDS awareness reported that 83 percent were aware of AIDS, and 59 percent "knew their chances of getting it were quite small."[21] It was also reported that people still felt it could be contracted through toilet seats. Doctors had discovered that "the virus believed to cause AIDS is transmitted to the fetus through the placenta,"[22] but some doctors also still felt that AIDS was caused by homosexuality.[23]

The director of the Quebec AIDS Committee reported that "'The disease doesn't seem to be spilling over into other groups.'"[24] At an inquest in

British Columbia, medical experts testified that for the "average Canadian," the risk of contracting AIDS from transfusions or blood products was almost zero. However, the medical director of the Red Cross's Blood Transfusion Service in British Columbia said he would not put warnings on U.S. blood products used by hemophiliacs because it would be insulting to tell hematologists how to use blood products: "We are not dealing with the great unwashed, we are dealing with a number of highly trained professionals."[25]

There seemed to be an increase in the perceived threat from AIDS towards the end of 1984, as reported in an item in the Canadian Press. Researchers were said to fear that hundreds of thousands of people could be carrying the virus responsible for AIDS; and another headline read that AIDS was more extensive than previously thought.[26] A headline stated that AIDS could be transmitted to others, but the first example used in the article was that of a drug-abusing mother.[27] Articles were still being published saying that the disease struck "promiscuous homosexuals."[28] And one of three articles published on December 7, 1984, goes on to say that the Atlanta Centre for Disease Control knew several people had contracted the disease prior to 1979 and "AIDS may be slowly spreading to other sectors of the population"; however, the women identified were working as prostitutes or were partners of intravenous drug users—readers were not provided with any information on the men.[29] Similarly, a headline published at the end of 1984 in the *Globe and Mail* pointed out that AIDS could be spread through "conventional sex" but the accompanying article was paired with a sidebar article entitled "Immune system of gays 'different.'"[30] Treichler (1987: 37) points out that as late as 1985, researchers were discussing the concepts of "vulnerable anus," "fragile urethra," and "rugged vagina," in a misinformed attempt to explain why AIDS could be transmitted through anal sex but not vaginal intercourse.

The consequence of associating AIDS with identity rather than behaviour is illustrated by an article in 1984, where it is reported that Manitoba's first confirmed case of AIDS was not initially recognized because the victim did not fit into any of the high-risk categories.[31] Through this period, newspaper reports lacked consensus. Some discounted the easy identity to disease link for Haitians, for example, and pointed to the startling conclusion that heterosexuals could not only contract but spread AIDS; other articles appeared to reaffirm the old homosexual-AIDS connection.[32] It appeared that the concept of "high-risk groups" versus the "general community" would not pass away easily.[33] Several years later articles were still being printed, like the one about "patient zero," that reinforced the conception that AIDS was spread by sociopathic marginals.[34]

Overall, AIDS is signified in a very particular way in these articles, associated especially with so-called "high-risk groups." Although the causes proposed for AIDS have been many and unusual—a plague from King Tut's tomb, a result of genetic mutations caused by "mixed marriages" (Treichler 1987), a plot by the U.S. government to undermine the former Soviet Union or destroy American ethnic minorities[35]—the more usual reporting around AIDS is far more mundane.

Misinformation continues about AIDS, but in some ways it is the early (mis)representation that is most important. Not only have marginal groups been stigmatized through their association with AIDS, but this signification makes people who do not identify themselves as members of those groups less likely to see themselves at risk, more likely to engage in unsafe practices and more likely to contract the disease. AIDS has been confused by the metaphors used, but understanding AIDS *as a disease* requires seeing what the metaphor elides. Though the label has changed, many still see it as the "gay plague."

The Commission of Inquiry on the Blood System in Canada began on November 22, 1993. It was named the Krever Inquiry after its chair, a court of appeals judge who had previously conducted an inquiry on the confidentiality of health records in Ontario in 1978–80 and had also served on the Royal Society of Canada study on AIDS in Canada in 1987–88. The inquiry's budget was set at $2.5 million and its mandate was to inquire into how the problems with the blood supply arose and how to reform the system.[36]

More than one million Canadians received transfusions between 1978 and 1985 and, of these, more than one thousand hemophiliacs and blood-transfusion recipients were infected with HIV before the mandatory testing and heat-treatment of blood was begun by the Red Cross in 1985.[37] Amidst allegations that Red Cross officials knew of the contaminated blood and yet refused to release safer products, an inquiry was timely and necessary.

Although the Krever Inquiry's mandate was to look into how blood-transfusion recipients contracted HIV, sexual orientation still arose as an issue. By characterizing transfusion recipients as "innocent victims," a line was drawn differentiating them from "others" who had contracted HIV, the implication being that the others had done so because of their lifestyle, by "choice."

In testimony at the inquiry, people recounted inadequate or incomplete advice from physicians, and also evidence which showed that it was assumed that only "certain people" got AIDS. For example, in testimony in Toronto, a hemophiliac said that when he asked his doctor in 1983–84 about AIDS, he was told "he didn't have anything to worry about." At that same day's hearings a woman testified, "I thought AIDS was something going around and killing gay men. I never thought it could be in the blood. It never hit me."[38] Witnesses said doctors and nurses had failed to inform them about "safer-sex practices," told them their partners were at no risk of contracting

HIV, refused them treatment, left their meals outside hospital room doors or said HIV was no worse than the common cold or chicken pox.[39]

In testimony at the inquiry, the chief medical officer for the city of Toronto from 1981 to 1988 made the point that it was impossible to apply the hindsight of 1994 to events of 1983. However, a report from the Centre for Disease Control in Atlanta on July 16, 1982, had said that "the occurrence (of AIDS) among the three hemophiliac cases suggests the possible transmission of an agent through blood products."[40] So though judging by hindsight might be unfair, clear warning signs were being ignored. Although that chief medical officer was among the first to see the possible risk to hemophiliacs from contaminated blood, he had formed a committee that did not see contact-tracing of gay and bisexual men as important.[41] Anonymous testing is now preferred to contact-tracing, because the latter discourages people from being tested, but at the time there was simply no interest in tracking down people to inform them that they might be at risk.

Homophobia is an important issue in such an inquiry, because it creates an image of what "type" of person is at risk of contracting the disease and what "type" isn't, which further affects testing and public reporting. In hearings in Toronto, Vancouver, Edmonton, Regina and Winnipeg, witnesses accused government officials of "joking" about reopening leper colonies for gay AIDS sufferers, and of denying funding to gay groups and hindering AIDS education.[42]

In hearings in Halifax, witnesses testified how the gay community had been ignored when AIDS had appeared in Halifax in 1983 and how health authorities were only interested in the threat to "the general public." The founder of the Nova Scotia Persons with AIDS Coalition testified that the former administrator of community health services had told him that "likely all the people at risk of contracting the AIDS virus were infected and would soon die, so there was no urgency to have a public health campaign," that the provincial epidemiologist felt that no more than twenty Nova Scotians would be affected by AIDS, and that a government official was rumoured to want to quarantine people with AIDS on an island in Halifax Harbour.[43] Gaetan Dugas, thought to be the first AIDS sufferer in North America, lived in Dartmouth between 1979 and 1983 but no one knew if he had the disease.[44]

The inquiry also heard how Red Cross officials felt it wasn't their job to warn hemophiliacs of contamination in blood products, and that national guidelines that allowed contaminated blood products to be sent to hospitals to be used by hemophiliacs were followed in 1985, while safe products were withheld.[45]

In commenting on his lack of action, the provincial epidemiologist in Nova Scotia from 1980 to 1988 is quoted to have said, "We were trying to find out more information about how the disease was spread. It appeared to be associated primarily with a certain type of lifestyle, mainly homosexuals."[46] He also said that in 1984 he had "changed his mind that 'AIDS was something that was over there and not coming to Nova Scotia'"; however, the community health services administrator said "that he wasn't worried AIDS would soon be sweeping Nova Scotia. He believed only five percent of the population was homosexual and the group of intravenous drug users was relatively small."[47]

In testimony in New Brunswick, the medical director of the provincial Red Cross said he had ignored a national directive to contact and warn the gay community, and that blood donated by men who appeared and acted "gay" was discarded by nurses. In commenting, he said their "action was entirely correct, moral, ethical, rational and sensible."[48]

In testimony after testimony, the Krever Inquiry heard how officials withheld safe blood products and knowingly distributed contaminated blood. The national organization was said to be inflexible, to have disregarded suggestions from provincial officials whom they accused of overstepping their authority, and to have saved heat-treated products for "virgin" hemophiliacs.[49]

As a columnist pointed out in a Halifax paper, the Krever Inquiry has highlighted the existence of a double standard: a special category of "innocent victims" deserves an answer as to why they got infected, unlike gays who may have contracted AIDS through sex. What is evident in the inquiry is that many people, including heterosexuals, contracted AIDS through sex. Moreover, many people contracted HIV through lack of accurate information and stereotyping on the part of authorities who felt that AIDS was a "gay disease." As the columnist quotes, "their attitude toward the gay community was 'It'll get rid of them, gays, and the intravenous [drug] users.' The alarm bells were not raised. It was, and is, institutionalized homophobia."[50]

At the beginning of 1993 the Atlanta centres for disease control and prevention revised the definition of acquired immune deficiency syndrome to include tuberculosis of the lungs, recurring pneumonia and invasive cervical cancer. These, along with twenty-three other conditions, and a new laboratory test for the immune system, define AIDS.[51] One consequence of the redefinition of the disease is increased recognition of how it affects women; the definition had originally been based on how it affected gay men. AIDS is one of the three main causes of death for women between fifteen and forty-four in the United States. And even though the media still reports cases where men contract HIV from prostitutes, studies indicate women are twelve to seventeen times more likely to have contracted the disease from a man than the reverse, and 80 percent of cases involve women of childbearing age.[52] Heterosexual sex accounts for 75 percent of AIDS infection cases worldwide and is estimated by the World Health Organization to account for 90 percent of new cases.[53]

Summary

A shift in social thinking has occurred. In slightly more than a decade, "society" has slowly progressed beyond thinking that AIDS is just a gay or otherwise marginal disease. However, early stereotyping created a long-lasting stigma, and many people contracted HIV because they felt and were treated as if they were not at risk. This stigma continues today through the shame and embarrassment associated with HIV testing and education. The disease itself does not care about a person's identity or sexual orientation, and although it is now known to be spread through high-risk behaviours rather than by high-risk people, it is the sad example of a disease that has been contracted in a climate of ignorance created by distorted social messages. The way the disease was signified contributed to its spread, and this misinformation was spread through the media.

Notes

1. "AIDS virus hits two heterosexual women in metro," *Daily News*, January 6, 1988.
2. "Spread virus, AIDS carrier jailed three years," *Globe and Mail*, December 9, 1989; "Wentzell says he's sorry, sentenced to three years," *Daily News*, December 9, 1989.
3. "HIV carrier released," *Globe and Mail*, December 24, 1991: A6, Brief.
4. "Wife can sue bisexual husband over AIDS risk, court rules," *Toronto Star*, June 26, 1993: A2.
5. "AIDS carrier denies having intercourse," *Globe and Mail*, April 5, 1991: A4; AIDS case prompts case for detention, Existing laws seen as no protection," *Globe and Mail*, April 6, 1991: A5; "Ontario debates no-sex orders," *Halifax Herald*, April 8, 1991: A4; "AIDS carrier arrested," *Globe and Mail*, June 20, 1991: A6; "HIV carrier arrested in B.C.," *Halifax Herald*, June 20, 1991: A2; "Man remains free," *Globe and Mail*, August 10, 1991: A5; "Woman with AIDS virus assails accused in court," *Globe and Mail*, April 7, 1993: A6; "Man told of AIDS before affair, MD urged accused to use condoms," *Globe and Mail*, April 8, 1993: A5; "AIDS doctor failed to test accused man in 1987, court told," *Toronto Star*, April 10, 1993: A18; "Women took AIDS risk trial told," *Toronto Star*, April 22, 1993: A28; "Accused in AIDS trial acquitted on 3 charges," *Toronto Star*, May 1, 1993: A22; "MD's assessment sought in AIDS trial," *Toronto Star*, May 13, 1993: A9; "AIDS case man doesn't suffer from stress disorder, trial told," *Toronto Star*, June 25,

1993: A20; "Verdict likely next month in AIDS trial," *Globe and Mail*, July 9, 1993: A4; "Accused dies; AIDS trial left in limbo," *Halifax Herald*, July 21, 1993: C20; "Decision on Ssenyonga verdict put off," *Globe and Mail*, August 5, 1993: A5; "Judge ponders verdict for dead AIDS carrier," *Toronto Star*, August 5, 1993: A2; "Judge won't give verdict in case of AIDS carrier," *Globe and Mail*, December 18, 1993: A3; "AIDS trial victims angry after no verdict given," *Toronto Star*, December 18, 1993: A22; "Crown won't fight lack of verdict in AIDS case," *Toronto Star*, January 16, 1994: A7; "AIDS in court," *Toronto Star*, January 17, 1994: A14, editorial; "AIDS carrier's victim compensated—and criticized," *Toronto Star*, February 8, 1994: A1; "State-supervised sex," *Toronto Star*, February 10, 1994: A18, editorial.

6. "Inmate with H.I.V. who bit guard loses appeal," *New York Times*, February 18, 1993: B7.

7. "Prisoner with AIDS bit jail guard," *Montreal Gazette*, November 2, 1991: A10.

8. "Jailing of Man with AIDS spurs legal debate," *New York Times*, January 18, 1993: B5.

9. "Robber with syringe uses threat of AIDS," *New York Times*, March 22, 1992: 22.

10. "Jilted lover injected me with HIV, man claims," *Halifax Herald*, July 19, 1993: A6; "Three charged in HIV injection," *Daily News*, July 19, 1993: 6; "Charges stayed against two in bizarre Edmonton case, Tycoon, private eye caught off guard by decision," *Globe and Mail*, November 13, 1993: A4; "Kiwi millionaire jovial after HIV-death case ends," *Daily News*, November 13, 1993: 8; "Bizarre HIV-injection case winds toward conclusion," *Halifax Herald*, November 15, 1993: C16; "Murder by HIV, Charges stayed, but case isn't dead, Alberta says," *Montreal Gazette*, November 15, 1993: A8.

11. "Top court rules blood donors with HIV can be prosecuted," *Globe and Mail*, June 5, 1993: A3.

12. "Anti-AIDS law tested in courts," *Washington Post*, November 18, 1992: A2.

13. "Judge bars AIDS tests of suspect," *Washington Post*, January 3, 1992: C1.

14. "Offenders may face AIDS tests," *Toronto Star*, March 22, 1994: A9.

15. "HIV sexual assault charges stayed," *Vancouver Sun*, February 19, 1992: B1.

16. "Punishment: No sex for five years," *USA Today*, October 31, 1991: A2.

17. "Something's wrong when we have 600 stories on AIDS and only six on arthritis," *Globe and Mail*, April 10, 1993: D8.

18. "Haitians hurt by Red Cross notice: experts," *Montreal Gazette*, September

27, 1994: A3.

19. "AIDS: The terror stalking Metro's gays, Killer illness has caused homosexuals to be less promiscuous," *Toronto Star,* August 26, 1983: A17; "AIDS Deadly mystery threatens Canada, Cases of syndrome that robs body of defences double every 6 months," *Toronto Star,* August 11, 1983: A15; "Killer disease linked to blood, Evidence points to contagious agent in mysterious illness," *Toronto Star,* January 15, 1983: A12;

20. "B.C. AIDS case prompts inquest," *Calgary Herald,* January 16, 1984: B5.

21. "AIDS optimism called premature," *Globe and Mail,* May 8, 1984: M2.

22. "Mother gives fetus AIDS," *Calgary Herald,* July 3, 1984: D6.

23. "Doctor: AIDS victims 'deserve what they get,'" *Montreal Gazette,* August 21, 1984: B1.

24. "AIDS news mixed," *Winnipeg Free Press,* August 28, 1984: 16.

25. "Risk of AIDS from transfusions said low," *Calgary Herald,* October 9, 1984: D7.

26. "AIDS more serious threat now than a year ago," *Calgary Herald,* December 7, 1984: F8; "AIDS more extensive, blood test indicates," *Winnipeg Free Press,* November 6, 1984: 33.

27. "AIDS virus can be passed on to others, scientists say," *Winnipeg Free Press,* November 15, 1984: 91.

28. "Researchers fear thousands carrying deadly AIDS virus," *Winnipeg Free Press,* December 7, 1984: 35.

29. "AIDS cases tripled in 1 year," *Toronto Star,* December 11, 1984: F6.

30. "Evidence is increasing on spread of AIDS through conventional sex," *Globe and Mail,* December 31, 1984: M7.

31. "First Manitoba AIDS case doesn't belong to high-risk groups," *Winnipeg Free Press,* April 28, 1984: 3.

32. "Haitians and AIDS: The facts and fictions," *Toronto Star,* September 29, 1984: B5; "Case shows heterosexuals can spread AIDS," *Calgary Herald,* January 6, 1984: C8; "Heterosexual transmission of AIDS may be possible," *Toronto Star,* February 3, 1984: F6; "New U.S. study pinpoints homosexual-AIDS link," *Toronto Star,* January 14, 1984: A15.

33. "Deadly AIDS may spread to heterosexuals, MDs report," *Toronto Star,* September 16, 1983: B15.

34. "Patient Zero, The airline steward who carried a disease and a grudge," *Toronto Star,* December 12, 1987: M1 and M20.

35. "The Evil Empire's Last Hurrah," *Village Voice,* February 2, 1993: 22; "Conspiracy Theories: J. Edgar Hoover to Spike Lee," *Village Voice,* January 26, 1993: 20.

36. "Judge opens probe into safety of blood supply," *Montreal Gazette*, November 22, 1993: A6.

37. "Blood inquiry testimony to begin Feb. 14, Hearings to be held in each province," *Globe and Mail*, January 20, 1994: A8; "Delays plague inquiry into safety of blood supply," *Toronto Star*, January 11, 1994: A2; "AIDS victims describe blood system nightmare, More than 1,000 got AIDS from tainted blood," *Halifax Herald*, February 23, 1994: D15.

38. "Nightmares recounted at tainted-blood inquiry, Told by doctor not to worry about AIDS, hemophiliac infected with HIV testifies," *Globe and Mail*, February 24, 1994: A8; "Anger, tears as victims tell of blood horror, Inquiry witnesses decry lack of warnings about HIV risk," *Globe and Mail*, February 22, 1994: A1.

39. "MD spurned boy's family over AIDS, probe told," *Toronto Star*, February 22, 1994: A2; "Wife dies soon after, man told not to worry, blood inquiry told," *Toronto Star*, February 25, 1994: A2; "AIDS status not learned for year, probe told," *Globe and Mail*, February 23, 1994: A6; "Hospital form letter told mom son had HIV, Hemophiliacs' parents testify at blood inquiry," *Toronto Star*, March 22, 1993: A1.

40. "Blood inquiry puts crisis in perspective, Evidence so far shows early warnings about AIDS entering blood supply didn't trigger immediate responses," *Toronto Star*, March 28, 1994: A17; "AIDS risk from transfusions once called 'extremely low,'" *Toronto Star*, March 9, 1994: A11.

41. "Fear of AIDS was 'rampant' official tells blood inquiry, Gays 'badly treated at Toronto hospitals' in '80s, probe told," *Toronto Star*, March 18, 1994: A5.

42. "Anti-gay attitudes common in government, inquiry told," *Halifax Herald*, June 4, 1994: A8.

43. "AIDS' impact on N.S. gays 'didn't matter' to officials—activist," *Daily News*, July 30, 1994: 4; "Rumour terrified N.S. gays, lawyer tells blood inquiry," *Globe and Mail*, July 28, 1994: A6.

44. "Major AIDS virus carrier went undetected," *Halifax Herald*, July 28 1994: A1; "'Patient Zero' lived in Dartmouth, AIDS group lawyer slams 'indifference,'" *Daily News*, July 28, 1994: 4.

45. "Not my job, official says, No warning made; Red Cross chief cites 'policy,'" *Daily News*, July 30, 1994: 4; "Safe products available but not used, inquiry told, Non-treated products for hemophiliacs sent to hospitals, Nova Scotia Red Cross official testifies," *Globe and Mail*, July 29, 1994: A5; "Untreated Factor 8 distributed in 1985," *Halifax Herald*, July 29, 1994: A1; "Dangerous blood sent to hospitals, Untreated products used after safe blood received," *Daily News*, July 29, 1994: 5.

46. "Tracing HIV transfusions 'hit and miss,' 'We could have done more,'"

Halifax Herald, July 27, 1994: A1.

47. "HIV: 23 lost N.S. victims, Search for tainted-blood recipients had no staff—health official," *Daily News,* July 27, 1994: 3.

48. "Red Cross knowingly gave out bad blood, inquiry hears," *Daily News,* July 16, 1994: 12.

49. "Red Cross inflexible, MD says, Inquiry told national body refused higher blood standards," *Globe and Mail,* July 15, 1994: A2; "Red Cross knew blood was unsafe, inquiry told," *Halifax Herald,* July 16, 1994: A1; "Rigid rules cited as reason unsafe blood released, New Brunswick Red Cross felt it couldn't disobey head office, inquiry is told," *Globe and Mail,* July 16, 1994: A3; "Tainted blood inquiry hears tales of misery, buck-passing officials," *Halifax Herald,* August 5, 1994: A6; "Hemophiliacs knew risks, blood inquiry told," *Halifax Herald,* August 4, 1994: A6; "Patients knew risk—Red Cross," *Daily News,* August 4, 1994: 8.

50. "Gay man says Krever inquiry reveals AIDS double standard," *Daily News,* August 5, 1994: 2, column.

51. "New definition for AIDS arrives, bringing new concerns," *New York Times,* January 6, 1993: B3; "Widened definition of AIDS leads to more reports of it," *New York Times,* April 30, 1993: A18.

52. "Revising the anatomy of an illness," *Globe and Mail,* July 9, 1991: A6; "AIDS isn't a woman's disease? The statistics might surprise you," *Daily News,* July 14, 1993: 2; "Paris hookers infecting clients daily with HIV," *Winnipeg Free Press,* December 14, 1991: B16; "Women less likely to transmit virus," *Globe and Mail,* December 9, 1991: A5; "Women more vulnerable to AIDS: Report," *Toronto Star,* January 4, 1992; "Breast milk can spread AIDS, study by doctors in Africa finds, Infected women urged to use bottled formula if available," *Globe and Mail,* August 29, 1991: A5; "AIDS cases from sex on rise for women," *New York Times,* July 23, 1993: A12; "Police warn of HIV prostitute, Woman's return puts johns at risk," *Daily News,* September 23 ,1994: 9; "Health warning issued about Dartmouth hooker with HIV," *Daily News,* September 11, 1993: 3; "Johns warned of AIDS danger," *Halifax Herald,* September 11, 1993: A1.

53. "'Ridiculous' to call AIDS 'gay disease,' expert says," *Daily News,* December 27, 1993: 4; "Heterosexual contact accounts for most new HIV cases," *Washington Post,* February 13, 1992: A10; "Heterosexual sex listed as cause in 75% of world's AIDS cases, 5,000 people infected daily, health organization states," *Globe and Mail,* November 12, 1991: A8.

6

The Halifax Race Riot:
Extralocality and Racism in the News

"Ethnocentrism" means seeing the world only from one's own ethnic or cultural point of view, thinking that other people should share that point of view and judging them by one's own cultural standards. Ethnocentrism can result in prejudice and discrimination, and when displayed in the media can reinforce a slanted view of the world. In this chapter the issue of ethnic sensitivity is taken up in the portrayal of "race relations" in the news. Joy Mannette recounts three cases from the news and discusses how race and ethnic issues are portrayed in ways that reinforce ethnic bias and display a lack of ethnic sensitivity.

Although the examples used are from Nova Scotia, the analysis can be applied to events in other parts of Canada—to Oka, Davis Inlet or Akwesasne, or to the concern over immigrant crime, discussed in another chapter—or to other countries as well—the L.A. riot, the Crown Heights riot, conflict in Lebanon, peace in the Gaza Strip, the Gulf War, the restoration of democracy in Haiti or the invasion of Panama. Ethnic bias is not always easy to see in news coverage and that is part of the problem.

In "Reading the news," specific examples are reproduced to show how lack of ethnic sensitivity and sometimes overt ethnocentrism play a part in the discussion of race and ethnic issues in the press. The main topic discussed here is the so-called 1991 Halifax race riot, with articles drawn largely from local papers. However, the underlying theme is that these messages are unaffected by distance and that, even in national papers, ethnic bias can be reproduced.

"Extralocality" is a term used here to describe how distance from events is inconsequential in modern society; today we receive news of events far from where they occur. In the "Analyzing the news" section, this process of disseminating news and reproducing particular ethnic relations is examined.

Given that much of what we know of the world comes through the media, we need to question how the news interprets the world in such a way that it comes to stand in for direct experience.

The talk—Joy Mannette

There is a Mi'kmaq word, "napite'lsit," that I think offers the nicest orientation to some of the things that I want to talk about in relation to the way in which race and ethnic issues get taken up and treated in the media. If I were proceeding in a typical Mi'kmaq fashion, I wouldn't tell you what it translates into in English, I would just leave you with this whole metaphoric presentation and let you figure it out for yourself.

I think that the special treatment of race and ethnic issues in media coverage is quite appalling and involves intolerable carelessness. I'd like to elaborate on how the politics of race gets treated in the media within the Canadian context and how I've seen that work out in some research that I've done. I'll focus on three particular race and ethnic incidents within the Nova Scotia context. The first was in the fall of 1968 in Halifax. We had a moral panic around the issue of black power centred around the October 1968 first human rights conference that was held there, and then in November and early December of 1968, the formation of the Black United Front of Nova Scotia.

The second thing that I would like to talk about is a bit more contemporary, and that has to do with a 1985 Weymouth Falls case. On June 8, 1985, a black man who lived in Weymouth Falls, Digby County, Graham Jarvis, sometimes known as Graham Cromwell, was shot and died as a result of a gunshot wound. The perpetrator of the shooting was accused of manslaughter and was acquitted.

The third thing that I want to talk about is the recent Mi'kmaq treaty trials here in Nova Scotia, beginning with the Mi'kmaq treaty moose harvest in the fall of 1988 and the ensuing trial process that was carried out in Sydney which focused around the thorny issue of the extent to which provisions under the 1752 treaty between the Crown and the Mi'kmaq nation are sustained today. Those are the incidents I'll talk about in terms of the politics of the special status of race.

Referring to the special status that race and ethnic reporting has within the media framework, if we look back at 1968, what we see is the creation of a moral panic in Halifax. We see a very deliberately orchestrated media campaign that transformed a series of relatively innocuous events within the black community into something close to insurrection. The media coverage focused on the threat attendant to the visit to Halifax in October of 1968 of Stokely Carmichael. The *Chronicle-Herald* had an interview with him at the airport when he was leaving but no coverage of what ensued while he was here.

It's also interesting to find the kind of stories that the *Chronicle-Herald* pulled from the wire during the fall of 1968 as it began to sort of shape its sense of the politics within the local black community. One of the stories that it pulled was a speech which has become a kind of benchmark for people who've looked at the way in which media treats race relations. Enid Powell, speaking in London, England, in the spring of 1968, prophesied that rivers of blood would run in the streets of Britain if black migration was to continue. That story showed up in the *Halifax Herald* coverage at the same time that the Black Panthers were in Halifax. That's the kind of wire service selection going on at the time.

The end result is that you have this construction of possible insurrection by the black Nova Scotia community which is simply not supported by the events going on within that community at the time. And it would also be possible to demonstrate that the October 1968 human rights conference bore the mark of what we might call "small l" liberal action as opposed to radical action, and yet it too was seen as a radical activity.

If we look at the question of unusual care being taken in relation to coverage of race and ethnic issues, we certainly couldn't apply that to the Weymouth Falls case. Indeed, the dominant media in Nova Scotia dealt with that issue by effectively silencing it. It was the tabloid format of the *Daily News* which covered the Weymouth Falls case through January of 1986; and the *Toronto Star* broke the case on December 27, 1985, with very sustained coverage. Excessive care was taken in the way in which that particular medium sought to examine the shooting of this black man, and the attendant circumstances around it.

If we look at the question of carelessness, however, we can see that widely represented in all media coverage of the Weymouth Falls case, for example, in confusion over people's names. It seemed very difficult for the media to understand that someone might be known popularly within a community in a way that's not reflected on their birth certificate; after all, the only kind of people who go by aliases are criminals. Also, persistent problems surrounded the accurate identification of various spokespersons or groups who were acting within the black community in agitating for a reexamination into Graham Jarvis's death.

In the more recent case of the Mi'kmaq treaty trials, reporters were assigned to cover situations about which they knew very little. I can tell you hardly anybody knew anything as they went into the Mi'kmaq treaty trials, and it was an on-the-job learning experience for almost everyone who was connected to it. Coverage of the Mi'kmaq treaty trials would have been much more prominently displayed had those treaty trials taken place in the city of Halifax as opposed to Sydney, a subregional bias that enters into media coverage, particularly around race/ethnic issues. Furthermore, the

Halifax-based media, in accessing legitimate spokespersons for the Mi'kmaq community, orients to the Confederacy of Mainland Micmacs, located at Schubenacadie [Truro]. Given that the Union of Nova Scotia Indians, which was very pivotal in organizing the treaty trial initiative, is located in Sydney, this was not inconsequential and represents a subregional carelessness on the part of media attention to race/ethnic issues.

What can we say about the characterization of race that emerged from these three incidents, given that you have various strategies designed to deflect attention from the issues the communities in question wanted to pursue, and as such refocused attention on issues that lent themselves to a much more reformist approach? In the first instance, if you peruse the dominant media coverage, we were given an understanding of race that was borrowed from the American context. The characterization of race relations that we received was one of violence, of a threat to the established order and of tremendous organizational instability within the minority organizations. That, I think, has been a persistent theme in the coverage of race and ethnic issues throughout the ensuing twenty-five years or so from the mid-1960s to the early 1990s.

We don't have a lot of reference within the Nova Scotia context to the racial politics of central Canada; instead we have remained stuck in this rut of referencing the American context. How that got played out in the sixties was in terms of equating black politics in Nova Scotia with what was going on in the U.S. In the 1980s, certainly in terms of black politics, you have a different effect taking place, one which revolves around the myth of black progress, which has sustained popular understanding and been widely disseminated in the media. As a result, in the Canadian context it is often assumed that the kind of problems that were associated with black communities in the 1960s no longer existed in the 1980s, that various affirmative action initiatives had corrected those problems. That certainly is the tone that underpins the situation of the 1985 Weymouth Falls case.

Now, it becomes difficult to talk about the overall understanding of race that comes out of the Mi'kmaq treaty trials because we have all had our racial consciousness raised as a result of the events at Kahnawake and Akwesasne in 1991. It's often tempting to look at the Mi'kmaq treaty moose harvest in 1988–89 and the ensuing trials in light of those events, but that would be fallacious. The Mi'kmaq treaty trials were a revelation within the Nova Scotia context, and they put the whole issue of aboriginal rights quite firmly on the agenda. However, the Mi'kmaq treaty trials came on the heels of the Marshall inquiry, which also put the issue of race on the public agenda even though it was based on an understanding of race as biogenetic characteristics, not culture or power.

So when we try to understand what it is that we learn about racism and race issues from media coverage, we must also understand that we are learning through the media about situations we never encounter in our daily lives. And that has to do with relative ethnic segregation, and we vicariously interact in a symbolic way through media coverage with communities and peoples that we know nothing about. We come to understand them as violent, we understand that their lives are messy and ill organized, and that they are increasingly making extravagant demands on the social order that is unprepared to deal with those demands.

The metaphor "napite'lsit" translates into English something like this: When you look at a situation or a person and you look at it with ill intentions in your mind, you attribute to that situation and that person the same ill intentions that you direct towards it."

Reading the news

The theme Joy Mannette develops is that the media does not handle race relations very well, but recreates various myths and ethnic prejudices. The underlying topic is that, because we get "information" about the world from what we read and watch in the media, we have very little control over these symbolic representations. This process of relying on externally produced, mediated information is called here "extralocality." (Smith 1990).

On July 19, 1991, the front-page banner headline of the afternoon edition of a Nova Scotia provincial paper read: "Race riot rocks downtown."[1] The Article said a local minister, characterized as a "black community leader," "pleaded with rioters and police to stay calm." Officials were quoted as saying that the violence was not surprising, and "representatives" of the black community said they would be planning boycotts and marches to combat racism and discrimination. The shocked headline, therefore, indicated deeper underlying problems.

As can be seen in Article 6.1, the "riot" at the centre of the controversy concerned a group of blacks being turned away from a bar, who then went through downtown streets assaulting white bystanders, vandalizing storefronts and getting involved in a confrontation with the police. The incident has been explained by the *Herald* as sparked by door policies at a bar which allegedly discriminated against blacks, but in this article it is said to have originated when a group of whites had attacked a black man (lines 14–16).

Article 6.1
15 hurt in early morning rampage
(*Daily News*, July 20, 1991: 4)

1 By Charlene Sadler—Racial tensions in Halifax's nightclub district burst into
2 violence early yesterday morning when a group made up mostly of blacks rioted in the

3   downtown core, assaulting bystanders, fighting with police and smashing windows.
4   Police said yesterday 15 people were injured and eight (four blacks and four
5   whites) were arrested. Four people have been charged so far. Six people were treated
6   and released from hospital.
7   As many as 150 people may have been involved before the incident ended around
8   5 a.m.
9   Gottingen street merchants estimate that 14 businesses in the area were vandalized,
10   but none was looted.
11   Halifax Police Chief Vince MacDonald said yesterday about 35 police, including
12   two car-loads of Dartmouth officers, responded in full riot gear, using nightsticks to quell
13   the riot.
14   Here is a breakdown of the events based on accounts of witnesses and police officials:
15   On Wednesday night a black man was attacked by a group of whites in Rosa's
16   Cantina on Argyle Street.
17   On Thursday afternoon, Rev. Darryl Gray, of the Cultural Awareness Youth Group,
18   received a call from Roger MacKinnon, the manager at Rosa's, who was concerned
19   about the tension, and asked him to intercede.
20   At 1.30 a.m., Gray was at the entrance to the bar with MacKinnon when they saw a
21   group of about 50 black men coming toward them. Gray asked MacKinnon and some
22   bouncers to go inside while he waited outside with police officers who were present in
23   anticipation of trouble.
24   Gray had some success reasoning with the crowd, but a group in the rear began
25   randomly assaulting whites.
26   MacDonald said police "were running with the crowd, in many cases, picking up
27   those that were injured and making contact with ambulances."
28   Police then confronted the crowd for about an hour near the Derby tavern, at the
29   corner of Gottingen Street and Portland Place.
30   Gray again tried to intervene. Several people began to move away from the Derby.
31   The police then approached the group again, still in riot gear.
32   He said the police moved in on the crowd, confronting both rioters and onlookers.
33   The group moved to Uniacke and Gottingen Streets where it remained for about
34   an hour, vandalizing the area until police and community leaders successfully intervened.
35   Businesses had plate glass windows smashed and the "Charlie Zone" police sub-
36   office lost a window when a white youth threw a trash can through it.
37   At a news conference yesterday MacDonald acknowledged the riot was racially
38   motivated.
39   Charged were: Louis Beales, of Preston, who pleaded guilty yesterday to charges
40   of assaulting an officer. Charges of disturbing the peace were dropped. He was fined
41   $440 in Halifax provincial court yesterday.
42   Peter Joseph Campbell, of Mulgrave Park, faces charges of obstruction and
43   resisting arrest; Angelo P. Downey, of North Preston, faces charges of causing a disturbance.
44   Both have been released.
45   A young offender was also charged.

Picture caption: The scene outside Rosa's yesterday.

The news media very quickly labelled the "rioting" on the streets as "racial tension," in part because it involved a violent confrontation between blacks and whites, but also because the alleged perpetrators were black. Despite the many references to race in Article 6.1 (lines 2, 4, 15, 21, 25, 36 and 37–38), there is no obvious reason to conclude that "racial tension" is the best explanation for the events. Race could simply be coincidental, but the article forcefully constructs this interpretation as the best one, particularly through the use of racial references and shocking words such as "rampage."

An editorial the following day used emotionally charged words such as "war zone . . . chaos . . . rampage . . . devastation . . . destruction . . . racial tensions . . . swarmed . . . rebellion . . . disorder . . . outrage . . . [and] malaise."[2] Arguably, these words are ethnocentric as well, because it is questionable whether similar actions by whites would be labelled in the same way. The director of the Black United Front and a local minister in the black community were the main sources used in the editorial. The event was clearly characterized as serious, and there was an attempt to view it as motivated by discrimination and as a series of violently criminal acts. It was not portrayed in an exaggerated way as merely a "race riot," but neither were the racial tensions underlying it discounted.

Coverage of the violence was extensive. There were innumerable front-page stories and editorials in the provincial *Halifax Herald* and *Daily News* on the riot, its causes, subsequent events and solutions.[3] The riot, the anti-racism march, the vow to crack down on racism by the mayor, and the inquiry into police relations all received intensive coverage. Many of the articles, like the one reproduced in Article 6.1, provide a concise version of the conflict. A reader can get much of the picture of "what happened" by reading any one of these articles. Smaller articles, such as Article 6.2, present parts of what happened. These articles depend on other articles to make sense but, because media coverage was prominent and extensive, that was unlikely to pose a problem.

Article 6.2
Man "couldn't talk to them"
(*Daily News*, July 20, 1991: 5)

1 By The Daily News Staff—Esmain Ahmadvand, 25, was walking home from working
2 at the Keg around 2 a.m. yesterday morning. Passing by the Metro Centre, Ahmadvand
3 said he was suddenly caught in the middle of a group of 40 to 50 black males who were
4 punching everybody who got in their way.
5   Ahmadvand said they attacked him without provocation.
6   "I couldn't talk to them. I didn't have time to talk to them," Ahmadvand said.
7   Ahmadvand, who immigrated from Iran 15 months ago to escape the turmoil there,
8 suffered a broken nose in the beating. He said he didn't understand why he was the
9 victim of a seemingly random attack.

A sense of the capriciousness of the violence is conveyed by this article describing one small incident in the riot. A man was walking home from work (lines 1–2), and was suddenly surrounded by a crowd of black men (lines 3–4) who were beating people at random (lines 3–4 and 8–9). They attacked him even though he hadn't done anything (line 5), and they wouldn't listen to reason (line 6). What made it even more ironic was that the victim was a recent refugee from violence in Iran (lines 7–8). The article, short as it is, anchors the categories of "vicious attackers" and "innocent victim."

The above is a typical "riot account." There were also accounts of how police officers "taunted a mob . . . were egging on the crowd . . . and [that the group were on their way home] when confronted by the police."[4] This is a more troublesome interpretation, as it is then possible to construct an alternate version of the events which happened that night. This "subversive" theme disrupted the "race riot" theme, and eventually grew to include an overarching criticism of the ethnic makeup of police personnel.

A report in the national news filed from Halifax included what had become the official version of events and of the racism that sparked it, and the concern that the police had exacerbated the situation. The headline, "Blacks say bars at centre of riot, Halifax police beef up patrols," however, fails to carry the connotation of police provocation.[5] A story two days later, filed from Halifax by the same reporter, explains the problem as stemming from a racial confrontation at a local high school two years earlier.[6] The charge of police provocation is relegated to the last paragraph, and the idea is attributed to "blacks who turned out for a weekend community meeting." This theme gradually faded from view as days passed, but was replaced with the idea that more minority representation is needed on the police force, a criticism some tried to stymie by saying too few blacks apply in the first place. Thus, competing interpretations of the riot can be read in the news.

The *Toronto Star* carried the story on the front page for four days, each article written by the same reporter in Halifax.[7] The first appeared on Saturday and got several facts wrong, including the night of the riot. It did report the insinuation of police provocation, but this is a small item in a story which starts "generations of racism exploded into violence . . . [this] has been building just like a powder keg, like a volcano and it has erupted."

The Sunday front-page article in the *Toronto Star* gives details of several confrontations between blacks and whites. People involved in fights are quoted, vowing revenge for harm done to them or their friends. The lead paragraph reads: "A crowd of angry blacks—estimated as at least 30—attacked a group of whites in a north-end housing project last night, breaking an uneasy calm after two nights of racial violence." On Monday the lead paragraph reads: "People in the neighbourhood where a white man was badly beaten Saturday night by angry black youths are calling for an end to the accelerating cycle of madness." It describes in great detail attacks against various people near housing projects, just as the previous day's account had. The fourth front-page article, on Tuesday, does not focus on violence, specific acts of discrimination or possible racist actions by police, but on systemic poverty: "From the concrete alleys that are children's playgrounds in Halifax's north-end housing projects to the dilapidated houses in remote rural areas, high drop-out rates and double-digit unemployment are the norm in Nova Scotia's black communities." By July 24, 1991, the *Toronto Star* had dropped its coverage of the race riot to page 4, where it was placed alongside an article about a "near riot" in Montreal occasioned by a confrontation between police and a group of blacks outside a bar. So, competing readings of the event occur in this extralocal newspaper as well.

The importance of the riot to the national media is highlighted by the fact that a week later, when a man was assaulted in a small Nova Scotian town, it made the *Globe and Mail* (Article 6.3) solely through its link, real or perceived, with the earlier racial violence in Halifax. This article also describes a white man beaten by a black in a racially motivated attack. It stands on its own as a crime report but was apparently included only because of earlier articles in the *Globe and Mail*.[9]

Article 6.3
Man beaten with bat
(*Globe and Mail*, July 29, 1991: A5, Canada in Brief)

1 Kentville, N.S. (CP)—A 27-year-old man was listed in critical condition in a Halifax
2 hospital yesterday after being beaten with a baseball bat. Kentville police said
3 Warren Frederick Bond's life was hanging in the balance after what witnesses called
4 a racially motivated fight outside a pizza shop. A police spokesman confirmed that a
5 17-year-old black youth was in custody. Mr. Bond is white. The youth is currently
6 charged with aggravated assault, said local police Chief Del Crowell.

After the initial flurry of shocked articles in the local papers, the retrospection began, looking to the past for causes of the "riot." This retrospection continued as a dominant theme in later articles, which raised the issues of discrimination, poverty, economic recession, previous incidents, racism in the police force, racism in the criminal justice system and so on. But in less than a week, the retrospective search for causes took a twist— there were concerns that the media itself had exaggerated or even contributed to the problem.[10] In an examination of the national news, the local media looked at how the national papers were treating the story. The Halifax police chief is quoted as saying that "the weekend was in fact pretty quiet." An editorial a day later suggested that the violence may not have been as widespread or bad as the media had conveyed. In an accompanying article, a tourism industry spokesperson said that television cameras can actually invite trouble. A local columnist wrote that the media exaggerated the racial element, and in a newspaper poll published the same day, some suggested there wouldn't have been as much trouble if the media had just ignored bad news. Two days later an article in the *Herald* worried about the effects on tourism. An editorial the next day slammed those who had said the media had exaggerated the problem, accusing them of "buck-passing and finger-pointing."

By the first of August the new story was the anti-racism march, where both whites and blacks marched to protest racism. By December the reports on the riot were out.[11] The police report found that the police had not acted with brutality or racial slurs. The report of a civilian group, however, charged that the police did not interview all witnesses, and that police themselves did not know about car-to-car police tapes. An editorial suggested that the civilian report "seems more in touch with the real world," and the front-page banner headline of the provincial paper, "Race reports worlds apart" stressed the gap between the two reports. By February the attorney general vowed action on race relations; there were comparisons with the L.A. riot; and the Race Relations Foundation was put on hold until funding was found.

To conclude, the coverage of the Halifax "race riot" was overwhelming and complicated. The initial barrage of articles eventually diminished in number, but the issue continued to be reported for months. The description of what had happened was at issue because interpretations of events were continually shifting and being debated.

Analyzing the news

The fact that the media could offer readers different interpretations of the "same event" shows how different points of view can be brought to bear on an issue. It also shows how newspaper articles are not in any simple sense factual but are, rather, open to debate. What this difference of opinion disguises, however, is this: news articles are not only interpreted by an active reader, but they create interpretations as well. Two issues will be taken up here: how a racial incident was discursively constructed and the phenomenon of the news' extralocality.

"Race riots" are both events in the world and events constructed in the news. The media can create social panic by sensationalizing and exaggerating an event, so from a reporter's point of view it is important to get the facts straight. But what are "facts" and what would "getting them straight" look like? For readers who did not directly experience an event (which is most of us most of the time), the media's account stands in for that experience.

Most people experience crime vicariously through the news. They cannot be where the news happens and they cannot even determine how factual media accounts are. The report of a "race riot," then, is not simply a report of an event in the world, it is an extralocal report written by people one will never meet, of events one will never witness in person. The report is treated as being one of an actual event, but it is at heart a social construction accomplished through discourse (Berger and Luckmann 1966; Schutz 1967; Smith 1987; Turner 1974; Atkinson 1978). The structural organization of the accounts is revealed in the following analysis.

Article 6.1, "15 hurt in early morning rampage," is not simply a factual account. The "facts" in the account may or may not be factual. Actually, there was successive controversy over what had really happened. If we suspend our usual view that the account is about an actual event, it can also be read as a set of instructions, a prescription. By putting aside the question of facticity for the moment, what is interesting is how the account constructs a description of events retrospectively. The account tells the reader how it is to be read as a report about a riot, after the fact. The chronological order, the apparently literal description of what happened as time passed, the use of authoritative sources, quotes from people who should know what happened, descriptions of the criminal charges and their disposition—all provide the reader with rules for the warrantability of the claim that a race riot indeed happened.

Article 6.1 is a reconstructive account that goes over the events of the previous day.

1   [Byline]—Racial tensions in Halifax's nightclub district burst into
2   violence early yesterday morning when a group made up mostly of blacks rioted in the
3   downtown core, assaulting bystanders, fighting with police and smashing windows.

"Racial tensions" are named as the cause of the violence at the very beginning of the article, providing a strong interpretation of what follows. By beginning in this way, the article directs the reader to read an account of a race riot, it provides rules for that reading, and it is difficult to construct an alternate reading from the account. The opening phrase is not equivocal or ambiguous—there is a place, a time, an action and an explanation. The criminal acts then mentioned throughout the article—rioting, assaults and vandalism—reinforce the sense that a race riot actually occurred.

4   Police said yesterday 15 people were injured and eight (four blacks and four
5   whites) were arrested. Four people have been charged so far. Six people were treated
6   and released from hospital.
7   As many as 150 people may have been involved before the incident ended around
8   5 a.m.

9   Gottingen street merchants estimate that 14 businesses in the area were vandalized,
10 but none was looted.
11   Halifax Police Chief Vince MacDonald said yesterday about 35 police, including
12 two car-loads of Dartmouth officers, responded in full riot gear, using nightsticks to quell
13 the riot.

This initial summary indicates that a large number of people were involved, the riot police were dispatched and there were a number of arrests and people charged (lines 4–13). This section serves as a preface for the account within an account that follows. The fact that the recounting of events (lines 15–36) reiterates the preface (lines 4–13) does not make the article repetitive but reinforces the facticity of the account.

15   On Wednesday night a black man was attacked by a group of whites in Rosa's
16 Cantina on Argyle Street.
17   On Thursday afternoon, Rev. Darryl Gray, of the Cultural Awareness Youth Group,
18 received a call from Roger MacKinnon, the manager at Rosa's, who was concerned
19 about the tension, and asked him to intercede.
20   At 1.30 a.m., Gray was at the entrance to the bar with MacKinnon when they saw
21 a group of about 50 black men coming toward them. Gray asked MacKinnon and some
22 bouncers to go inside while he waited outside with police officers who were present in
23 anticipation of trouble.
24   Gray had some success reasoning with the crowd, but a group in the rear began
25 randomly assaulting whites.
26   MacDonald said police "were running with the crowd, in many cases, picking up
27 those that were injured and making contact with ambulances."
28   Police then confronted the crowd for about an hour near the Derby tavern, at the
29 corner of Gottingen Street and Portland Place.
30   Gray again tried to intervene. Several people began to move away from the Derby.
31 The police then approached the group again, still in riot gear.
32   He said the police moved in on the crowd, confronting both rioters and onlookers.
33   The group moved to Uniacke and Gottingen Streets where it remained for about
34 an hour, vandalizing the area until police and community leaders successfully intervened.
35   Businesses had plate glass windows smashed and the "Charlie Zone" police sub-
36 office lost a window when a white youth threw a trash can through it.

This account is chronological, as an account of a happening has to be, detailing the initial incident (lines 15–16), the subsequent tension (lines 17–19), the attempts to defuse the situation (lines 20–25) and the interwoven street violence and actions of the police (lines 26–36).

The bulk of the article recounting the "events" (lines 15–36) is bracketed by introductory and concluding phrases. The sentence at line 14 promises that what will follow is a description of what happened, based on trustworthy reports from eyewitnesses and the authorities.

14   Here is a breakdown of the events based on accounts of witnesses and police officials:

The admission from the police chief (lines 37–38) that racial violence is the reason for the incident also einforces the preferred reading of the previous facts. The facts are only facts, however, through being labelled as such by these two lines.

37   At a news conference yesterday MacDonald acknowledged the riot was racially
38   motivated.

Ten explicit references to race are made throughout the article (lines 1, 2, 4, 15, 21, 25, 36 and 37), of which five are in the middle section of the article. There are six more subtle references to "black areas" (lines 9, 28, 29, 30, 33 and 43), of which four are also in the middle section of the article.

All these various elements—the tensions, the violence, the police—work together to create the interpretation that a "race riot" actually occurred. These elements are more than simply factual descriptions of what happened—they are facts by virtue of being embedded into a rendition of an event, and the event recursively becomes real through the inclusion of such facts. The account concludes with a report that various people had been charged with assaulting an officer, disturbing the peace, obstruction and resisting arrest, and causing a disturbance (lines 39–45), further substantiating the events—there was no mistake.

39   Charged were: Louis Beales, of Preston, who pleaded guilty yesterday to charges
40   of assaulting an officer. Charges of disturbing the peace were dropped. He was fined
41      $440 in Halifax provincial court yesterday.
42   Peter Joseph Campbell, of Mulgrave Park, faces charges of obstruction and
43   resisting arrest; Angelo P. Downey, of North Preston, faces charges of causing a
44   disturbance. Both have been released.
45   A young offender was also charged.

Subsequent media accounts used expressions such as "race riot," "racial violence," "violence not surprising," "racial tensions," "street violence," "renewed violence," "rampage," "rage" and so on. Through the use of such terms the incident was further reified as an event, linked to past events and deeper underlying problems and made to meet the description of a racial problem. The "race riot" was both a "thing" in the world and an event constructed through the news. The question of whether there was a race riot, however, was a source of contention, because there were those who said the media had focused unfairly on racial violence, failing to see it as evidence of deeper problems and exaggerating it in a way that was harmful, for example, to tourism. Both criticisms point to the effect that words can have.

A consequent criticism of how the riot was handled in the media was that "black" was used as a defining term in a way that "white" never is. In a parallel incident in Sydney, for example, approximately seven hundred people clashed in the street and, even though it was reported that racial epithets were used, it was not termed a race riot in the headline and that interpretation was specifically denied in the text.[12] Months later, in a similar incident in Shelburne, Nova Scotia, a police chief was quoted as saying that racial names were used by both sides but there was no indication of a racial problem. In neither case did the media use the term "race riot," even though there was evidence that racism was involved; perhaps the difference was that most of the protagonists were white.

There are various other situations where the media has been criticized as contributing to ethnic discrimination as well.[13] It is difficult to cover news stories of the various ethnic groups in Canada today, especially when the structure of news gathering relies on reporters sitting in meetings, deciding on stories and then going out to gather information. The problem with that scenario is that news is not defined within these communities themselves. It is easy to reinvest time-honoured stereotypes linking ethnicity to drug trafficking or violent crime.[14] As witness to this, look at the concern over immigrant crime in 1994 that flamed up after the shootings of Georgina Leimonis at the Just Desserts Cafe and of Constable Todd Baylis of the metropolitan police force, both in Toronto. These shootings and, more importantly, their media coverage led to concern that immigrants were committing a disproportionate amount of crime and that crime statistics should be collected by "race."

The construction of the "race riot" in Halifax analyzed here was accomplished extralocally through the news. The story was picked up by, at least, the *Globe and Mail*, the *Montreal Gazette* and the *Toronto Star*. Given the medium of newswires and on-the-spot reporters, it is no accident that the portrayal of events in the out-of-province newspapers was similar to that in the Nova Scotia media—place did not matter in the news one got in this case. People with no direct experience of the event get the "facts" in the news. The initial riot, the subsequent interpretation of events and the eventual findings of the committees to investigate the police handling of the incident, all were available through the news network. In many places and for most readers, extralocality replaces experience.

It is important, then, to look at interpretations of events found in the news and how they change over time. Explanations for the riot shifted from mob violence to provocative actions by the police, to discriminatory policies at local bars, to years of discrimination, to poverty and recession, to racism in general and so on. The final note that concluded media coverage of the riot months later was that the problem can be solved through minority hiring by the police force. This solution is a remedial and in some ways superficial one, but it provided closure.

Extralocality is a feature of the news which provides readers with interpretations of "events" far from the original. This is an issue for sociologists who attempt to determine who controls the information that creates the dominant interpretations (Grenier 1992; Holmes and Taras 1992; Romanow and Soderlund 1992). However, in Nova Scotia, the accounts of the Halifax race riot in the local and national papers highlight the problem of extralocality in a different way—the credibility of the information that readers use in the course of their everyday lives becomes questionable. The events were said to be reported in a way that made the situation seem "worse than it really was." Canadian and American newspapers both repeated the erroneous information that a man was stabbed. The Halifax police chief topicalized the problem: "'If I was in another part of this county and read what I had read, I would be wondering whether I should call my relatives in Halifax to see if they were OK down there,' MacDonald said. 'It just sounded so intense—"Another night of racial tension, a black man gets his throat slit." . . . [the message] It sends out about our community that I don't think is really the truth of the matter.' The weekend was in fact pretty quiet, [the police chief] said."[15]

It is not simply that papers outside Nova Scotia got some details wrong, reporting erroneous information and exaggerating the scope and the seriousness of the problem. It is not simply that perhaps many of the accounts were factually correct. This reporting highlights the fact that our news is secondhand, channeled through the medium of news reporting. Even for people living in Halifax, the main source of information about the events was the news. The local media's analysis of the reporting at the national level makes it seem that if the media could only get its facts straight, there wouldn't be a problem. However, extralocality is an issue whether the facts are straight or not.

Ruling relations in modern society are made up of professional organizations that transcend any particular location and experience. The media is by nature extralocal, able to take up and transform our experiences through the form of accounts available to it, while those very experiences are informed through the knowledge that we live in a mediated world. The media transforms experiences into news and, at the same time, experiences are informed by the news. The knowledge we have of the world is put together from myriad bits of information about farflung places we'll never see, by people we'll never meet. It is diffuse ideology (Chomsky 1989).

The media takes up experience and transforms it into factual accounts; we then experience the world as secondhand but immediate. As an example of this dual aspect of the news, I came upon a massive car pile-up on a main highway outside the city of Halifax late one night. The traffic had suddenly slowed and stopped and, after a long wait, tow trucks and police cars slowly moved through the lanes of traffic. After more than an hour the traffic slowly resumed, and less than a kilometre ahead there were dozens of cars off the road with broken lights, crumpled fenders and so on. The area was lit with the flashing lights of tow trucks, police cars and ambulances; people were milling around, television crews were in the middle of the road. I had the feeling that I was in the middle of something "exciting," and it was clear what had happened, but I also felt that I should get home as quickly as possible to turn on the television and find out what had "really" happened. I didn't find the story on the television, but I did see it in the newspapers the next day.[16]

Interest in race relations and the criminal justice system is increasing and, although much has been written, much more work needs to be done (Harris 1990a; Manette 1992; Manitoba 1991; Nova Scotia 1989). Those in the media are themselves part of the problem when they unreflectingly reproduce dominant ways of thinking about minority groups.

Summary

This chapter began with the idea that the news sometimes puts a "spin" on race and ethnic issues. The speaker mentions several examples that bear out this idea. Ethnocentrism and racism are said to inform such media accounts, and the media can reproduce a dominant, discriminatory point of view. The Halifax race riot of 1991 was then analyzed to see how reporting developed on that event. Race was highlighted in the papers as at the root of the problem, but in a variety of ways: racism in bars, racism by the police, racism and poverty, and so on. The shifting accounts of what happened bring home the idea that interpretation is central to the understanding of an event.

The issue of interpretation was taken apart further in the analysis section, where we looked at an initial account of the event to see how it was constructed through discourse. The account was found to have a structure that enables an interpretation of what happened as a race riot. Not every news article on racial conflict is going to have such a structure, of course, but the structure of this one leads a reasonable reader to "see" that a race riot occurred. The importance of looking at how media discourse portrays the world becomes more apparent when we realize the extent to which our knowledge of the world is extralocal and known only through the news. More than one person, myself included, had relatives phone from Toronto because they thought Halifax was in flames, burning in a racial conflagration.

Notes

1. *Halifax Herald*, July 19, 1991: A1.
2. "In search of solutions," *Halifax Herald*, July 20, 1991: A6, editorial.
3. "Racial tensions reignite," *Halifax Herald*, July 20, 1991: A1; "Blacks lack confidence in police—Gray," *Halifax Herald*, July 22, 1991: A1; "More black police urged," *Halifax Herald*, July 23, 1991: A1; "Black applicants rare, say Halifax police," *Halifax Herald*, July 24, 1991: A1; "Police commission to look at job equity," *Halifax Herald*, July 25, 1991: A1; "Blacks consider boycotts, marches," *Halifax Herald*, July 26, 1991: A1; "Racism probe launched, Report expected Sept. 1," *Halifax Herald*, July 27, 1991: A1; "Minister's comments blamed for reduced Africville turnout," *Halifax Herald*, July 29, 1991: A1; "In search of solutions," *Halifax Herald*, July 20, 1991: A6, editorial; "Fighting racism now," *Halifax Herald*, July 27, 1991: A6, editorial; "Stabbing sparks renewed violence," *Daily News*, July 20, 1991: A1; "Youths bloodied in assault," *Daily News*, July 21, 1991: A1; "HPD urged to recruit more black officers," *Daily News*, July 23, 1991: A1; "Mayor admits racism in city," *Daily News*, July 25, 1991: A1; "AG vows to take on racist Halifax bars," *Daily News*, July 26, 1991: A1; "City needs catalyst for racial change," *Daily News*, July 23, 1991: 16, editorial; "Mayor out of touch with Halifax realities," *Daily News*, July 26, 1991: 20; "Discouraging start," *Daily News*, July 29, 1991: 12, editorial.
4. "Violence flares for second night," *Daily News*, July 20, 1991: 4; "Police attacked crowd—witness," *Daily News*, July 20, 1991: 4.
5. "Blacks say bars at centre of riot, Halifax police beef up patrols," *Globe and Mail*, July 20, 1991: A3.
6. "Weekend of racial tensions, Rumours link Halifax riot to school brawl two years ago," *Globe and Mail*, July 22, 1991: A4.
7. "Blacks call for action after riot in Halifax," *Toronto Star*, July 20, 1991: A1; "Racial violence flares again in Halifax," *Toronto Star*, July 21, 1991: A1; "Stop cycle of violence, Halifax residents plead" *Toronto Star*, July 22, 1991: A1; "Nova Scotia blacks have 350-year history but feel 'like strangers,'" *Toronto Star*, July 23, 1991: A1.
8. "Halifax blacks, whites plan march against racism," *Toronto Star*, July 24, 1991: A4.
9. "Weekend of racial tensions, Rumours link Halifax riot to school brawl two years ago," *Globe and Mail*, July 22, 1991: A4; "Nova Scotia blacks demand solutions to discrimination," *Globe and Mail*, July 23, 1991: A1; "Recession adds to racial tension in cities, MP says," *Globe and Mail*, July 25, 1991: A3; "Quota system urged, N.S. official backs minority hiring," *Globe and Mail*, July 27, 1991: A4; "Black culture

sold short by tourist brochures," *Globe and Mail*, August 1, 1991: A3; "Blacks, whites join in anti-racism march," *Globe and Mail*, August 2, 1991: A4; "Probe of racial brawl faulted, Halifax police accused of not fully investigating officers' conduct," *Globe and Mail*, December 20, 1991: A3.

10. "City's image takes drubbing in national press coverage," *Daily News*, July 22, 1991: 3; "City needs catalyst for racial change," *Daily News*, July 23, 1991: 16, editorial; "Wide publicity about violence worries tourism operators," *Daily News*, July 23, 1991: 5; "The media spread the message of racial fear and confrontation," *Daily News*, July 24, 1991: 2, column; "Tourism officials slam media reports of racial violence," *Halifax Herald*, July 26, 1991: C1; "Self-serving reporters," *Halifax Herald*, July 27, 1991: A7, letter to the editor; "Fighting racism now," *Halifax Herald*, July 27, 1991: A6, editorial; "Negative media images of blacks help make the perception a reality," *Halifax Herald*, August 1, 1991: C1, column; "Media: it's time to redefine 'news,'" *Daily News*, August 4, 1991: 21; "Media watch group to be formed," *Halifax Herald*, nd.

11. "Riot report splits police, civilians," *Daily News*, December 20, 1991: 3; "Police-black relations not helped in report," *Daily News*, December 20, 1991: 18; "Riot reports worlds apart," *Halifax Herald*, December 20, 1991: A1; "AG vows report will spur progress on race relations," *Daily News*, May 5, 1992: 5.

12. "Leaders call for calm after Sydney," *Halifax Herald*, July 29, 1991: A1; "It's remarkable how many times racism 'isn't a factor' in N.S.," *Daily News*, February 12, 1992: 2.

13. "Media accused of 'inflaming' conflicts of language and race," *Toronto Star*, May 30, 1991: A9; "Media: it's time to redefine 'news,'" *Daily News*, August 4, 1991: 21, column.

14. "Narcotic-trade stigma burden on innocent," *Globe and Mail*, November 22, 1994: A1; "What's your reaction to these faces?" *Toronto Star*, April 9, 1994: B2, editorial; "Don't blame me; work with me, Black community not to blame for Just Desserts shooting," *Toronto Star*, April 19, 1994: A21.

15. "City's image takes drubbing in national press coverage," *Daily News*, July 22, 1991: 3.

16. "Icy roads cause traffic havoc on BiHi," *Daily News*, December 16, 1991: 3; "Quick freeze wreaks highway havoc, No serious injuries reported," *Halifax Herald*, December 16, 1991: A3.

THE LAW AND THE MEDIA

Reality and Anxiety: Crime and the Fear of It."
(*New York Times*, February 18, 1993: A14)

"Judiciary, media clash over limits on crime reporting."
(*Globe and Mail*, June 4, 1993: A4)

"Inquiry report impugns newspaper's fairness."
(*Globe and Mail*, December 14, 1990: A8)

"All the news that's fit to fake."
(*Globe and Mail*, February 15, 1993: A17)

"Cannibal Killer's Kinky Confession—
It's So Sick Cops Kept it Top Secret."
(*Globe*, September 17, 1991)

"Dahmer created zombies to sate his lust, defence says."
(*Montreal Gazette*, January 31, 1992: A9)

"Milwaukee Cannibal Kills His Cellmate!"
(*Weekly World News*, February 11, 1992)

"Cannibal Dahmer collects $12,000 from pen pals."
(*Halifax Herald*, March 7, 1994: A2)

"Moon Landing Was a Hoax!"
(*Weekly World News*, March 5, 1991: A1)

"Andrei the cannibal:
Russian charged with killing, mutilating 53 people."
(*Montreal Gazette*, April 25, 1992: A11)

7

Crime Rates and Crime Fear:
Portraying Crime out of Control

*C*arjackings and home invasions show that crime is out of control; the crime rate is up; violent crime is on the increase; young offenders laugh at the law—these are all contemporary ways of expressing what is becoming an everyday fear about crime. Is crime really on the increase or is it just media hype? This chapter begins with a talk by Paul MacDonald, a former media relations officer for the Halifax city police. He describes some of the difficulties inherent in the job: releasing information about crimes that have been committed, dealing with reporters who are sometimes unfamiliar with police procedures and making sure that the public gets the correct impression of crime so there isn't a social panic.

"Reading the news" looks at examples of how crime is reported in the news, focusing specifically on stories about the increase in crime and crime rates, and the need to "do something about crime." During 1994 several highly publicized violent crimes occurred in Canada, and many news articles asked whether there had been an increase in crime or not. On the basis of these stories, it seems that the media often sensationalizes and exaggerates crime out of proportion to its actual incidence, exactly one of the problems identified by Constable MacDonald.

"Analyzing the news" takes up the idea that the newspapers have to "get the story right," but in order to develop a different idea, the media perhaps creates its own knowledge about the world that doesn't need to exactly mirror "reality." Most people get their knowledge about crime from the media; if they get a distorted view that crime is out of control, their fear of crime might not reflect their actual possibility of victimization. However, although an unreasonable fear has unfortunate consequences for how people live their lives, it is still very real and reflects how a knowledge of the world constructed and obtained through the media is practical knowledge "for all intents and purposes"—fear is discursively produced.

The topic of this chapter is fear of crime, but the underlying theme is that fear of crime is constructed socially, through the media. A social panic unfounded in reality may not simply be a media exaggeration, but it can serve a real purpose in society. A media relations person may have a very difficult job helping reporters "get it right" if there are strong pressures to present a picture of crime out of control and the need for new laws to do something about it.

The talk—Paul MacDonald

I'm the media relations officer with the Halifax police, and I've been on the force since 1966. Approximately six years ago we got involved with community-based policing, and from that I ended up in the job I'm doing now. To start, I had on-the-job training from people who were in this job before. I was sent off to Ottawa to the RCMP school media relations course. When I first came back, naturally I had a phone and a little desk, and I sat there and I waited for the phone to ring. And unless there was actually a news-breaking story, I was never getting any phone calls. Now today, about three years later, the phone is ringing continuously, there are always people coming in to see me, and I created a very, very busy position. I must ask some of the media people what did they do before I came along because they seem to be using me continuously for stories.

Police stories are one of the main staples of the media because they make good reading. A good story is where you have conflict, you have a hero, you have a villain, you have somebody overcoming obstacles. I believe quite often most people, and probably myself included, have read a book or read a story where we empathize with the criminal. The person was smarter than the system, he was victorious in the end, and this makes a very interesting type of newspaper story. So what we have to do as police departments is realize that we are going to be one of the main features, that we have to be able to communicate with the media and try to get our point across, so that the general public understands what police work is all about.

Now just last week we had a police-media workshop. We had members from all the local media attend a one-day workshop. What we tried to focus on was our policies, and for the management people to understand where the media are coming from, because we have to realize that the media today is the watchdog for all of us. People today are just too busy; they don't have time to watch what's going on with all the government agencies, with different industries, with the environment, pollution, people trying to skim money, or wrongdoing.

The police realize that we have an enormous responsibility. We have enormous authority, and along with that goes accountability. One of the main areas where you're going to get accountability is through the media, and I can verify that wholeheartedly. The hardest thing is if a police officer is involved in some type of wrongdoing, having made either a human error or a criminal error, to stand up and say, "Oh yes, we did that. That's one of our people. Yes, he did this." You always want to try to fluff it over, you want to say, "Well, maybe I can get back to you tomorrow." It's human nature that you'll try to say, well, maybe this'll go away. But with our policy that we were discussing with the media, and that we've implemented, what we're attempting to do is become more forthcoming, more outward. Why, start off with something that leaks to the media and it ends up on page seven today, a small little brief; then two days later it's on page three, by Saturday it's a front-page story, and each day people are following it as it progressively gets worse and worse. Instead of coming out, have your whole front-page story that day, let everybody judge what happened. There are incidents where it may look like it's completely wrong, and sometimes you'll get the sympathy or the understanding from the general public to say, "Oh, I see why this happened." But if you just stonewall, say "no comment," if you try to pretend it doesn't exist, then you're going to end up putting in the minds of the investigating reporter that there is more to this than meets the eye. But if you give everything out, then you're going to end up with a front-page story naturally, but it's going to come and go. And try to get into your story why this happened, and what's going to be done to try to prevent it from happening again.

So I don't know why anybody in the world wants to be a reporter, they have to be crazy. I mean how do you go to work and be a police reporter today, tomorrow you're working on pollution in the harbour, the next day you're talking to some lawyers about some fraud cases, and the next day you're talking to somebody about the environment. You have to be an expert in every field that I can think of, and one of my main jobs is clarity. I have to explain everything. I mean, even though I feel that they know what I'm talking about, I have to double-check. Because quite often what they'll do, they'll put a junior person on as a police reporter, especially when you're busy.

I'll give you an example that happened just the other day. A reporter asked me about a certain case, and I said, "Yes, the person will be arraigned in court tomorrow morning on weapons charges." And the reporter said, "What do you mean?" I said "What do you mean what do I mean?" And they said, "Arraigned, what's that?" And I said "Oh." And you have to go back and explain.

I'll just give you another example. A while back a reporter called and said, "Do you have any suspects in the motorcycle-rapist incident?" This was about three months into the investigation. And I can't say, "Yes, we have a suspect," because for example, if we do have a suspect the person may flee the area. If we say we don't have a suspect, the person says, "Oh they don't know who I am," and maybe encourage the person to do it again. So I really don't say if we do have or don't have suspects. So I said to the reporter, "We do not have any warrants out for any particular person's arrest. There has been no arrest in this case, it's still under investigation." The headline the next day said "Police have no suspects in motorcycle-rapist case." And we did have a suspect, we knew exactly pretty well who it was, we were preparing the case to go to court, so the investigator at that time comes running up with the newspaper and demanding, "Why did you tell them there was no suspect, I'm going to lay charges, you know." So I called the reporter and I said, "Well, I didn't tell you there was no suspect." "Well, you said there were no warrants. And you said there were no charges. So there can't be any suspects."

So that's where you have to get into clarity. For how does a person be a reporter and talk to me one day, and talk to somebody from the Nova Scotia Power Commission the next day about gridlocks and power lines, and try to understand exactly what that person's talking about?

I think one of the main issues is who is going to make the decision on what information is going to be used. The media would like to come in and look at all the police reports, read them, and say "OK, we'll use this and this." The police are looking at all the reports and they're saying to the media, "You can't have this, you can't have this, you can't have this, but we'll give you this." So we're trying to come to some type of a compromise. We have the responsibility to the person who made the complaint not to identify that person. We have the responsibility to the person, if there is a charge, that they have a fair trial. We have to stay away from opinions. We have to stay away from past records of people. There are a number of issues that we have to try to stay away from. And if you look at it, I am the person that ends up making the press release.

If you look at the media structure also, you have the news editors, the assignment editors. They receive the information from the reporter, it follows back down to the person who is reading the news. And somebody has made the decision that it was a suicide. We're not going to show this. However, this person was very prominent; he tied up 5,000 people going home on the bridge. So now we're going to use his name. So somebody in their hierarchy makes that decision. Somebody in our management makes the decision of "No, we're not going to do this, we'll do this and this." And that's where I think it's important that the police and the media try to understand each other. Not so much for the fact that, yes, we want a better image.

I can guarantee you if I send out a press release or I contact every media outlet and say we have a great new crime prevention campaign, and would you meet us here tomorrow morning and we'll reveal it, we'd have maybe three or four reporters. If there was a major crime happened here, you wouldn't even have to call the reporters. You would have every reporter dying to get into the place because crime prevention programs aren't really that interesting.

To sum it up, what we have to get back to with our department and with all our departments, is with the community-based policing, and the media is the major problem. The media can give a perspective on crime, sometimes they're right, sometimes they're wrong. The media can give a perspective that every house in the south end is a potential target. You better lock your doors and put chains and get guard dogs. They can heighten fear or they can lessen fear. And being the police, we have to be very careful how we approach or we can heighten the fear of crime or take it down to lower than it actually is.

Reading the news

Paul MacDonald raises several concerns about the interaction between police and reporters, echoing some of the points that will be brought up later. He says it is important to make sure the media gets the information right, to avoid misinterpretations and misinforming the public. The risk of sensationalizing crime, for example, is that it can both feed into and increase the fear of crime in the community (Leyton, O'Grady and Overton 1992). Here I shall addresses how the media topicalizes that fear, specifically how the media portrays increases or decreases in the crime rate, and how it represents people's fear of crime. Articles 7.1 and 7.2 topicalize the widespread concern that kids are getting away with murder.

Article 7.1
Bill would get tough with young criminals
(*Halifax Herald*, May 13, 1993: D9, Capsule)

Ottawa (CP)—Youths as young as 10 could be prosecuted for crimes and young murderers would face up to 10 years in prison under a private member's bill introduced Wednesday by Liberal MP John Nunziata.

"Presently a 10- or 11-year-old can commit murder and literally get away with it," said Nunziata, who represents a Toronto riding.

His proposals would also push 16- and 17-year-old offenders into adult court, instead of youth court where they usually end up under the current Young Offenders Act.

"It's time we stop treating 16-and 17-year-olds like babies," said Nunziata.

"If we prosecute them in adult court, it would act as a deterrent to criminal behaviour for themselves and their peers."

Private members' bills rarely become law.

Justice Minister Pierre Blais has said he is considering some changes to the Young Offenders Act—including altering the minimum and maximum ages—but has not introduced any specific proposals.

Article 7.2
MP's bill tough on young offenders
(*Winnipeg Free Press*, May 13, 1993: A15, by Bob Cox, Canadian Press)

Ottawa—Youths as young as 10 could be prosecuted for crimes and young murderers would face up to 10 years in prison under a private member's bill introduced yesterday by Liberal MP John Nunziata.

"Presently a 10- or 11-year-old can commit murder and literally get away with it," said Nunziata, who represents a Toronto riding.

His proposals would also push 16- and 17-year-old offenders into adult court, instead of youth court where they usually end up under the current Young Offenders Act.

"It's time we stop treating 16-and 17-year-olds like babies," said Nunziata.

"If we prosecute them in adult court, it would act as deterrent to criminal behaviour for themselves and their peers."

Private members' bills rarely become law.

Justice Minister Pierre Blais has said he is considering some changes to the Young Offenders Act—including altering the minimum and maximum ages—but has not introduced any specific proposals.[Ω]

Nunziata introduced the bill the same day as David Andrew Fraser, 16, of Calgary, pleaded guilty in adult court to fatally stabbing teenager Ryan Garroch in a schoolyard a year ago.

Fraser faces life imprisonment, but will eventually be eligible for parole.

Garroch's family, concerned that Fraser might give a maximum five years in prison, spent much of the last year lobbying for changes that would toughen the Young Offenders Act.

Nunziata says the Act is seriously flawed and requires fundamental changes.

"At present the (act) is an invitation to certain young people to break the law," said Nunziata. "It's a joke in a lot of cases."

His bill would:
- Make the act cover children aged 10 to 15. The current act covers those aged 12 to 17. Younger children cannot face a charge. Older teenagers can be sent to adult court for more serious crimes.
- Raise the maximum penalty for first-and second-degree murder to 10 years from the current five.
- Allow for the publication of young offenders' names after a second conviction for a serious offence.

The bill is one of many introduced by MPs on criminal justice issues recently.

In this chapter's notes, the newswire source is indicated to show how broadly available the stories are—CP (Canadian Press), AP (Associated Press) and so on. The newswire is a vital source of stories that can be re-edited to fulfil the daily requirement of putting out a small or local newspaper without large resources. The result, however, is homogenized news, universally available and extralocally produced, such as the two preceeding articles published on the same day in Halifax and Winnipeg.

Articles 7.1 and 7.2 are quite typical of the concern over crime reported in 1993. The original story was made available across Canada through the CP newswire and included quotes from the MP sponsoring it. One thing immediately apparent about these two articles is that the first 156 words are identical and cover in detail the changes the MP's bill would make. At that point (identified with an omega symbol: Ω), the *Winnipeg Free Press* article includes material not found in the first, referencing a particularly violent youth crime in Calgary and lobbying by the victim's parents for changes in the law.

The titles of these articles presume that there is a problem with young offenders that is currently not adequately dealt with by the criminal justice system. Liberal MP Nunziata says that youths who commit murder "get away with it," that the current law treats some juvenile offenders "like babies" and that toughening the law will "act as a deterrent." However, the article glosses over deeper questions of how often murder is committed by youths, whether there is actually an increase in youth crime and whether increasing penalties would increase deterrence. Independent of other evidence, a reader could be lead to the conclusion that there is a problem and that it is necessary to do something about it.

Article 7.2 especially conveys the intractability of youth crime, citing a relatively rare example of youth violence where one teenager stabbed another. The victim's family is said to have lobbied for changes to the law that would make sentences longer and "toughen the Young Offenders Act" (YOA). Nunziata says the YOA is "seriously flawed" but is not quoted with respect to what these flaws are. He is quoted as saying that the YOA is a "joke" and "an invitation . . . to break the law." The proposed bill would lower the age of youths the Act covers to ten, double the maximum penalty for murder and partially remove the publication ban that currently protects the identity of young offenders.

The perception that youth crime is escalating in our society and that the law is too soft on young offenders is created by many such news articles, commentaries, and opinion and editorial pieces. However, it is not easy to know whether the problem they describe is exaggerated or not; many of the news reports are as innocuous as Article 7.3.

Article 7.3
Youths keep police busy on weekend
(*Halifax Herald,* November 15, 1993: A1)

1   Two groups of youths kept Halifax police busy on the weekend.
2   Friday night, 10-15 teenagers were involved in a fight outside a home on Regent
3   Road around 9:30.
4   Police said five males were questioned and released that night.
5   One youth left the scene with a broken nose. Another had some teeth knocked out
6   and suffered other facial injuries.
7   Police said some of the youths wielded baseball bats during the fight and police
8   also found two steak knives outside the house.
9   Close to 15 officers were called to the scene.
10   A spokesman said police will consult with the Crown prosecutor's office concerning
11   charges.
12   In another incident late Saturday, 25-50 youths aged 13-18 threw rocks at several
13   houses in the Lacewood Drive area and broke a couple of windows, police said.
14   The group then went to Sybyl Court and tipped a car on to its roof.
15   A spokesman said there were no arrests and police are still looking for suspects
16   in the incident.
17   The two incidents are unrelated, he said.

This article relates crimes committed by youths: violent assaults involving weapons (lines 2–11) and unrelated incidents of vandalism and mischief (lines 12–17). There is no commentary or editorializing, seemingly just a description of the facts. However, the account textually organizes the facts and the events are told from a police point of view, citing details from police sources: "five males were questioned and released" (line 4), baseball bats and knives were used as weapons (lines 7–8), charges may be laid (lines 10–11), there was a second group of youths (lines 12–13) and, although no arrests were made, police are still looking for suspects (lines 15–16).

This story appeared on the front page, and "placement" is one way to gauge the relative importance of a issue. By themselves, these events cannot rank alongside international terrorism, corporate crime or political corruption. The article is interesting, however, for how it reports relatively minor incidents involving youths that can be construed to be part of a much bigger problem facing today's society. The article trades on and reinforces a "social panic" about the link between youths and crime, and the attention these youth crimes receive might be out of proportion with reality. Relying on the police as the main source of information reinforces the seriousness of the crimes.

In contrast, Article 7.4 disputes and downplays the sense that crime is out of control. Readers are told that Canadians were not any more likely to be victims of violent crime in 1993 than they were in 1988 (lines 1–3). The research on which this report is based comes from a survey on personal risk, part of the General Social Survey program that involved telephone interviews of approximately ten thousand adult Canadians (line 4). Twenty-five percent of those surveyed had been victimized by crime over the preceding year, the same proportion as in 1988 (lines 4–6). And a majority of these crimes were not reported to the police (lines 18–28), perhaps because they were felt not to be serious enough. Crime was highest in urban areas, with women and the young suffering the highest rates of victimization (lines 29–34). A criminologist from the University of Toronto puts crime "into perspective," saying that the view that crime is out of control is "hype," presumably caused by the media (lines 7–12). Because the study surveyed more than ten thousand people and found that their likelihood of victimization had remained unchanged from 1988 to 1993, the "almost half of us" who thought crime had increased (lines 2 and 13–15) must simply be wrong, victims of distorted information.

Article 7.4
Crime not up, but concern is—StatsCan
(*Daily News*, June 14, 1994: 8)

1 **Ottawa (Southam)**—Canadians are no more likely to be victims of crime than
2 they were five years ago, yet almost half of us think crime has increased since
3 1988, according to Statistics Canada figures released yesterday.
4   About one-quarter of the more than 10,000 Canadians surveyed in 1993 said they
5 had been victims of at least one crime in the preceding year, the same number
6 found in a 1988 survey.
7   While the figure shouldn't make us complacent about crime, it should put it into
8 perspective, said University of Toronto criminologist Anthony Doob, who co-
9 authored the survey report.
10   "The kind of hype that crime is out of control should be questioned seriously," he
11 said. The survey results "allow us to look more reasonably and rationally at crime
12 policy."
13   A total of 46 percent of Canadians thought crime in their neighbourhoods had
14 increased, yet few thought their communities had more crime than other places in
15 Canada.
16   "Crime may be perceived to be a problem—but for the most part, most of us see
17 it as being located somewhere else," the survey report said.
18   The study also revealed that 90 percent of sexual assaults are not reported to
19 police, while 68 percent of other assaults go unreported.
20   And in 30 percent of the sexual assaults and 20 percent of the non-sexual
21 assaults, fear of revenge or reprisals was among the reasons victims gave for not
22 reporting the crime.
23   But Doob cautioned that many of the sexual and non-sexual assaults were
24 considered by the victim to be too minor to report, a personal matter or best handled
25 another way.

26   In about half the cases, victims said they didn't want to get involved with police.
27   "People are making individual, strategic decisions about reporting crime," Doob
28   said. "They're in effect saying, does it make sense for me to report this crime."
29   Crime victims were most likely to be young, urban dwellers and women who are
30   single, separated or divorced.
31   People aged 15 to 24 were three times more likely to be victims than those over
32   age 24. Urban dwellers were victims 44 percent more often than rural dwellers.
33   And separated or divorced women had the highest incidence of being victims—
34   twice as high as for separated or divorced men.
35   As in the past, the majority of sexual assaults and assaults were committed by
36   people known to the victim.

This Southam News article both topicalizes and dismisses crime fear. The concern about crime is clearly up, yet based on people's own reports of victimization, the experts can find no empirical justification for it—leaving people's feeling that crime has increased without any real basis. No consideration is given to the idea that there may be other good reasons for people to think that crime had increased: that people could be more aware of crime, people could be concerned that the criminal justice system is not dealing adequately with crime, or the media may have created the fear in the first place. And no consideration was given to the possibility that a personal sense of victimization can change over time, as people become more desensitized to crime. And, finally, why should fear be rational? It is difficult to know what is being measured here.

This story was printed as a national front-page story, and in smaller papers as well.[1] The articles were similar, citing various statistics to buoy the claim that victimization rates had not increased, even though people had the apparently erroneous perception that crime had increased. Another article in the *Globe and Mail* proclaimed that light had been shed on Canadian crime, and its draw read "Law and Order. Canadians' growing fears of assault and intrusion result from increased reporting of anti-social acts. In fact, the numbers show that violent crimes such as murder are not on the increase."[2]

A similar article from the United States compared public fear of crime with police crime statistics.[3] This report was not based on a victimization survey but on police statistics, which are based upon people's willingness to report incidents to the police in the first place and thus are generally felt to underreport crime (Jackson and Griffiths 1991; Linden 1987). The article began with "Contradicting a widespread perception that New York City is more violent than ever, the Police Department released its official 1993 crime statistics yesterday, which show that reported incidents of violent crime decreased modestly for the third year in a row." This is the only reference to public fear, while the rest of the article deals solely with the statistics. The question of whether crime has actually decreased or reports to the police have simply dropped is not addressed. No reference is made to who said there was widespread fear, what evidence this statement was based on or what could account for it. The notion that public fear is widespread yet groundless seems to be a common theme in the media, just like the contradictory theme, that crime is increasing. It is puzzling.

The 1992–93 period witnessed a spate of articles on the fear of crime.[4] A *Globe and Mail* editorial cartoon even showed Santa Claus in an army surplus store holding a newspaper headlined "Fear of Violent Crime Growing," asking for a red bulletproof vest with white fur trim![5]

At the same time as official surveys are being published showing that victimization trends are unchanged or decreasing, there are reports that Canadians are not only afraid but angry. The results of an Angus Reid poll reflects a growing law and order approach to crime.[6] Respondents are quoted as favouring the return of the death penalty in certain cases, tougher rules on parole and manual labour for young offenders. Not only does the public seem to want tougher measures against crime, politicians are taking those measures.

The shooting of metropolitan Toronto police constable Todd Baylis in June 1994 became a focus of concern about immigration.[7] Editorials called for changes to the process, because the accused had been able to stay in Canada for two years after he had been ordered deported following a criminal conviction for drugs and weapons. When arrested, he was found to have two loaded semi-automatic handguns in his possession.[8]

The fallout from this particular murder and the femicide in April 1994 of Georgina Leimonis at the Just Desserts cafe in Toronto created demands for a review of immigration policies.[9] The immigration minister responded with a policy to deport immigrant criminal offenders and was quoted as saying "[I] will not allow people to make a mockery of our laws and [I] will not put Canadians at risk."[10]

The immigration minister was quickly criticized for assigning only a twenty-member RCMP task force to the job of tracking down and deporting immigrant criminals, for indicating confusion in immigration policies in general, for contributing to members of minority ethnic groups being unfairly targeted as criminals, for unfairly targetting immigrants who have been on welfare perhaps through no fault of their own and for allowing failed claimants to become landed immigrants if they can avoid deportation for three years.[11]

In an unusually public statement, a metropolitan Toronto police officer said there should be better controls on immigrants who come to Canada— controls that in any other situation would be considered an infringement of one's constitutional rights, an invasion of privacy and a violation of the right to be presumed innocent. In Article 7.5, this police officer comes out in support of what critics call a conservative law and order approach.

Article 7.5
All immigrants should be fingerprinted, cop says
(*Halifax Herald*, July 14, 1994: D24, Nation in Brief)

1 **TORONTO (CP)**—Immigrants should be required to carry photo I.D. cards bearing
2 their fingerprints, says a senior police officer who was on duty the night a fellow cop
3 was shot to death.
4   "If people want to come into this country, they shouldn't mind being fingerprinted
5 and having those prints kept on file," said Sgt. John Evans, who works at 12 Division,
6 the suburban station where Const. Todd Baylis worked.
7   "It means trampling on some civil rights." Evans, 51, said he's speaking out
8 because he plans to retire from the force.

A study conducted by Statistics Canada and released in July 1994 showed that immigrants are more hardworking, better educated and more stable than native-born Canadians, countering the view that the immigration system lets in criminals.[12] The "immigrant" who killed Constable Baylis had come to Canada from Jamaica at age eight and was only in a narrowly bureaucratic sense Jamaica's problem. In July 1994 the prime minister of Jamaica said in a speech in Ottawa that the deportation of immigrants would be no solution for Canada's social problems, and that the number of deportees returning to Jamaica was contributing to a rising crime rate there.[13]

Getting tough on crime, then, seems on the surface to be a response to a failure to control crime, especially crime committed by immigrants and youths. But at the same time measures are being introduced against these groups, Statistics Canada is saying that crime rates are actually not increasing. Why has a National Crime Prevention Council been formed to combat the social causes of crime if there is no crime epidemic?[14] Why not set up a National Crime Fear Prevention Council to reassure the public that the government is doing its utmost to protect them from harm?

When one reads the newspapers, it seems difficult to ascertain if the public's fear of crime is misplaced or if there really is an escalating crime problem that requires tough solutions. If there is such an urgent problem to require tougher legislation, then perhaps the public perception is correct. But if the fear of crime is simply exaggerated, then what are the new crime control measures designed to correct? The media seems to be sending out contradictory messages, that crime is on the rise, but the public's fears are unreasonable. However, asking such questions presupposes that the framework of "crime rate stable but fear rises" is the correct one. Why compare perceptions to official rates of crime? These questions are taken up in the next section.

Analyzing the news

One wonders what an unreasonable fear of crime would look like. One 1994 article began with the phrase, "Canada has not become more violent and crime against individuals is not on the upswing, but many Canadians nevertheless believe the crime rate is rising, a Statistics Canada report says."[15] Based on victimization studies, this *Globe and Mail* article continues to say there is no greater risk of crimes such as robbery, assault, theft and sexual assault in 1993 than in 1988. The public's fear of crime is made to seem exaggerated in comparison to the "objective reality" of crime statistics, and a co-author of the report is quoted as saying that "There is still a crime problem . . . but let's not be hysterical about it." The explanation for the "hysteria" is presented as this: "politicians and the media are to blame for the public perception that the crime rate is escalating."

The news report states that, comparing 1988 and 1993, the assault rate remained the same at 67 per 1,000 respondents, robbery declined from 13 to 9 per 1,000, and theft of personal property dropped from 59 to 51 per 1,000. No other comparative numbers on criminal victimization are given. In 1993, the chance of urban household victimization was 222 per 1,000, compared to a rural rate of 133. The urban victimization rate for women was reported as 20 percent higher than for men, which the co-author says results from underreporting that probably occurred in the past, making current numbers seem artificially high in comparison.

The actual study the newspaper report is based on is a large victimization survey, which has two measurements of crime and one measure of the fear of crime (Gartner and Doob 1994). The first measure of crime is the rate of victimization reported to researchers, which shows not much overall increase. The figures reported in the news article are reproduced in Table 7.1.

The second measure of crime shows that the official rate of crime reported to the police has increased. For example, sexual assault increased from 1.0 per 1,000 people in 1988 to 1.2 per 1,000 in 1993; and theft increased from 28.9 to 30.2 per 1,000. The other categories of crime exhibited similar modest increases. Rather than attributing these numbers to an increase in crime, which would contradict the previous results, they are explained by the researchers as resulting from a simple increase in reporting and not to any real increase in crime itself, a conclusion which is defensible, but arguable because it is difficult to know whether reporting "really" goes up or not.

The news article says only that 46 percent of people surveyed think that crime has increased, and that women were four times as likely as men to say

Table 7.1
Personal victimization rates per 1,000 population

	theft	—	sexual assault		robbery	—	assault	—
	1988	1993	1988	1993	1988	1993	1988	1993
Canada	59	51	—	17	13	9	68	67
urban	70	57	—	18	14	9	72	72
rural	46	36	—	14	—	—	56	53
15-24	123	93	—	48	39	23	145	155
25-44	65	61	—	17	10	9	80	69
45-64	22	29	—	—	—	—	19	38
male	58	51	—	—	17	12	74	68
female	61	51	—	29	10	6	63	66

Source: Gartner and Doob (1994).

they felt unsafe walking in their neighbourhoods alone after dark. Neither of these "facts" shows an obvious increase in fear, let alone an unfounded one. We do not know if the perception of an increase in crime is higher than in 1988; and a fear of crime is not the same as fear of being victimized. For example, I am not more afraid for my own personal safety, but I think there is more crime in general in society.

In terms of the perceived change in the level of crime, it's evident that it isn't really sufficient to say that 46 percent of Canadians think crime has increased—the Juristat survey itself (Gartner and Doob 1994) says that 43 percent believe crime has stayed the same, and 4 percent think it's decreased! The highest perception of an increase was in urban areas, with 48 percent believing crime had increased, while in rural areas 56 percent believed it had decreased or stayed the same, as Table 7.2 shows. This is certainly not hysteria, as the media account would have us believe.

Table 7.2
Perceived change in neighbourhood crime in the past five years (%)

	increased	decreased	same	don't know
all	46	4	43	8
urban	48	4	41	8
rural	40	4	52	4

Source: Gartner and Doob (1994)

Another "fear fact" cited in the news story is that the number of women who felt unsafe increased from 39 to 42 percent, but it is difficult to see this as hysteria because the numbers aren't there to support it. If we look at violence against women, it would seem there is good "objective evidence" to justify being afraid to walk alone at night, even though the study points out that most sexual assaults are committed by people known to the victim. Perhaps the level of fear is higher in 1993 because there was not as much awareness of violence against women in 1988; perhaps the higher fear of victimization comes from women being less likely to think it can't happen to them; or perhaps women's fear is based in their knowledge that the criminal justice system has not always acted in the interests of women.

A second news article on this study pointed out that the percentage of respondents saying they felt "very safe" walking alone in their neighbourhood after dark went down from 40 percent in 1988 to 32 percent in 1993.[16] This decline in confidence is not the same as a rise in fear, but what exactly did the justice minister mean when he said media coverage may be to blame, and how are we meant to "keep it in perspective"? The whole problem is not really knowing what to believe about crime, so what would it be like to "keep it in perspective?" The hightened "law and order attitude on crime" may signal frustration with the criminal justice system more than fear.[17] Are both frustration and fear supposed to mirror the rate of criminal victimization? Are emotions supposed to be reasonable and match official statistics?

The official crime rate generated by the police and reflected in the Uniform Crime Reporting (UCR) statistics depends on crime reported by the public. The victimization rate generated by the General Social Survey (GSS) depends on crime reported to researchers. The second will reflect a higher incidence of crime in society than the official rate simply because people are often reluctant to step forward and report crime to the police. The third crime rate we deal with here is people's subjective impressions of crime increase. To compare this with objective information collected from the GSS or UCR statistics is unfair and misleading. Although police and government researchers know more about victims and criminals than most of us, they do not necessarily know more about being a victim or a criminal, and their knowledge that crime is not increasing does not mean that the "perception" that it is is false. The crime and victimization rates do not tell the whole story.

The difference between the crime (UCR) and victimization (GSS) rates and what I call the fear/frustration rate (FFR) is there is no apparent reason to expect that they should be the same—they are all social constructions. Even the best statistics reflect the quality of the questions researchers ask, or the character of police work. As mentioned, people can have a general perception that crime has increased, even though their direct experiences do not bear this out, because they also have a "mediated" experience of crime in society obtained extralocally, through the media. The fear of crime and the perception that the criminal justice system needs to do something about it is a socially constructed experience refracted through the media.

Crime coverage is prominent. The *Toronto Star,* for example, indexed on the Canadian Business and Current Affairs (CBCA) CD-ROM database, lists 135 articles on crime for 1991, 163 for 1992 and 185 for 1993, an increase of 37 percent. The coverage on young offenders has increased as well. The *Canadian Index* lists 32 citations on young offenders (27) and their legal status (5) for 1991; 50 citations on young offenders (38) and their legal status (12) for 1992; and 177 citations on young offenders (110) and their legal status (67) for 1993—an increase of 453 percent!

Articles on young offenders were prominent in the Canadian news in 1993.[18] Many articles are available across Canada through the Canadian Press and are published virtually unchanged in newspapers as geographically diverse as the *Vancouver Sun* and the *Chronicle-Herald.* And although there was some equivocation about whether the rate of youth crime was increasing or not, the overall perception in 1993 seems to have been that it was out of control, a perception enhanced in no small measure by the crime-control platforms adopted by the national political parties in the fall election.

It is difficult to keep things in perspective when the news constantly reflects the fear that crime is on the increase. There are stories about violent youths, the growing use of guns in violent crimes, and the new crimes of home invasion and carjacking, and there is continual debate over whether crime rates are really going up or not. The list is virtually endless.[19]

The revised immigration policy is only part of a growing turn towards a law and order approach to crime. In March 1993 it was announced that the federal and provincial governments had been in talks to amend the Young Offenders Act but had failed to reach an agreement. Changes tabled to the YOA in June 1994, however, included doubling the sentence for first-degree murder to ten years; trying sixteen- and seventeen-year olds charged with serious violent crimes in adult court; sharing information on young offenders with police, school officials and child welfare agencies; using victim impact statements in court; and publicizing information on young offenders where there was a perceived threat to public safety. The issue of lowering the minimum age of responsibility to ten years of age was referred to a Commons committee for further study.[20]

As Kenneth Whyte pointed out in a column for the *Globe and Mail,* however, "the facts argue against an increase in teen criminality . . . the rise in the number of charges laid is due to nothing so much as society's increasing reliance on the courts and constabulary . . . the number of youths convicted of truly violent crime is stable . . . fighting a phantom crime wave can be quite expensive."[21]

Whether crime is actually out of control and on the rise or not is arguable, and perhaps irrelevant, for there is a general *concern* internationally that crime is out of control. The United States passed a $30-billion anticrime bill in 1994 that included extending the death penalty to fifty federal offenses, adding 100,000 new police officers to city streets, banning the sale and possession of certain assault weapons, building state prisons and boot camps, and increasing the range of life sentences.[22] The opening speech of the British government in 1993 proposed the need to curb rising crime, and in 1994 resulted in a bill to restrict the traditional rights of the individual.[23] The German government has also tabled a package of laws to combat violent crime.[24] And in addition to the changes suggested in immigration policy and for young offenders, Canada has proposed to toughen penalties for certain drug crimes.[25]

Given the negative news on crime, and the increasing harshness of the law, that a law and order agenda seems to be sweeping the land. It is possible that the negative reporting around crime is simply the result of bad reporting; or it could be that it is the readers who are unable to "put it all into perspective." However, rather than seeing reporting and reading as "apprentice activities," where what is reported and what is read are objective realities which simply have to be transmitted in the right way, perhaps something else is going on.

Fear of crime serves the interest of a law and order agenda. It is irrelevant at one level whether crime is really increasing or not. If crime is perceived to be out of control, then there is pressure to do something about it. Protestations that crime is actually stable or decreasing have little effect because the tendency of the media is to highlight dramatic and violent crimes. Politicians appear to be quite willing to climb onto the law and order bandwagon and pledge to "do something about crime" as a political manoeuvre. The law and order agenda is part of a larger conservative ideology that is constructed through the discursive reality of the media. So despite whether the topic is "crime out of control" or the "fear of crime is exaggerated," the images displayed in the media promote the same reformist strategy— something has to be done to control crime and assuage fears.

Summary

This chapter began with a police media relations officer describing the work of dealing with the media on a day-to-day basis. This is not an easy job, given very practical difficulties, such as dealing with reporters who might not be crime-literate or who inadvertently distort or exaggerate crime news.

Then various news articles on crime were examined to see how they might contribute to an unreasonable fear on the part of the public. And, in fact, in 1993 there were various news stories on how the fear of crime cannot be said to be based in reality when it is compared with official statistics from the government and police.

However, if people believe in something, then that "practical knowledge" affects their day-to-day living in the world. Fear of crime drives people to lock their doors, buy security equipment and take self-defence courses. And while these are all very understandable responses to a fear of crime, they might not be based in any actual possibility of victimization. But that doesn't matter.

In 1993 and 1994, Canada and other countries passed crime bills which promised tougher sentences for offenders, more minimum mandatory sentences, more use of incarceration, more prisons, more police on the streets, more investment in surveillance technologies, more restrictions on the rights of the individual, and so on. People are willing to go along with these measures because they believe crime is on the increase and/or they believe not enough is being done about it. Does the tail wag the dog, or vice versa; are law reforms driven by public perception, or the other way around? They certainly go together.

News reports fit into a textually constructed reality, where public perception and official policy are part of a loop. The more stories people read about crime, especially of events they can't control, the more likely they are to think crime is out of control, which will produce more stories and generate interest in legal reform, a condition promoting the production of crime news in the first place.

The work of "getting it right" is a lot harder than at first sight, whether one is a police media relations officer, a reporter or a reader.

Notes

1. "Violence not up, Statscan finds, Despite own experience, many Canadians believe crime rate is increasing," *Globe and Mail*, June 14, 1994: A1; "Fear of crime rising—study," *Halifax Herald*, June 14, 1994: A19, CP.

2. "Shedding light on Canadian crime," *Globe and Mail*, September 27, 1993: A9; "Crime drop in Metro," *Toronto Star*, July 22, 1994: A20, editorial; "Crime-rate dip is biggest ever," *Montreal Gazette*, August 24, 1994: A1; "Crime up? Stats show we just think it is," *Toronto Star*, June 14, 1994: A3; "Measuring crime," *Toronto Star*, June 21, 1994: A20, editorial; "Crime rate falling—study," *Daily News*, August 24, 1994: 9, CP; "Any crime too much, says Rock," *Halifax Herald*, August 26, 1994: A10, CP; "Murder rate drops by more than 20%," *Toronto Star*, August 24, 1994: A3.

3. "Crime levels fell in 1992, report says, New York city figures contradict perceptions," *New York Times*, April 2, 1994: 21.

4. "Prisoners on passes little threat, panel says, Program 'works amazingly well,' chairwoman says," *Globe and Mail*, March 18, 1992: A8; "Fear rises as crime storms havens," *Globe and Mail*, October 3, 1992: A1; "Fear stokes debate on release of sexual offenders, State can lock up predators indefinitely," *Globe and Mail*, December 11, 1992: A1, Wall Street Journal; "Media crime coverage under fire as alarmist," *Halifax Herald*, April 1, 1993: A2, CP; "Victoria crime down despite poll fear," *Victoria Times-Colonist*, October 29, 1993: np; "Call for action, Both the right and left want something, Crime the issue with U.S. voters," *Globe and Mail*, November 5, 1993: A16, Minneapolis-St. Paul Star Tribune; "Canadians being 'conned,' Crime wave a 'myth': academics," *Winnipeg Free Press*, November 19, 1993: np, CP; "Canadians warned against buying into crime wave 'myth,'" *Halifax Herald*, November 19, 1993: A7, CP; "Crime fears a 'con,' experts say," *Daily News*, November 19, 1993: 12, CP; "Don't panic over crimes, Rock says," *Toronto Star*, August 21, 1994: A12; "Don't cave in to outcry over crime, judge told," *Toronto Star*, May 3, 1994: A11; "Crime stats contradict public perception," *Globe and Mail*, May 16, 1994: A3; "Let's get tough on criminals, not guns, Reform party says," *Daily News*, May 17, 1994: 12, CP; "Crime tops municipal leaders' agenda, Statistics belie public perception that gun use is on rise," *Globe and Mail*, June 8, 1994: A3; "Fear of crime rising—study," *Halifax Herald*, June 14, 1994: A19, CP; "Murderers walk the streets, fearful Hotline callers say," *Daily News*, June 20, 1994: 5.
5. *Globe and Mail*, December 23, 1993: A16, editorial cartoon.
6. "Canadians want to get tough on crime, poll says, Majority supports death penalty for cop-killers," *Daily News*, June 9, 1994: 10, Southam.
7. "Staff cuts leave crooks loose—paper," *Daily News,* June 20, 1994: 10, CP; "Immigration ignoring dangerous criminals, newspaper reports," *Halifax Herald*, June 20, 1994: A10, CP; "Official defends release of accused cop killer," *Halifax Herald*, June 24, 1994: A15, CP; "Accused cop killer 'fell through cracks,'" *Daily News*, June 29, 1994: 10, CP.
8. "Doing time for immigrant crime," *Globe and Mail*, June 21, 1994: A20; "Immigrant crime reveals goofs," *Daily News*, June 24, 1994: 24; "Immigration officials take heat in review of cop-killing case," *Halifax Herald*, June 29, 1994: C17, CP; "Paperwork kept cop-killing accused from being booted," *Daily News*, June 21, 1994: 11, CP; "Murder suspect faces drug charge, Crack, illegal gun found, police say," *Globe and Mail*, June 20, 1994: A7.
9. "Faster deportation promised," *Halifax Herald*, June 21, 1994: A9, CP; "Round 'em up, Cops want RCMP to nab dangerous aliens," *Toronto Sun*, June 26, 1994: 4; "Flubbed deportation typical, Immigration

Department a real mess, internal studies say," *Daily News*, July 4, 1994: 9, CP; "Tougher deportation rules planned," *Halifax Herald*, July 4, 1994: A10, CP.

10. "Immigration policy aims to please everybody," *Daily News*, July 7, 1994: 9, CP; "Deportation crackdown unveiled, Foreign criminals head exit list, entry eased for some refugees," *Globe and Mail*, July 8, 1994: A1; "Marchi cracks down on criminal immigrants," *Halifax Herald*, July 8, 1994: B7, CP.

11. "Marchi-ing to an offbeat drummer," *Halifax Herald*, July 9, 1994: C1, editorial; "Mr. Marchi's immigration mess," *Globe and Mail*, July 13, 1994: A2; "The face of crime is colorless, Yet security agencies persist in labelling minority groups," *Toronto Star*, March 7, 1994: A19; "Crackdown on criminal immigrants found wanting," *Daily News*, July 8, 1994: 9, CP; "Assessing Mr. Marchi's immigration prescriptions," *Globe and Mail*, July 8, 1994: np; "Marchi 'crackdown' actually a permanent amnesty program for deportees," *Globe and Mail*, July 9, 1994: D6; "Responsible immigration," *Globe and Mail*, July 16, 1994: np.

12. "Study debunks immigrant myths, Harder working, better educated than Canadian-born, Statscan says," *Globe and Mail*, July 13, 1994: A1.

13. "Crime not our fault, Jamaican PM says," *Globe and Mail*, July 15, 1994: A3; "Deportation of lawbreakers no answer—Jamaican PM," *Halifax Herald*, July 15, 1994: C18, CP.

14. "Grits form $4-million crime panel," *Daily News*, July 6, 1994: 37, CP.

15. "Violence not up, Statscan finds," *Globe and Mail*, June 14, 1994: A1.

16. "Fear of crime rising—study," *Halifax Herald*, June 14, 1994: A19, CP.

17. "Canadians want to get tough on crime, poll says," *Daily News*, June 9, 1994: 10, Southam.

18. "More students carrying weapons to school," *Vancouver Sun*, March 2, 1993: A6, CP; "Youth violence is on the rise," *Calgary Herald*, March 2, 1993: A8, CP; "Silence cloaks young sex offenders, Expert estimates only a few youths are ever charged," *Calgary Herald*, March 31, 1993: B1; "Defiance of the law brings claim Young Offenders Act too limited," *Vancouver Sun*, April 16, 1993: A4; "Young scofflaw's bravado fuels law-and-order debate," *Winnipeg Free Press*, April 16, 1993: A2, CP; "MP's bill tough on young offenders," *Winnipeg Free Press*, May 13, 1993: A15, CP; "Bill would get tough with young criminals," *Halifax Herald*, May 13, 1993: D9, CP; "Law can't touch young attackers, Police frustrated, parents furious," *Winnipeg Free Press*, June 25, 1993: A9, CP; "Report says murder rate stable, Youth

crime nothing new," *Winnipeg Free Press,* August 18, 1993: A3, CP; "Youth crime not soaring, study says," *Toronto Star,* August 18, 1993: A2, CP; "Youth crime 'not on the rise,'" *Vancouver Sun,* August 18, 1993: A1, CP; "Worries aside, youth crime not on rise," *Halifax Herald,* August 18, 1993: D16, CP; "Campbell vows stiffer terms for youth crimes," *Vancouver Sun,* August 31, 1993: A4, CP; "Young Offender's Act: Where Canada's parties stand," *Halifax Herald,* September 14, 1993: B16, CP; "Law-and-order mood worries criminologists," *Vancouver Sun,* September 15, 1993: A1, A2; "Teen violence soaring: report, MUC police urged to help combat delinquency," *Montreal Gazette,* October 22, 1993: A1, A2; "More youths face violence charges," *Winnipeg Free Press,* December 22, 1993: A3, CP; "Violent youth cases up 9%, study finds," *Toronto Star,* December 22, 1993: A14, CP; "Number of youth violence cases jumps," *Halifax Herald,* December 22, 1993: A14, CP.

19. "Violent youth cases up 9%, study finds," *Toronto Star,* December 22, 1993: A14, CP; "Metro murders decrease, but use of guns is growing," *Toronto Star,* January 1, 1994: A1; "World-class crime rate," *Toronto Sun,* April 29, 1994: 18; "Metro police dispute StatsCan findings of decrease in crime," *Toronto Star,* August 31, 1993: A9; "Crime rate dispute baffling statisticians, Police, federal experts busy checking figures," *Toronto Star,* September 2, 1993: A6; "StatsCan crime rate was wrong," *Toronto Star,* September 4, 1993: A4; "Shedding light on Canadian crime," *Globe and Mail,* September 27, 1993: A9; "U.S. crime declines but violence still 'shocking,'" *Daily News,* October 3, 1993: 18, AP; "Reality and Anxiety: Crime and the Fear of It," *New York Times,* February 18, 1993: A14; "Crime in D.C. shocks Clinton, 'This is crazy,' President says," *Globe and Mail,* August 5, 1993: A1.

20. "Ottawa backs off on young offenders, No agreement with provinces on amending law," *Toronto Star,* March 25, 1994: A13; "Rock on a roll," *Halifax Herald,* June 3, 1994: C1, editorial; "Rocksolid: Justice Minister Allan Rock, superstar," *Daily News,* June 10, 1994: 25, Southam News.

21. "There's no reason for more stringent controls on youth crime," *Globe and Mail,* June 4, 1994: D2; also see Fasiolo and Leckie (1993).

22. "President urges law officers to press for an anticrime bill," *New York Times,* April 12, 1994: A14; "House takes up crime bill and votes tough measures," *New York Times,* April 20, 1994: A16; "House approves crime bill after days of bargaining, giving victory to Clinton," *New York Times,* August 22, 1994: A1.

23. "British Tories push law and order agenda," *Halifax Herald,* November 19, 1993: C15, CP; "Britannia overrules a crime wave, A crackdown

aimed at youths is altering a centuries-old justice system," *Washington Post National Weekly Edition*, November 21-27, 1994: 17.
24. "Anti-crime law planned," *Daily News*, May 16, 1994: 12, Brief, AP.
25. "Tough anti-drug bill bashed," *Halifax Herald*, February 19, 1994: A10, CP.

8

Crime Stoppers and the Police: The Ideological Construction of Community

*C*rime Stoppers is a relatively innocuous form of crime reporting, where the police publish the particulars of a crime and solicit the assistance of the public to solve it. These items are examined in this chapter within the context of the relationship between the police and the media in modern society. Tony Thomson introduces the issue by looking at how the police have come to be interested in the media as a vehicle for public relations and crime control. He sees the growing use of the media by the police as a way to enhance their own image and extend their control into the community. The point he makes is a critical one, that the police are interested in using the media to their own advantage, not simply in providing a public service. Historically the police have shied away from being too open with the media, but in modern society the media can be used to solicit help from the public, to warn people about crime in their community and to promote the need for more police resources around budget time.

In "Reading the news," some examples of Crime Stoppers are reproduced to show how the police have used this form of crime reporting for crime control. The Crime Stoppers program has been prominent in soliciting public help in solving crimes, and there has been much publicity surrounding its successes. In these examples the emphasis will be on what type of discourse they employ and what types of crime they publicize.

In "Analyzing the news," the Crime Stoppers program is linked to other efforts to extend the role of the police, such as a trend broadly known as "community policing," a movement that promises to reform the character of police–community relations. Community policing arises from a broad-based social movement that has criticized the police for not being responsive to the diverse needs of all groups in society. It has also become a way for the police to defuse criticism and increase their effectiveness. In this section the more critical issue of who defines "community" and threats to its safety is considered. Crime is as much an ideological construction as a real threat, and whoever controls the definition of crime is in a powerful position to manipulate public opinion. Crime Stoppers gives us a very particular representation of crime, one that emphasizes public, violent crime committed by strangers, and that increases fear in the very community the police help define.

The talk—Tony Thomson

I'm not much of an expert, certainly not on the media, but I want to relate to you a particular kind of interest in the subject. What I've been doing for the last little while is studying policing—RCMP and small town policing. I haven't particularly focused on the relations of the police to the media. I want to come at it from the other way. I want to look at how the police use the media. So it's more from the point of view of the interests of the police than of the media.

I want to present an overview first of the traditional image of the RCMP and the process which led temporarily to the undermining of some of the respect and admiration for the force in Canada. In the 1970s the RCMP became more conscious of the need to manipulate public opinion in their favour, to create a positive public image. And in the process of that the relationship between the police and the media had to change. So I'm going to look at how that relationship was developed and how I think it's inherently problematic.

The RCMP had in the past distanced itself from the public and the media—they didn't have a conscious strategy aimed at influencing the public to their benefit. In large measure this was because the desired effect was actually being achieved without their trying to do it. The RCMP had become a national symbol quite early in the century, with the beaver and the maple leaf. The myth of the RCMP had its origins in the taming of the west and the Arctic, in exotic locales and the clash of cultures. Some of this positive propaganda was consciously created: the musical ride, Mounties in red serge, hagiographies written by Mounties about what it was like to police at the turn of the century. So all of this creates a very positive public image of the police which is propagated by the media.

There was a similarity at the time with the creation of the FBI in the United States. Under J. Edgar Hoover the FBI was reorganized in the 1920s, and he was astute in his political use of the media to depict criminals and the FBI agents who rounded them up. There are interesting echoes of the same kind of process, even in Nova Scotia. In the 1920s we hardly had any roads, hardly any automobiles, but we did have an automobile gang. There were a series of break-ins in Colchester and Pictou counties by a gang which was depicted in the media as terrorizing the rural population in the summer of 1921. This made headlines and was very similar to the kind of crime stories that were coming out of the United States. So they're not in the headlines for long and, after they're captured, the *Halifax Herald* make it clear in its account that it was keeping quiet about a very significant development in this case—the RCMP had been involved in the investigation and to the RCMP was given the credit for breaking this rural terror.

Support for the RCMP was not unanimous—for example, liquor laws were being violated in small communities, but many people did not see this as immoral. There's one other example of policing violating standards in the communities, and that's the militant workers in Cape Breton who had provincial police repressing their strikes in the 1920s. Eventually the RCMP move in, but the RCMP is seen by these more militant workers as worse than the local alternative because they're outsiders, they don't represent the community, and they're seen as at the beck and call of the politicians of Ottawa and Halifax, and therefore of the business interests behind them. But that wasn't the dominant view, even in the 1920s and '30s.

The RCMP wanted a different image of themselves. They wanted the outsider image, apart from society—that was the construction that they were trying to cultivate. A view of equitable law enforcement, an end to favouritism, this is the image the RCMP wanted to present, and the mainstream media was willing to go along—an end to favouritism and corruption, a police force which would not be run by the mayor or his cronies in a small town. Close ties with people in the community was not the norm in the RCMP; frequent transfers were. Get them out of the community, don't let them develop close ties. The force was highly militaristic in its discipline: young recruits who have to be unmarried when they join, unmarried for a certain length of time, lived in barracks. In these respects it's not an exaggeration to compare the RCMP to an occupying army. And not surprisingly, the Northwest Mounted Police were modelled after the Royal Irish Constabulary. This is how they were seen certainly by certain groups in Nova Scotia in the 1920s and '30s.

OK, that's the myth, unmade temporarily in the 1960s. I don't need to dwell a great deal on what the sixties meant to policing. Again, if you look south of the border you can find civil rights workers being harassed and murdered by local police officers, minorities in the north trying to defend themselves against police attacks, municipal policing earning the epitaph "pig."

Minorities in Canada were less demonstrative in support of their rights and against the police. There was one exception in Canada—the FLQ. In the process of repressing the liberation movement in Quebec, the RCMP shattered their own mythology. Within the mandate of the RCMP was a domestic spying division. Shortly after the apprehended insurrection details began to leak out about RCMP wrongdoing, and here you see the role of the press. It took a royal commission to detail these particular crimes, the arson, the break-ins, the mail openings and the other illegal activities. And it was very damaging to the RCMP in terms of its reputation for incorruptibility and efficiency. That reputation was badly tattered.

In response to this debacle there were several processes. In the first place the reputation of the entire force had been tarnished by a single division. So the decision was made to civilianize the spy force, to remove it from the RCMP. In fact, what you end up with is a more autonomous organization. It may contain the same personnel, but it has a different letterhead. And more importantly, any blunders cannot be placed at the foot of the RCMP.

Secondly, the RCMP has to become more proactive in the manipulation of its own image. A new posting was created called the police–community relations crime-prevention officer.

There was a third equally important development outside the force to which the RCMP had to respond and that was the advent of community groups demanding more local control over schooling, over politicians, over social services and inevitably over the police. So the important social issue that emerges in the early 1970s regarding the police is accountability. To whom are the police accountable? The RCMP were accountable to the attorney general, to their supervisors, and in general they were accountable to the philosophy of equitable policing.

So there's several models of policing. There's the RCMP occupying-force model. The alternative model appeared to be municipal policing and that was worse. Municipal policing was at the beck and call of local elites of the time. There's a story in one small town that every morning the mayor walked into the police station to give the police chief his orders for the day. With respect to this model of policing, the RCMP were better.

There is also a third model beyond the occupying force or three-tiered policing which is what you had in the towns, and that's community control, police accountability to the community. This is what emerged in the 1970s, but there's a real sociological problem with this third model. The problem as I see it is that "the community" is very hard to define. Who is the community first of all? Ultimately, the community is composed of divergent groups and different class interests. Who represents the community? Who decides who represents the community? These are very important political issues which emerged in the 1970s and certainly now worked themselves out in the newest development which is community-based policing. So who gets defined as representatives of the community is a highly political issue.

From the point of view of the RCMP, who also turned to community-based policing, it meant a new relationship with the media. The RCMP's relationship with the media up to this point had been minimalist: they wanted to give the least possible information, especially about particular crimes. From the point of view of the media, however, what sells newspapers is crime stories. So you had a slight problem. What the media wanted the RCMP didn't want to give. However, now when the RCMP and other police forces go into community-based policing, they want to use the media for their own image. Much of the community-based policing model, in terms of its effectiveness, has to do with positive public perceptions of the police force.

So an unintended consequence is that on the one hand you have the media wanting dramatic crime stories, but you have the police force not wanting to give many details. On the other hand, you have the police force wanting to give positive crime prevention stories which would boost their image in the communities, and yet the reporters and the newspapers had very little interest in crime prevention. When the cop on the street asks the crime prevention officer, "How many crimes have been prevented today?" the answer is "Who knows?" When a reporter is asked the same question, the answer is "Who cares?" Crime prevention is not newsworthy and it doesn't make good coverage. So I see that as one of the fundamental problems in terms of community-based policing in relation to the media.

I want to raise one other issue very quickly, and that is the media's desire to show crimes. In its desire to show crimes and traumatization, it's not going to stop at where the badge is. It's just as interested in showing police misconduct, police deviance, maybe more so. Maybe that's an even hotter crime story, so there is that antagonistic interest. And the police in some ways are feeding into that, particularly in small towns.

And here, I want to raise the question of the training that's appropriate for small-town police officers. There's a firearms training system that comes out of Los Angeles, California. Nova Scotia officers are learning from videos with scenarios of crimes, and they're supposed to role-play in them. They're all Spanish-speaking, and the video inhabits a violent world where guns are everywhere, where no one is to be trusted, where every casual encounter that you might have is fraught with danger. Now the philosophy of this is street survival. You have to approach every situation as if it is imminently dangerous. Now, however appropriate this may be for an occupying army, and the police in Los Angeles may be an occupying army, I'm not so sure it's appropriate in small towns. I think it goes completely contrary to community-based policing, to the kind of interaction that police should have with citizens. You approach citizens in every situation suspiciously. You stop a car and you have to assume it's a high-risk stop. You approach like this, you peer in, this is how you're taught to stop cars in a small town where it's a little old lady or the next-door neighbour. Maybe once in their lifetime the police officers are going to have a life-threatening situation, and maybe that justifies it. But I'm not so sure it does. And it certainly doesn't justify it in community-based policing. My last remark here is this: this kind of firearms training system is actually going to feed into the media because it's going to lead to civilians being killed. It's going to lead to civilians with three in the chest or one in the forehead, even in a small town.

Reading the news

Tony Thomson raises several issues concerning the relationship between the police and the media. One is that traditionally the police have had an adversarial relationship with the fourth estate, perhaps because they saw the press as interfering with the role of the police in fighting crime. Reporters ask nosey questions, sometimes embarrassing the police about unsolved crimes, and could release information that would interfere with an investigation. In this way, reporting can get in the way of policing.

The RCMP in particular, however, have come to see that creating a positive media image can actually aid them in their job. Although it is to the advantage of the police to have a positive image in and of itself, on a deeper level it could also aid in law enforcement. An image of a professional, autonomous, independent police force, for example, builds trust and confidence among the public. At one level the police have to repair the damage created by a traditional image of corruption and political interference in policing; on another level, however, the police can actually turn manipulation of their media image to their advantage. Add to this the modern development of community policing and there is accountability, independence and news control.

How the police use the news to serve their interests in policing is the focus of this section. Crime Stoppers news articles have the potential to broaden the sources of information available to the police to solve a crime. Crime Stoppers represents a movement of the police back out into the community, represented by projects such as Neighbourhood Watch, Community Policing and Coastal Watch, where tips from people are used to detect drug smugglers. The police see the media as something that can be used towards the broader goal of crime detection and prevention, but this can create another type of antagonistic relationship between the police and reporters because crime prevention does not necessarily interest reporters.

Underneath these various programs is a deeper issue: the use of the media by the police to control and prevent crime. It is arguable whether these programs are actually successful, but there are those who think the police should not be in the business of controlling the news, that is too high a cost to pay in order to control crime, and that perhaps crime cannot be so easily controlled in the first place.

Article 8.1 is a typical Crime Stoppers article. The police are soliciting the public to help them in the investigation of an armed robbery. The crime occurred late at night and involved three youths. Framed in different terms, there was a crime, a location, a victim and three perpetrators. Anyone with information is asked to call the number given.

Article 8.1
Police seek help finding suspects
(*Halifax Herald,* November 20, 1992: A12)

1   Police are asking for the public's help in finding three teenagers suspected of robbing
2   a man in Bedford at knifepoint last month. The Oct. 15 robbery occurred on
3   Meadowbrook Drive at 11:15 p.m. One of the suspects was wearing a baseball cap.
4   Anyone with information on the crime is asked to call Bedford police at 494-8900
5   or Crime Stoppers at 422-8477.

The crime in this Crime Stoppers article is framed in official terms as a "robbery." A robbery is not simply the action of stealing or taking through force, it is also a bureaucratic category that enables the processing of an action as a crime and identifies it for the public as against the law. The described event is not framed as a disagreement, a lost wager, or a loan, but as a robbery. The crime violates the sense of "fair play" because three assailants have attacked one person, and it feeds into the current fear that youth crime is out of control. The article presents a "normal" version of a crime through the discourse used to describe the event. This discourse anticipates and creates an unequivocal interpretation for the reader that a crime has been committed. This item is similar to many such articles that appear in local and provincial newspapers.[1]

Article 8.2 desribes another crime, in this case "the theft of a substantial number of lobsters." The lobsters presumably have not wandered away or been misplaced—they have been taken. It is defined as a theft, although it could also have been a liberation. This incident has even less information— the crime, the location, no description of the perpetrator(s), and a request for anyone with information to call the police, although no phone number is given. This event is also framed in official discourse.

Article 8.2
RCMP investigating theft of lobsters
(*Halifax Herald*, December 11, 1992: A4, A20)

1   LUNENBURG—Lunenburg RCMP are investigating the theft of a substantial number of
2   lobsters Monday night from holding crates in the Blue Rocks area.
3   St. Rod Dove said the lobsters were taken from a mooring. Anyone with information
4   is asked to call the Lunenburg RCMP or Crime Stoppers.

Articles 8.1 and 8.2 are short, contain the barest of information and represent requests on the part of the police for information from the public that may help solve these crimes. That seems pretty straightforward. The articles assume that citizens will be willing to help the police. Neither tell the reader much about the work of Crime Stoppers itself, but they follow the standard pattern of reporting a crime and its location and requesting information.

Article 8.3 contains more "affective" information, details that confirm that a crime has occurred and convey a sense of outrage. The victim, a woman, was working alone at night in a convenience store. The offender, a young black male, entered the store and beat her so viciously that she lost consciousness. To affirm the senselessness of the crime, the amount of money stolen is said to be small. There is a sense that no one could approve of such a crime, that it is beyond the bounds of acceptable behaviour.

Article 8.3
Man sought in beating, robbery
(*Halifax Herald*, November 29, 1993: A4)

1   Crime Stoppers is asking for the public's help in finding a man who viciously beat a
2   Dartmouth convenience store clerk on Nov. 21.
3   The clerk, at F&S Grocery, 99 Woodlawn Rd., was working alone at 10:15 p.m.
4   when a man suddenly entered the store and started punching her in the face.
5   The clerk can't remember how many times she was struck because she was
6   knocked unconscious. She was taken to the hospital.
7   The thief stole a small amount of cash from the store's register.
8   He is a black male, 16 to 18 years old, five foot to five foot two, with an average
9   build. He was wearing a light, grey, hooded sweatshirt.
10   Crime Stoppers will pay up to $2,000 for information leading to his arrest.
11   Information concerning this crime, or any other serious crime in Nova Scotia, can be
12   phoned anonymously to Crime Stoppers at 422-TIPS (422-8477). Outside metro, the
13   number is 1-800-565-TIPS (1-800-565-8477). On the MT&T Mobile Cellular network, the
14   number is (TNN) TIPS.
15   Crime Stoppers does not tape or trace calls. Callers will not be identified and will
16   not have to testify in court.

There is perhaps no obvious reason for this article to be more extensive, but the length and detail reflect and create the relative seriousness of the crime. After the initial request for assistance (line 1), and the date and type of crime (lines 1–2), there is an extensive description of the robbery and assault (lines 3–7), a description of the perpetrator (lines 8–9), several numbers to call with information (lines 10–14) and the assurance of anonymity (lines 15–16).

This article is both a description of a crime and a request for assistance; it can also be said to be an advertisement placed by the police. The information in the article is strictly controlled: there is nothing about the stage of the investigation or possible suspects. There are no interviews with neighbours and no pictures. No experts have been consulted to comment on the crime or to argue over its seriousness. There is no contextual information to determine whether this crime fits into a pattern or not. The article is solely about the crime in question and gives us enough information to form a basis for assistance. It is very unlike most newspaper articles on crime.

Many Crime Stoppers articles appear in local newspapers. In 1992 the *Halifax Herald* had almost 150 references to Crime Stoppers listed, and in 1993 almost the same. By themselves such articles do not enhance or detract from the reputation or image of the police; there is no reason to think they tell the reader the police are or are not doing their job. Crime Stoppers does, however, represent a way the media can be used by the police to their advantage. The public can be enlisted to detect criminals and solve crimes, and to affirm that crime exists and something must be done about it.

Moreover, there are articles that applaud the success of the Crime Stoppers program and praise the police for their efforts. For example, in a *Halifax Herald* article from June 1992, a RCMP constable is quoted as saying, "We want to have an open line of communication between the community and detachments ... it's imperative we become involved with the community ... crimes cannot be solved without [public] assistance. Our success rate is much higher when we have the public's co-operation."[2]

An article from November 1992 written by the police reporter for the *Halifax Herald* overviews the Crime Stoppers program in Nova Scotia and praises its success: since 1987 it is said to have been responsible for 1,207 successfully concluded cases, the recovery of almost $1 million in stolen goods and almost $500,000 in illegal drugs. Paying up to $2,000 for information if the culprit is caught and tried, and based on more than 16,000 calls, Crime Stoppers is said to have had a 99 percent arrest rate for the cases featured in newspapers.[3] An editorial in the *Herald* a few days later repeated much of the same information, adding its praises.[4] These "advertorials" are a common feature in the newspapers.

In an editorial published in the *Halifax Herald* in February 1993 and reproduced as Article 8.4, a reader receives a pithy overview of the success of the Crime Stoppers program. The language is interesting, with its images of citizens battling crime (line 7) and crime-fighting partnerships (line 10). The editorial constructs the sense of a "community" which agrees on what crime is and unites together to fight it. This construction and reference to "community" creates a boundary between the law-abiding and the law-breaking. Most readers can identify with a group of others who are "doing something about crime."

Article 8.4
Playing a Part
(*Halifax Herald,* February 3, 1993: B1, editorial)

1 THE GOOD news in recently released 1992 crime statistics for Halifax was that total
2 offences dropped by eight per cent and that there was a marked reduction in the number
3 of break and enters.
4   Credit for such progress belongs in no small measure to the police.
5   Other factors, however, must not be ignored. Among them are programs such as
6 Neighbourhood Watch, Crime Stoppers and others which awaken awareness and
7 which encourage citizens to battle crime. Such efforts helped improve the security of
8 residents and visitors last year and may be partly responsible for increased reporting
9 of crimes like assault and/or sexual assault.
10   It just shows what can be done when partnerships are formed to fight crime in the
11 community.

The editorial attributes the decease in crime primarily to the efforts of the police, and also to programs such as Neighbourhood Watch and Crime Stoppers. With no evidence cited to support such a claim, the editorial is an "advertorial" to promote the police and their programs. Crime rates decrease for all kinds of reasons, some of them very mundane: crime may be reported less, police activity may be down because of decreases in funding and staffing, or crime may have actually fallen. The point of raising objections to the editorial's claim that crimefighting stopped crime is to show that the editorial is not simply a rendition of facts but a construction that offers an interpretation of those facts and may or may not be true. It is the editor's assertion that Crime Stoppers is partly responsible for the decrease in crime.

A different tone was evident in an article from April 1993 where the lead sentence was, "The public deserves much of the credit for a reduction in crime last year in Queens County."[5] An RCMP staff sergeant, speaking to the Queens County Municipal Council, grouped Crime Stoppers with Block Parents, Neighbourhood Watch and Marine Watch. Where the police sergeant attributed "much" of the credit to the public, however, an editorial a day later said that the drop in the crime rate was attributable in "some degree" to the public.[6] The editorial concludes, "There may be any number of reasons for these figures, but one may be sure that good work of the police and law enforcement agents is a prime factor." My point is not simply that the success of the programs in fighting crime is characterized in different ways, but that the solution to crime is characterized as due to "effort" rather than coincidence, public goodwill, or something else. Both articles, regardless of where they place the credit, certainly present the police in a positive light.

The newspaper seems to have no question that Crime Stoppers has been a success. It is said to have been helpful in solving many cases and to have recovered almost fourteen times more in stolen property than was paid out in awards. The awards are funded by local organizations and many are not claimed, a testimony to public altruism. Most of the calls are reactive, providing information immediately after the crime, but in some cases about crimes that occurred in the more distant past. By the end of 1993 it was estimated that more than a million dollars in stolen property had been recovered, that arson cases estimated at $333,900 had been solved and that $750,000 in drugs had been seized.[7]

Analyzing the news

Let us examine more critically the degree to which Crime Stoppers aids police work and crime detection and begin to deconstruct the discourse used in Crime Stoppers articles.

Crime Stoppers is an institutional response to the problem of crime control and is sponsored by dominant institutions—the mass media, the police and private corporations. Crime Stoppers is not based on an official fear that crime is out of control, or on the desire of people at the community level to develop a local initiative to fight crime, but is part of a broader effort to bring the police and citizens closer together. Crime Stoppers articles are emotional portrayals that generate sympathy for the victim and moral outrage against the offender and are often coupled with stories about the program's success, embodied in "discourses of effectiveness and affectiveness" (Carriere and Ericson 1989).

An example of a "discourse of effectiveness" is the article, "'93 pays off for Crime Stoppers," from the *Halifax Herald* of December 22, 1993. Here the media, independently or by quoting the police, commented on the success of a Crime Stoppers program. Such articles are often self-congratulatory, offer little statistical support for claims made, and praise the efforts of police to reach out to the community and generate support for fighting crime. These articles validate the success of the programs and thus legitimate the work of the police. Questions are seldom asked about the moral rightness of the programs, the police are not blamed for not doing their job well and criticisms are not raised about issues such as using citizens as informants.

An example of a "discourse of affectiveness" is Article 8.3. In this article the public comes to identify with the store clerk and to sympathetically see her as the victim of a violent and unprovoked attack. People should be safe to work, walk on the street and otherwise live without the fear of becoming the victim of violent crime. There is no suggestion of sympathy for the offender or of mitigating circumstances, just the portrayal of a vicious act.

In an informal analysis of fifty-two Crime Stoppers articles, I found cases of the police asking for help from the public in solving crime in a variety of newspapers: the *Edmonton Journal, Ottawa Citizen,* and *Halifax Herald,* for example, among others. After screening out articles that editorialized on the success of the programs, the items were categorized by type of criminal offence, location and perpetrator/victim relationship. The main categories of offences depicted in the Crime Stoppers articles were armed robbery (35 percent), sexual assault (15 percent) and break and enter with theft (15 percent). Most of the offences took place in public places (67 percent), such as the street or parking lots, and convenience stores or banks. The perpetrators for which information was available were predominantly strangers, usually white males in their teens or early twenties. The articles generally received prominent placement, appearing on average before page five of the newspaper.

The overall impression created by these items is of public, violent crime committed by strangers. In a more extensive analysis, the complete set of Crime Stoppers citations for the *Halifax Herald* was downloaded from CD-ROM for 1992–93, a total of 332 articles. The results are shown in Table 8.1.

Several patterns can be found in the table. In the top half, all the Crime Stoppers articles are divided into major Criminal Code crime categories to reflect predominant crimes; "other" comprises 115 citations of the total (332) and is an indeterminate category that includes a wide variety of offences, each too small to list separately. When "other" and "advertorials" are factored out, as they have been in the bottom half of the table, we find that break and enter (BE)/theft" accounts for 51 percent of the offences, with "armed robbery" trailing a close second at 38 percent, and 10 percent are sexual assaults. Of the total offences indexed by location (172), 36 percent (61) were "public" and 53 percent (91) were "private." The proportions erroneously make it seem like most crimes occur in the home. However, of the "public" offences 77 percent (47) were armed robberies, 71 percent (65) of the "private" offences were break and enter/theft crimes, and in 12 percent (20) of the cases the location was not known. This makes it clearer that crimes reported in the newspapers as having occurred at a residence are

Table 8.1.
Crime Stoppers news articles[8]

Offence	Location			Relationship			Total
—all offences	public	private	na	strange	known	na	
armed/robbery	47	17	3	61	0	6	67
sexual assault	7	9	2	16	2	0	18
BE/theft	7	65	15	1	4	82	87
other	49	25	41	14	16	85	115
advertorials	na			na			45
total	110	116	61	92	22	173	332
—selected offences							
armed robbery	47	17	3	61	0	6	67 (38%)
sexual assault	7	9	2	16	2	0	18 (11%)
BE/theft	7	65	15	1	4	82	87 (51%)
total	61	91	20	78	6	88	172
% by major category	(36%)	(53%)	(12%)	(45%)	(3%)	(51%)	

Source: *Halifax Herald*, CD-ROM, 1992–93

not primarily intrafamilial crimes where the victim knows the offender. Of the total selected offences indexed by relationship (172), 45 percent (78) were committed by strangers, 3 percent (6) were committed by someone known, and in 51 percent (98) of the cases the identity of the perpetrator was not available.

From a criminological standpoint, what drives these statistics is criminal activity and the nature of police work. Armed robberies make up a significant percentage of public crimes, but break and enters by their nature tend to occur in private. The identity of the perpetrators in either of these groups is usually unknown or they are strangers to the victim; these are not generally acquaintance-victimization types of crimes. Both of these crimes are more likely to be good candidates to appear in Crime Stoppers than sexual assault, precisely because there are less likely to be independent leads for the police to go on. It is less apparent, however, that these crimes do not represent all crime but only crimes for which Crime Stoppers is a useful venue. Crime Stoppers is not intended to be a public information service but is a service for the police. Crime Stoppers articles present a skewed representation of crime because they advertise only crimes for which the police require assistance.

At face value, the impression created by these articles is of violence committed in public places and invasions of one's home by strangers. The victims are largely faceless and could be anyone going about their lives. There is no sense that the victims precipitated the offences in any way, that these were not real offenses, that the perpetrators were objects of discrimination, or so on. At face value, the message readers get is that dangerous people threaten normal law-abiding people and thus constitute a threat to the community. The explicit message of the Crime Stoppers items, that people in the community can help solve these crimes, is thus anchored by the implicit message that crime is an outside force that threatens the community itself.

It is possible that publicizing such crimes, and the high profile of such programs, can actually sensitize people to crime in their neighbourhoods and increase their role in crime detection, but they can also make people more afraid of the possibility of crime as well. The number of elderly, women and urban dwellers who are afraid to walk in their own neighbourhoods at night is growing, and a predominant number of Canadians think crime is increasing.[9] As discussed in another chapter, these trends in the fear of crime are not unequivocal, but they are not trivial either. Fear of victimization is linked to perceived vulnerability and is not necessarily connected to actual risk—it is a social construction. The media is certainly a source of misleading information, but publicity intended to raise awareness can have the unintended consequence of increasing fear of crime and concerns about personal safety. As discussed, the majority of Crime Stoppers articles are about violent public crimes committed by strangers; although these simply might be the types of crimes for which it is most useful to ask for public assistance, one unintended consequence might be to alarm the public and increase its fear of crime.

Many of the Crime Stoppers articles surveyed were not long and did not contain extensive descriptions of violent offences. Most, moreover, did not explicitly exhibit the "discourses of effectiveness or affectiveness"—they did not comment on the overall effectiveness of the program or seek to elicit public outrage—most were concise, with a description of the crime and the offender. The conciseness of the articles, however, did not make them less effective as communicators of the crime-control message. Their abbreviated and technical air added to their official character. There was nothing equivocal or ambiguous about them.

Crime Stoppers is part of a broader effort to bring police and citizens closer together that is generally called community policing (Kelling 1993; Mastrofski 1993; Garofalo and McLeod 1993; Rosenbaum 1993). In part, community policing programs have been instituted to make the police more responsive to the community, as the police have in the past been criticized

173

for not representing the needs of the poor, ethnic minorities and women (Linden 1987). Yet the immediate observation this criticism raises is that there is no one "community"—it is very diverse and divided along class, ethnic and gender lines. Making policing more responsive to the needs of the community is also based on the simple recognition that much of police work consists of calls for service (Reiner 1992). The police do not engage in much proactive crime prevention but rely instead on calls from the public for assistance. In combination, then, the argument is that making the police more responsive to the needs of the public(s), and the public more willing to help the police, will result in more effective policing and crime control. However, the shift from a professional to a community-based model is as much ideological as practical, and the effectiveness of its results are mixed (Hornick, Leighton and Burrows 1993).

Community-based policing involves some reorganization of police structures and duties; and allied programs of a similar prevention or public-service nature are various: Neighbourhood Watch, Operation Identification, the Block Parent Program, Victim Service/Crisis Intervention, Youth Intervention, Sexual Assault Awareness and others (Forcese 1992). Though these programs might be effective in deterring or preventing crime, the public relations benefits are important as well. The police benefit from a positive public image. Moreover, these programs do not necessarily require much change in the traditional method of policing and, because they are overseen by the police, they remain under police control. These initiatives do not challenge police authority or the overall definition of crime.

Crime Stoppers is reactive in nature. The police select the crimes to be published, which are then written up by newspapers to fit their publishing requirements. As media events, these items remain under the control of the police. In that sense, they are exercises in "news control." The consequence of selecting predominantly public, violent crimes committed by strangers is that a view of the world is constructed that serves the interests of the institutional powers behind the Crime Stoppers program: the police, the media and the businesses that provide support.

The view of the world constructed by Crime Stoppers reports is explicitly one of anonymous violent offenders committing crimes in public; the implicit message is that the media can enlist the public's help to aid the police, who are best equipped to deal with these threats to personal safety and property. This is an example of hegemony, of those who are in a position to benefit influencing public opinion. It can of course be argued that the whole community benefits from crime prevention and detection, but in this case there is no reshaping or redistribution of power. The police retain their legitimacy as agents of social control and members of the public are placed into a secondary role as unpaid informants through the vehicle of crime discourse.

The program reinvents the dominant relation between the police and citizens, through media construction of the law-abiding "community" and the portrayal of crime as a threat. The notion of community and the definition of crime are thus constructed by the news articles. In this way, an ideological view of the world is created by texts that create interpretations about safety and danger for the reader, and social control is reinforced.

Summary

The notion that "news control is crime control" does not mean the police actually control the news media—there is no need. The police are in a position to control the flow of information to the media about crime in general: the description of each crime, the stages of criminal investigation, the laying of charges and so on. Reporters are dependent on good relationships with the police and on not negatively provoking what is often their sole source of crime information. It is only when a case enters the court system that the police lose their power to define it, as the press turns to lawyers and court reporters for information on judicial proceedings. Reporting on these subsequent stages of a crime, however, is less common than on initial crime reports and investigations anyway.

The police have come to use the media in their own interests, as can be seen in the specific topics of Crime Stoppers reports. The notion of "community" is explicitly invoked as a way to involve citizens in detecting crime and as a way to enhance the image of the police as crimefighters. This creation of a"crimefighting partnership" between the police and the community is possible in a society where the media constructs social relations and is the dominant source of information about crime in the world.

There is nothing inherently wrong with programs such as Crime Stoppers, but we need to see them in the context of broader historical developments. The police have moved into a much less antagonistic relationship with the media. The consequence has been a subtle distortion of crime news to ideologically reflect the point of view of the police, who are then able to further extend themselves into the community they discursively construct.

Notes

1. "Crime Stoppers seeks abductor," *Daily News*, September 15, 1992: 7; "Crime Stoppers seeks help in finding robbery suspect," *Halifax Herald*, September 14, 1992: A3; "5 on Metro most wanted list," *Toronto Star*, March 3, 1994: A6; "Assault suspect sought," *Edmonton Journal,* January 25, 1992: C3; "Man tortured to death," *Ottawa Citizen*, January

27, 1992: C2; "Bandit hit milk store with a bat," *Toronto Sun*, February 24, 1992: 42.

2. "'Open line' to communities key to new RCMP program," *Halifax Herald*, June 20, 1992: D8.

3. "Crime Stoppers saves N.S. police forces 'a lot of footwork,'" *Halifax Herald*, November 21, 1992: A4, A10.

4. "A Word or Two: Five Good Years," *Halifax Herald*, November 24, 1992: C1, editorial.

5. "RCMP credit public for drop in Queens County crime rate," *Halifax Herald*, April 28, 1993: A5.

6. "A Word or Two: Welcome Trend," *Halifax Herald*, February 29, 1993: C1, editorial.

7. "N.S. Crime Stoppers tops $1 million mark," *Halifax Herald*, May 4, 1993: A6; "Crime Stoppers pays—in money and in crime reduction, Anonymity encourages callers," *Halifax Herald*, July 30, 1993: A8; "Program aids police," *Halifax Herald*, July 30, 1993: A8; "Anonymous phone tip credited for arrest," *Halifax Herald*, August 21, 1993: A3; "$1M in goods recovered through Crime Stoppers," *Halifax Herald*, October 19, 1993: A5; "A Word or Two: Crime Busters," *Halifax Herald*, October 20, 1993: C1; "'93 pays off for Crime Stoppers," *Halifax Herald*, December 22, 1993: A6; "A Word or Two: Stopper Success," *Halifax Herald*, December 27, 1993: B1.

8. These cases were initially coded by headline, date and page, type of crime, location and time, and suspect and victim relationship. The cases were then indexed by criminal offence, location (public or private) and relationship (stranger or known). Not all cases were publicized with the same information, so in cases where the police were looking for an offender, they might state his or her name and the offence committed but not the particulars of the location or the relationship to the victim. Such absences of information were categorized as "n.a." (not available). In some cases the type of offence makes some information unavailable, for example, in break and enters where no one had seen the perpetrator to determine whether they were known or not. Such offences are more likely to be stranger-related than a crime such as assault, but they also have a low investigative priority for the police, which results in less information being gathered about these crimes. The "other" category includes crimes as diverse as arson, fraud, drug charges, missing persons, property damage, vandalism and homicide. Restaurants, convenience stores and banks are categorized as public, but other businesses and residences are seen as private.

9. The 1993 General Social Survey found that 57% of Canadians 65 and over felt somewhat or very unsafe walking alone in their own neighborhoods

after dark, 16% higher than the second highest group, 45-64 year olds; of women aged 15-24, only 14% felt very safe walking in their own neighbourhoods after dark, compared to 50% in the same age category for men (Rosemary Gartner and Anthony N. Doob (1994), *Trends in Criminal Victimization: 1988-1993*, Juristat Service Bulletin 14: 13).

9

Lawyers and Serial Killers:
The Press and Sensationalism

Death, doom and destruction—this chapter deals with sensationalism in the news. The media is constantly full of disturbing stories of tragedy and violence in the world. People become sensitized and callous to it at the same time—news of disasters, genocide, war—all bring the world closer to home while exposing events that, after all, are happening to "them." One of the most chilling examples in modern society has to be the theme of the serial killer, which captures the alienated urban imagination in a way that many other crimes cannot (Leyton 1986; Hickey 1991; Ressler 1992; Sears 1991; Holmes 1988).

As background on the issue of press sensationalism, Darrel Pink describes some of his difficulties as a lawyer in dealing with the media. In his position, he routinely issues press releases and fields requests from the media to provide information on criminal proceedings. One of the difficulties he has found in interfacing with the media is that journalists often lack much of the specialized knowledge of criminal proceedings that is necessary to report on them. His criticism is that reporters are more oriented towards the "30-second bite" than to an in-depth analysis of crime issues. This criticism has come up in other chapters as well.

Reporters are not necessarily inept, but they are perhaps more oriented towards sensationalism than education, which is unfortunate when a story involves something as serious as informing the public about legal issues. In "Reading the news," examples of sensationalism, specifically on serial killers, are provided to ground that point. It may seem extreme to focus on such horrific crimes, but these stories are selected to make the strongest case possible. In these articles readers see horrific details sensationalized, exaggerated and glamourized. Such articles do not educate us about the law or about crime but are simply gruesomely "entertaining" in some macabre fashion.

In "Analyzing the news," the idea of sensationalism is discussed at a deeper level. Whereas Pink advances the idea that sensationalism gets in the way of good reporting, I suggest that it depends on what purpose reporting has in society. The premise that the media has done a bad job means that they could do a better job. Perhaps the problem is not that reporters simply cannot represent the complexities of lawyering (which privileges one form of knowledge over another), but that the purpose of the media is something other than to educate us about the law.

The talk—Darrel Pink

I'd like to pose a series of questions from the perspective of dealing with the media. As executive director of the bar society, I now deal with the media on a regular basis. In terms of the legal system, the courts and lawyers, interest in the media is really heightened at the present time, and whatever is happening in the courts is fair game. But there's somewhat of a paradox in saying that, because five years ago the number of reporters assigned to the courts in Halifax was about four times as great as it is today. In other words, what's happened is the economy has declined and there's increased pressure on the media outlets. They have taken reporters who were formerly assigned the court as a regular beat and have taken them out of that system and they'll do a court story today and a pollution story tomorrow. So rather than developing a pool of expert reporters who have knowledge about the court system and the justice system through its entire breadth, we have a very small number of reporters today that know anything about the justice system and the criminal justice system in particular.

The second initial comment is I think we have to distinguish between the high profile case and what I'll call the mundane case. Around here, in Canada as well, there are a number of cases which have really been pursued and broken by the media. When the story broke on the Donald Marshall case in 1982, the media was literally one day behind the police as the reinvestigation was ongoing. And, but for the media, the story never would have taken on the legion proportions that it did, let alone the public inquiry which eventually resulted; it never would have happened without ongoing media attention.

The Patricia Starr scandal in Ontario was also broken as a media event. The initial disclosures about what she had allegedly done came out of the work of reporters, and it was only the police that followed up and did the same thing. The ultimate charges in Mount Cashel also resulted from the work of reporters. The original police investigation in 1976 led to nothing, it eventually broke in the late 1980s again as a result of disclosure through the media, and public pressure then resulted in a public inquiry and charges being laid.

So in the high profile case, media concentration has and can produce very positive results. There's a down side to that, because the media often are quick to use names inappropriately, throw around allegations that are not well founded, and the libel and defamation laws don't provide a lot of protection because all that does is emphasize the public's attention on the issue, rather than really acquitting the person who may not have been properly charged in the media.

My third opening comment is, I was reading a public relations report that was done for another law society in Canada and I was struck by the comment, "There is value to a suspicious media chasing after the secrets of people and organizations in a position of trust." Well, I dare say there's no place in Canada that can say there's more truth to that statement than Nova Scotia. The events of the last several weeks in this province, in terms of our former premier, have really heightened the role of the media in doing the digging. Four weeks ago the former premier said there were no trust funds, and all of a sudden over the last several weeks, through both disclosures from the party and from disclosures in the media from the public record, the fact of trust funds has developed. I think that those of us that work in the justice system have to be willing to accept that the media is there, is going to continue to be there, and we have to have an open attitude toward them.

Well, just to wrap up the paradox that I started off with, though the media has now been reduced in terms of the number of people that are concentrating on the justice system, the response of the system in an institutional sense has been to create people to deal with the media. The attorney general's department has created a spokesperson, a media relations person, whose job is to act as the go-between. The police have done it as well. The courts have done it, there is an executive assistant to the chief justices, a person that the media can contact. Even in the bar society, when I took over my job one of the things I did was to be available to the media.

The justice system lived for years behind a barricade and gave no information to anybody and acted in this kind of secret method, and the media had to probe and push and poke to get any information. Now the system is attempting to open up, and the question is whether this is really opening up in a way that is going to satisfy the public. The media really is the funnel for the public. What we say, what we do, is screened to the public through the media.

If I issue a media release today, I have no guarantee that it will be given out to the public in the way that I produce it, because it goes through editors and producers and reporters. I had a recent experience where, rather than putting out a media release, I gave a fairly detailed report to the media, six pages long, about a certain thing that had taken place, and the media got it absolutely wrong. They referred to numbers that in no way were reflected in the report, they referred to what was between the lines. Our effort to be honest and open backfired colossally because people said, you're not being honest and open, there must be something that is subtle there that you're not telling us and therefore they speculated and got it wrong.

So one of the crucial factors here, as we use the media as that sieve, is the knowledge of the people in the media. I mean, are reporters knowledgeable about what they're reporting on? They don't know what an arraignment is, for example. Three weeks ago, when Thornhill appeared before the courts, everyone went in and said Thornhill pleaded not guilty. Well, anybody who knows anything about the criminal justice system knows that Thornhill didn't plea anything. He elected to be tried by judge and jury, he didn't enter a plea. He'll enter a plea before the court before whom he's tried. But you can tell the media that, you can repeat it six times, and they will continually get it wrong.

So the attempt to simplify the system can sometimes have devastating results because it leads to misinformation. And although we who are in the system sometimes rely upon the media to describe, to interpret, [and] to make understandable what we're doing, we often do so at our own peril because that information will often be changed and inaccurately reported. The issue of accuracy is very important, aside from the question of knowledge [and] do they know what the system is about. And what do you do when they get it wrong, when not because of ignorance they get it wrong, but they just make a mistake. Do you attempt to correct misimpressions that are left with the public as a result of the story?

One of the big problems I have is, I read the newspapers and watch and monitor the electronic media regularly, but I feel that I'm absolutely unable to objectively respond to what is there, especially if I'm involved in it. I can no longer say what does the public, I mean what does my mother, think about that? And so that's always the problem: do you attempt to correct misinformation?

We have become slaves of the thirty-second clip. For some reason there is a belief among the electronic media, in particular, that things have to be digested in such a way that they can have a sound bite for radio or a video clip for television, and it's got to be short and crisp. Now if I as a spokesperson have to make statements from time to time, if I really want to abuse the system, then I will perfect that thirty-second clip. I'll find the right comment that will summarize, either accurately or inaccurately, what I want to say. It's of no relevance, if it's catchy they'll use it, if it's provocative it will get used. And unfortunately much of what we're dealing with in terms of crime and the justice system and policing and legal issues don't easily allow for that thirty-second clip.

I don't know quite how you do it, but I am convinced that there is a disservice done when the big case of the week is reported in a total of five minutes over five days. That doesn't apply just to justice issues, of course, that applies to all major issues. The media has forced us to break up our thinking into little bites, to deal with it that way.

Another issue that I am very concerned about in terms of the criminal justice system is sensationalization. With regard to crime, if there's no blood and gore, or there's no sex, it's not newsworthy. And if it falls into the category of being newsworthy, then they have to show the dead body. They've got to show the corpse. One of the issues that has been dealt with recently in terms of access to the courts is, how does the media get hold of exhibits? Can they see the pictures that the police have produced of the crime scene? Can they see the bodies? Can they put the body on TV? Well, the jury sees the body, why can't the public see the body? Well, the effect of that in my view is that we are increasingly desensitizing the public to crime. The break and enter of your house is no longer significant, as nobody cares about break and entries, regardless of what the statistics are. The violation of your space, of your property, of your person as a result of break and enter is a very serious matter for the victims. But no blood, no guts, no sex, the media don't cover it.

The final thing is what role should lawyers, law professors and criminologists, the larger group of people who can act as resources to the media, play in interpreting the system to the public? I find the media is not willing, because they don't have the time or the resources, to really go and get good background help. They won't talk to people who can really give them information. They've got to deal with this story because their deadline is two o'clock this afternoon to get on the evening news.

A second concern about the role of lawyers is whether lawyers involved in cases can ever provide an objective opinion. I believe they cannot. Ethically, lawyers are quite limited in terms of the comments they can make to the media while a case is ongoing. But what I'm often concerned about is the desire of the media to talk to the lawyer who is in the front ranks. Some lawyers have an approach that they will talk to the media, and they talk to the media appropriately. There are other lawyers who can abuse the media. I've seen and I've watched lawyers use the media to their advantage, often to the disservice of the public, because the lawyer is using the media to give information that they think that they want out there. And sometimes they want cases argued through the court of public opinion, rather than before the court or tribunal.

I was involved in the Donald Marshall inquiry, and we would often sit back and chuckle at how some reporters, in the break in the morning proceedings, would form a scrum around particular lawyers. After a while, many of the people in the media realized that they were being used by the lawyers who were conducting the scrum, because the lawyer was trying to get something out through them that they may not have been able to get out otherwise. That is a real risk for the media. When the media get too close to lawyers, they can lose their sense of objectivity.

Reading the news

Darrel Pink makes many comments about the relationship between lawyers and the media. He mentions the important role the media has in exposing crime, and yet the difficulty reporters often have in understanding criminal justice procedures. He points out how lawyers run the risk of being misunderstood and misinterpreted by reporters, while at the same time some lawyers use the media to their own advantage. Many organizations rely on the media to inform the public, but the media's focus on the "soundbite" makes it difficult to cover complicated issues properly. These are all important topics related to the relationship between the legal profession and the media.

Sensationalism is another feature of reporting that also distorts stories on criminal cases. Although much crime reporting is innocuous and exhibits the problems pointed out above to a fairly low degree, there are also cases where inaccuracies and the wish to capitalize on the gory are obvious. Sensationalism caters to the worst tendencies of sloppy reporting—to get the scoop, to grab attention, to make a big splash without being careful about all the facts. Sensationalism flourishes in an enterprise where Donald Trump's divorce can mean bigger business than Nelson Mandela's release from prison (Kurtz 1994).

To make a point, the cases of serial killers used here reveal perhaps the strongest examples of sensational reporting possible. Homicide tends to be a heavily reported crime in the news media in the first place, and serial killers especially so. After looking simply at what sensationalism is, in a very highly reported crime, the significance of that style of reporting will be examined more closely.

The "House of Horror" story, Article 9.1, epitomizes the fear of serial killers: they live alongside other people who see them as "affable," "really nice" blokes (lines 29–30), neighbours who never suspect the evil in their midst, in this case one of the worst serial killers in British history (line 3).

Article 9.1
British police find eighth body in "House of Horror"
(*Daily News*, March 9, 1994: 17)

1   **Gloucester, England (Reuter)**—Britain's House of Horror yielded another body
2   yesterday, its eighth, and police said they are digging for more victims in one of the

3   country's worst suspected serial killings.
4   A grim-faced policeman emerged from the ordinary-looking home in the western
5   English city of Gloucester carrying boxes the size of a television set, draped with black
6   cloth to hide the contents from hundreds of prying eyes.
7   The latest remains, dug out of the foundations of the bathroom, were taken to
8   forensic laboratories but police, who are extending their search to other sites, admitted
9   they may never be able to identify all the victims.
10   Over a two-week period three other bodies were dug out of the garden and four
11   from the house.
12   "This brings the total we have found to eight," Chief Insp. Colin Handy said outside
13   25 Cromwell St.
14   Frederick West, a 52-year-old builder who lived in the house, was charged last
15   week with killing his daughter Heather, who vanished seven years ago at aged 16, and
16   two other girls.
17   Some officers say the final toll of bodies, some of which are two decades old, could
18   reach double figures and possibly make it Britain's worst serial killing.
19   All over Britain, families of young women reported missing over the last quarter of
20   a century now fear they could be entombed in the house.
21   It is sure to take its place in criminal history alongside London's 10 Rillington
22   Place— where sexual psychopath John Christie's victims were found under floorboards,
23   in the garden and in a papered-over cupboard—and 23 Cranley Gardens, where Dennis
24   Nilsen chopped up homeless men and buried them.
25   Christie was hanged in 1953 for killing his wife and at least five other women.
26   Nilsen, who confessed to strangling 15 men, was jailed for life in 1983.
27   West's neighbors, many of them young single people in an area full of cheap
28   apartments whose transient population has little sense of community, remember an
29   affable man who chatted little.
30   "He was a really nice bloke," said salesman Chris Dyer.

Picture caption: Police remove remains.

The article dramatically recounts "grim-faced" policemen carrying
remains out of the "House of Horror" in shrouded boxes while hundreds of
people look on (lines 4–6). The bodies, many of them unidentified, were dug
out of the basement and bathroom, some of them decades old (lines 7–18).
The perpetrator of the crime is likened to other infamous serial murderers
who preyed on harmless women and homeless men (lines 21–26), which
makes it part of a pattern. The neighbourhood in which the offender lived
is lower class, with "little sense of community," where young single people
and transients live (lines 27–28). That lack of community, despite the fact
that people knew the murderer, further anchors the moral repulsion of the
crime and the sense that it is linked to depravity and poverty.

There is nothing in the article about the law or the legal procedures
Frederick West will now face; there is nothing to explain the motivation for
the crimes, just the horror of the killings and their discovery. The dead

bodies allegedly killed by the accused over the years retrospectively enables the label "serial killer," even thought he has been charged with only one death. The linking of this case to other infamous cases, one more than forty years old, grounds the claim that this crime is "one of the worst." All these features are embedded in a text that replays the unexamined proposition "you just never know."

In comparison to the previous news story, Article 9.2 is more prurient in its treatment. The "House of Horror" article simply said there had been a series of slayings and is notably reticent with details: whether, for example, torture was involved or whether these were "sex slayings." The next article, however, is about a serial killer reportedly "terrorizing London's gay community." It speculates that the victims may have been strangled or suffocated after involvement in sadomasochistic sex (lines 6–7). The victims are thus directly portrayed as having been involved in "immoral" behaviour, in a way the victims in the first article were not. Furthermore, the victims' sexual orientation is topicalized indirectly, whereas sexual orientation does not seem to be important in the first article. The police are pursuing leads (lines 9–13), but there is no indication of why the murders could have continued on for so long.

Whereas the "House of Horror" article plays more on the "traditional" aspect of serial murder, the second article topicalizes a "deviant" sexual angle. This is part of the sensationalism, layering the illicit over the explicit. It makes the victims less innocent, but the assailant no less evil.

Article 9.2
U.K. pathologist to compare bodies of 4 murdered gays
(*Toronto Star*, June 21, 1993: A12)

1   **London (Reuter)**—A top British pathologist plans to re-examine the bodies of four of
2   the five victims of a killer terrorizing London's gay community.
3   Dr. Iain West will be the first pathologist to compare all the available bodies when
4   he examines them today. One of the victims has already been cremated.
5   Victims frequented bars and clubs in London's gay scene and are thought to have
6   been strangled or suffocated, some possibly after involvement in sadomasochistic sex
7   at the victims' homes.
8   The killer has vowed in telephone calls to police to kill one gay man a week.
9   Police said they are pursuing leads provided by some of the 50,000 marchers in
10 London's Gay Pride rally Saturday.
11   There were 400 posters of the victims along the march's route, while 10,000 leaflets
12 were handed out bearing photographs of the victims and asking for anyone who knew
13 them to come forward.
14   "The whole gay community is aware and we have been issuing advice that if you
15 meet someone new, make sure someone else is introduced to him, too," said Bill Walshe,
16 who organized Saturday's march.

In Article 9.3, more of the art of reporting is displayed in one of the most sensationalized cases in Canada—the trials of Paul Teale and Karla Homolka. Originally reported in a series of unconnected articles on unexplained deaths in southern Ontario, the cases involve the "sex slayings" of three young women, and a series of sexual assaults. The trial of Homolka was subject to a sweeping court-ordered ban, although information was still widely published in newspapers and magazines, on television shows and on the Internet.[1]

Article 9.3
The Ghoul Next Door: Choirgirl's crimes are so savage judge keeps details secret as cops target her yuppie hubby
(*Globe*, September 28, 1993: 24–25)

They were the picture-perfect pair.

Karla Homolka Teale, a stunning 23-year-old veterinarian's assistant ... long blonde hair and blue eyes ... peaches and cream complexion ... wouldn't hurt a fly.

Hubby Paul Teale, 26 ... accountant ... tall ... charming ... handsome enough to melt a young girl's heart.

But behind the Ken and Barbie masks lurked the face of grotesque evil.

Karla is now serving two 12-year manslaughter sentences for her part in the grizzly sex slayings of two young girls.

Parts of 14-year-old Leslie Mahaffy's body were found in a concrete tomb at the bottom of a lake.

Fifteen-year-old Kristen French's nude corpse turned up on a country road two weeks after she vanished on the way to school.

Paul Teale now stands accused of two charges of first-degree murder and 43 separate counts of sexual assault.

Police are also investigating his possible involvement in the disappearance of other teenage girls—and in the mysterious death of his wife's young sister.

The facts of Canada's most sensational sex-murder case are so sickeningly gruesome that Ontario judge Francis Kovacs wrapped them in a cloak of total secrecy. To ensure that Paul gets a fair trial, his stifling gag order even forbids revealing whether Karla pleaded guilty!

WE CAN SAY that as Karla sat stone-faced, the prosecutor read a chilling statement chronicling in painfully gory detail her role in the terrible deaths of the two girls.

WE CAN REVEAL that gasps of horror filled the courtroom.

After her sentence was handed down—she could be free in four years—Paul's attorney said the prosecution may have "made a deal with the devil" in return for her testimony.

WE DO KNOW that rumors swirled and were denied ... tales of torture and sex "snuff" videos in which the young victims were raped and killed for the camera.

The Toronto Sun has also reported that cops seized a homemade video showing Karla engaged in a sex act with another woman and that dozens of other tapes were taken from the Teale's St. Catharines, Ontario home.

And *The Hamilton Spectator* wrote: "Sources have said police focused on at least two tapes and were trying to enhance images on one. Two sources confirm that experts have been working on enhancing the hand of a girl, whose face is not shown to determine the identity."

At the time of her death, pretty Leslie Mahaffy was a ninth-grader. She was last seen by friends in the early hours of the morning.

Two weeks later—on the same day that Karla and Paul were married in a lavish wedding ceremony—parts of Leslie's body were found encased in concrete in Lake Gibson, a reservoir outside St. Catharines.

"With the death of Leslie I lost part of my future," says her anguished mom Debbie. "Even the happy memories I have of her are bittersweet."

Ten months after Leslie's body was discovered, Kristen French was snatched while she was walking home from school. Her naked body was found two weeks later on a remote country road.

Police reveal that both girls had been sexually assaulted, and Kristen had been kept alive for 13 horrible days after she disappeared.

"I went to the same school as Kristen," says Daniel Castellan, a friend of the slain teen. "I saw her two minutes before she was abducted. But I never noticed anything."

Cops are now reopening the investigation into the bizarre death of Karla's own 15-year-old sister Tammy. She choked on her own vomit during a family gathering.

Paul was also present.

Friends of the model yuppie couple are in shock, unable to accept that they could commit the unspeakable acts with which they were charged.

"Karla would get mad if someone would even try to kill a fly," says Kevin Jacobi, who has known her since the ninth grade. "Or she'd get mad if anyone tried to hurt an animal. She was a fanatic about that."

The striking blonde is the daughter of Czechoslovakian refugees, the oldest of three sisters. She attended the best schools, and sang in the choir. She was well-mannered, well-brought up.

Then, when she was just 17, Karla met and fell head over heels for dashing university student Paul Bernardo, who later had his name legally changed to Teale.

"She was in love," says a former teacher. "She used to go see him in Toronto during the week and every weekend."

The lovebirds finally married. The affair was extravagant, complete with horse-drawn carriage, and a pheasant dinner.

They seemed the ideal couple, with everything going for them.

But last January, their marriage and lives suddenly went crashing down in flames—after Paul was charged with assaulting his beautiful bride with a flashlight.

Then the other bombshells burst. Paul was charged with a spree of sexual assaults in a Toronto suburb. Next, he was slapped with murder charges in the deaths of Leslie and Kristen.

But while Karla sits behind bars in the grim Kingston Prison for Women, legal experts predict her husband might not come to trial until 1995. Meanwhile, the sick sex-snuff rumors still swirl.

Cover caption: Canada's Most Shocking Killings. The untold story of an unspeakable crime
Picture caption: She had breeding, beauty, the best schools—and a taste for sex that ended in the brutal death of 2 young girls
Picture caption: Guilty. Karla sat stone-faced as the prosecutor detailed her role in the gruesome deaths

Picture caption: Victim. Leslie Mahaffy, 14, was sexually assaulted-then brutally chopped into bits
Picture caption: Victim. Kristen French, 15, was kept alive for 13 horrible days after she disappeared

The media ban caused newspapers as respected as the *Washington Post* to be barred from Canada, although that didn't necessarily stop people from obtaining copies. As noted elsewhere, the cases started out with incidents that are all too commonplace, a series of violent sexual assaults in 1987 (Davey 1994). By the time the "Ghoul Next Door" article was published, the situation had spun further out of control, and a young couple was charged with the murders of two young women. This article is long, but included in its entirety because it combines so many of the aspects of serial murder sensationalism already mentioned: seriality, a connection to other crimes of that type, evil hidden underneath a conventional exterior, and sexuality.

The text of the court ruling by Justice Kovacs in the Homolka case was issued on July 5, 1993, and although it does not ban specific media stories, it bans several details of the case from publication: the circumstances of the deaths of any persons referred to during the trial; the plea by the accused; and the transcript of the trial proceedings.[2] Newspapers and magazines were stopped at the border, confiscated from store shelves, and in some cases shredded. The article used here, however, was sold openly in Canada and is not known to have been subject to any legal enforcement.

The "serial killer" image is constructed in a way similar to that found in the "House of Horror" article above. Karla Homolka and Paul Teale are like "Ken and Barbie"; and the use of these doll names underscores the theme that "you just never know," that there can be "evil in our midst." Throughout the article, the theme of the "picture-perfect pair" is played, but from the very first we read that "behind the Ken and Barbie masks lurked the face of grotesque evil," that they committed a series of gruesome sex crimes and slayings while appearing to be the perfect couple.

Various other themes are played out as well. There is the reconstruction of seriality; the link to other cases; there is the "you just never know" theme anchored by the Barbie and Ken mythology; and there is the sexual element that recurs again and again in the text, with melodramatic terms such as "grizzly sex slayings" and "sex 'snuff' videos." The article goes beyond simply describing the facts of sex assault and homicide, and caters to the prurient interests of the reader, as in the "gay serial killer" article above.

Part of the reason certain elements of this story were banned in Canada was that details from Karla's case might influence Paul's right to a fair trial. But reporting that Karla had "made a deal with the devil" by giving evidence against her husband is reporting that must be deconstructed, not hidden;

such talk becomes even more sensationalistic when it is whispered. Mounting a publication ban only serves to restrict 'legitimate' publications from publishing details of the case, while the field is left open for tabloid speculation.

Read as a literal description of events, the account is gruesome, describing mutilation, sexual assault, torture and murder. Read as metaphor, however, the language takes on a different character: can one have sex with an unwilling or unconscious person; are these crimes of lust and sexual urges or violence; what does it mean to say that there was a "pact with the devil"? The article is a drama, a morality play about danger within the community. It is an example of sensationalist reporting that is bizarre, extreme and irresponsible, yellow journalism at its worst.

Cases of serial killers are by nature sensational, but the media hypes them beyond recognition, distorts the immorality of the killers and often plays upon the moral innocence of the victims. Serial murder sensationalism can be seen to have a discursive structure which can be reconstructed, which means looking for the specific textual devices that convey the features of seriality, danger and sexuality. The articles have several common features: the killers exist unrecognized amidst ordinary people; they prey on innocent or deviant victims; the language used melodramatizes the crimes; and there is little or no account of law and legal procedures.

Analyzing the news

Let us look at the consequence of banning mainstream newspapers from covering a sensationalistic serial killer case, and speculate on the usefulness of sensationalism overall.

Much had been written on the trial of Karla Homolka and the upcoming trial of Paul Teale. There were probably more newspaper articles, editorials, columns, television shows and other media stories on the ban itself than on the actual crimes. When the *Buffalo News* published the story, and the *Toronto Star* printed a front-page photograph, the Ontario attorney general investigated to see if there had been a violation of the ban.[3] Libraries debated whether to display copies of newspapers carrying banned information, and in some cases actually clipped out the offending pieces until they received legal advice that shelving the papers did not constitute publication.[4] A retired police officer in Guelph, Ontario, was found guilty of contempt of court for mailing copies of stories from the *Sunday Mirror* and the *Washington Post*.[5] A U.S. cable show, "A Current Affair," was blacked out twice in Canada, despite CRTC regulations.[6] Details of the crimes were posted on the Internet faster than newslists and discussion groups could be shut down, contributing to the spread of rumours.[7] A December 1993 poll done by Angus Reid reported that despite the media ban, 25 percent of Ontario residents had learned banned details of the trial, but 35 percent weren't even aware of the case at all!

The ban was an interesting exercise in locking the barn door after the horse has bolted. Initial newspaper accounts of the 1991 and 1992 murders detailed evidence of the crimes that would later be banned from publication.[8] Furthermore, in imposing the ban after the short, two-hour trial of Karla Homolka in 1993, the trial judge was quoted in the newspapers as saying, "No sentence that I could impose would adequately reflect the revulsion of the community against the accused for the death of two completely innocent young girls. . . . The accused did not personally inflict the deaths, although she was responsible in law and in fact."[9] Given that the ban was apparently to ensure a fair trial for Paul Teale, slated for 1995, the judge's comments are puzzling because they seem prejudicial. And it is difficult to see why there would be a ban on the details of the presumed plea bargain, unless it would be to relieve the legal process of scrutiny in such a horrific case.

Whether it is ordinary crime stories or cases of serial killers, the charge that reporters often "get it wrong" in their search for a story is a technical complaint. Anyone can complain that what they do is not represented accurately by reporters. Reporters may not be interested in or able to synthesize long-winded, complicated professional, academic and legalistic discourses. To expect that reporters *could* get it right would assume they were able to just report the facts, like a tape-recorder. It assumes that reporters would not have another agenda.

The charge that reporters capitalize on the gory crimes of serial and other killers is more of a moral issue. Certainly the media has been heavily criticized for its interest in the Homolka-Teale cases. The idea that sensationalism is voyeuristic, that reporters are just interested in getting a picture of a corpse implies something sleazy about the profession. Maybe there is, but maybe that's more than just a failing.

Both the technical and the moral complaints presume that reporters get it wrong. Both complaints rely on a privileged viewpoint that the reportage could be better, that the lawyer or other professional has it right but is often misquoted in the media. (This does describe the daily lives of professionals who work with the media, but that's another issue). And the moral complaint, especially, implies that the reporter should rise above the commonplace.

Alternately, instead of simply seeing ignorance and sensationalism as inherently wrong, let us question the purpose they play in the larger social order. Is there a purpose both serve? The story found in Article 9.3 was not banned in Canada. Some of the headlines, articles and ads in that issue that give a sense of the context of the story are shown in Figure 9.1.

Figure 9.1
Tabloid news

Headlines of unusual events:

> **"Seaquest Stephanie: Housework keeps me slim and sexy at 46"**
>
> **"Powerful Pygmy potion ends drug addiction!"**
>
> **"Miracle Boy Learns to Walk—after years in a wheelchair!"**

Articles about famous people:

> **"Oprah's heart is solid gold!"**
>
> **"Webster runs for cover in Jacko video shocker"**
>
> **"Secret heartache Raymond Burr took to his grave"**

Advertisements for lucky charms:

> **"3 Wishes Voo Doo Doll with Magic Wand"**
>
> **"Loans By Mail"**
>
> **"Know Your Future. Live Personal Psychic"**
>
> **"Love, Money, Success"**

These are not stories about ordinary people, but about people who have "overcome" incredible odds, discovered unusual things or are famous and exceptional stars. The advertisements promise the reader wealth, success, love and knowledge of future events. Do you want unlimited credit, do you want to know the direction of your life, do you want to know secrets to get the sex partner of your dreams—this is all available through the ads of *Globe* magazine. The overall tone of the tabloid is of incredible events and special people who live in a mysterious world where luck and fortune play a role in determining their future.

It is not a question of "who" reads the garbage in tabloids, what is important here is "what" they are reading. What messages are people getting when they read tabloids, when they read sensationalism? When tabloids cover serial killers, they of course do it in a very sensationalistic and melodramatic way, only different by degree from how the mainstream newspapers cover the story. The murder case becomes part of the incredible universe peopled by stars, lucky people and lucky charms. The point is that this tabloid newspaper, because of its context, was allowed to report on the Homolka-Teale case in a far more sensationalistic way than newspapers that were banned.

Reporters do not simply get it wrong, the distortion of events is a part of our reality. The media is part of the institutional process through which we do or do not learn about crime. By imposing a court ban on such stories, the field is left open to the sensationalistic. But the story is going to have an effect whether it is reported well or not. That is the trick: the consequence of misreporting a story can be the creation of a myth, a falsehood. But myths have an effect on the practices people engage in and the lives they live. Sensationalism in itself is not a problem, but being misinformed about crime and the criminal justice system is. That is the deep complaint. If the mainstream press had been free to report on the trial and its outcome, readers would have had access to more responsible reporting than they were otherwise able to receive.

As a footnote to the Teale case, the media took the ban to court, appealing it.[10] Lawyers representing the *Toronto Star*, the *Globe and Mail*, the *Toronto Sun* and the Canadian Broadcasting Corporation (CBC) sought a formal order outlining reasons for the ban from Judge Kovacs in October 1993, prior to an appeal heard before the Ontario Court of Appeal in January 1994. Meanwhile the Supreme Court of Canada heard appeals of court-ordered media bans over the airing of the "The Boys of St. Vincent" and in the sexual abuse trial in Martensville, Saskatchewan. The Ontario Court of Appeal eventually reserved judgement in the case but was eclipsed by future events. On December 8, 1994, the Supreme Court of Canada ruled that the right of the news media to inform readers of the proceedings of jury trials is as important as the right of an accused to a fair trial.[11] This decision will encourage more responsible journalism, quell rumours and enable the media to inform the public about the proceedings of criminal trials.

Summary

In this chapter a lawyer concerned with the relationship between the legal profession and the media commented on the difficulty of dealing with reporters. His concerns involve reporters who are commonly not well versed in the procedures of the criminal justice system, lawyers who abuse the media in pursuit of advantage for their clients, and so on. These are common complaints, and anyone who deals with the media in a professional capacity probably has dealt with the problem of the ten-minute interview at two o'clock in the afternoon that has to make it to the evening news.

One specific complaint is that the media is oriented towards the thirty-second clip, to the most sensational story. And in a highly competitive market this is a way to grab the attention of the reader. The topic of serial killers was taken up as perhaps the most outstanding example of sensationalism, in order to reconstruct what sensationalism actually looks like. These accounts were found to emphasize certain distinctive themes: violence, sexuality and seriality; as well as the sense that these crimes go hidden, they could happen anywhere and they often involve innocent victims. There is, then, a deeply moral element to these articles.

The examination of these accounts yields a detailed understanding of sensationalism; the subsequent analysis shows how sensationalistic accounts act as tabloids do, reinforcing ignorance about the world and perpetuating the view that the world is a mysterious place where weird and unusual events occur. The example of an article on the Karla Homolka trial in Ontario is examined, as are the consequences of leaving the field to tabloids while imposing a ban on responsible reporting. Though the analysis ends up a long way from where the speaker starts, the point is made that sensationalism does a disservice by misinforming readers about the world in which they live. And this is not simply bad reporting; some would say that keeping people misinformed about how the world works serves a purpose. And that is perhaps the irony about court-ordered media bans, that people are kept in the dark about legal processes.

Notes

1. "Killer Ken and Barbie's Video of Horror," *Sunday Mirror*, September 19, 1993; "The Ghoul Next Door: Choirgirl's crimes are so savage judge keeps details secret as cops target her yuppie husband," *Globe*, September 28, 1993: 24–25; "Karla's Tragic Trail of Death," *Globe*, October 12, 1993: 43; "The story the Canadian government doesn't want you to see," *A Current Affair* (U.S.), October 26, 1993; "Unspeakable Crimes: This story can't be told in Canada, And so all Canada is talking about it," *Washington Post*, November 23, 1993: B1; "Canadians shocked by sex crime allegations against couple," *Boston Globe*, November 26, 1993: 6–7; "Canada finds a gruesome secret in its heartland," *Sunday Times*, December 5, 1993: 18; "The Barbie-Ken Murders, Canada: Blacking out a horror story," *Newsweek* (U.S.), December 6, 1993: 36; "Media stir latent Canada/US tension," *Manchester Guardian Weekly*, December 12, 1993: 18; "The Paul Teale/Karla Homolka Frequently Asked Questions List (FAQ), Version 2.2," March 30, 1994; "Blood Wedding," *Elle* (Britain), March 1994: 71–76; "In Canada, right to fair trial wins out over rights of press," *Independent* (London), nd.
2. *R. v. Bernardo*, O.J. No. 2047, Action No. 125/93, Ontario Court of Justice—General Division, St. Catharines, Ontario, Kovacs, J., July 5, 1993: paragraphs 140–42.
3. "Lid blown off ban," *Toronto Star*, December 1, 1993: A1; "Province investigating if The Star broke Homolka publication ban," *Toronto Star*, December 2, 1993: A1.
4. "Halifax Library cuts Teale article," *Daily News*, December 8, 1993: 3; "Two more libraries censor Teale article," *Daily News*, December 9, 1993: 3; "Library defies Homolka ban," *Toronto Star*, December 18, 1993: A24; "Homolka trial details available in Halifax: Article in U.S.

newspaper reinstated after library obtains legal opinion," *Globe and Mail,* December 18, 1993: A5; "Halifax library makes Teale story available," *Halifax Herald,* December 20, 1993: A3; "Local libraries rapped for clipping Teale tale," *Daily News,* December 21, 1993: 6; "End the ban on Homolka, libraries urge," *Toronto Star,* December 21, 1993: A11; "Halifax library honored for keeping information available to public," *Daily News,* July 2, 1994: 2.

5. "Ex-officer charged with violating ban, Gordon Domm gets wish to fight gag order in Homolka trial," *Toronto Star,* December 3, 1993: A4; "Ex-officer has hearing in his fight of court ban," *Toronto Star,* March 31, 1994: A8; "Contempt charges to stick," *Globe and Mail,* May 17, 1994: A4; "Retired police officer guilty of breaching Homolka court ban," *Winnipeg Free Press,* May 21, 1994: A3; "Ex-officer fined $4,000 for defying publication ban," *Toronto Star,* July 1, 1994: A9; "Ministry quiet on U.S. show on Homolka," *Toronto Star,* July 29, 1994: A16.

6. "Time to reassess jury system," *Toronto Star,* October 28, 1993: A24, editorial; "Is technology rewriting the justice system?" *Toronto Star,* November 9, 1993: A17; "Homolka blackouts contravene regulations, CRTC says," *Toronto Star,* December 4, 1993: A2; "The Current Affair," *Globe and Mail,* December 4, 1993: D1; "U.S. TV show set to air expose on new details in Bernardo case," *Toronto Star,* July 25, 1994: A6; "Show on Homolka claims inside look, Cable firms to black out local reception," *Toronto Star,* July 27, 1994: A5; "U.S. show airs banned Bernardo case data," *Halifax Herald,* July 28, 1994: A18.

7. "Computer links break trial ban," *Toronto Star,* July 31, 1993: A1; "Dal computer chief drops Teale ban breaker," *Daily News,* December 3, 1993: 8; "Plug pulled on computer access to banned details of Teale trial," *Halifax Herald,* December 8, 1993: A5; "Confessions of a ban-breaker," *Daily News,* December 1, 1993: 2, column; "Wired World," *Maclean's,* January 17, 1994, cover story; "Dal bans troublemakers on Internet," *Gazette,* January 13, 1994: np; "Judges' panel on Teale ban made irrelevant by Internet," *Daily News,* January 30, 1994: 2.

8. "Police seek help in body-parts case," *Halifax Herald,* July 5, 1991: A16; "Body in concrete identified as girl, 14—from Burlington," *Toronto Star,* July 11, 1991: A1; "Murder victim buried," *Daily News,* July 26, 1991: 10; "Aftermath: 'It keeps going through your mind, Who's next?'" *Globe and Mail,* July 20, 1991: D3; "Investigation ongoing into death of teen," *Halifax Herald,* August 20, 1991: C18, capsule; "'They found it was Kristie,' her father says," *Toronto Star,* May 1, 1992: A3; "Kristen lived 10 days after kidnap: police," *Toronto Star,* May 2, 1992: A1; "Did Kristen's killer attack once again?" *Toronto Star,* June 19 1992; "Professed killer called 911 to taunt police

about Kristen," *Toronto Star*, July 23, 1992: A1.

9. "Bernardo and wife charged in slayings, Homolka accused of manslaughter in Mahaffy, French cases," *Toronto Star*, May 19, 1993: A1; "Tell us Karlas' 'deal,' lawyer insists," *Toronto Star*, June 29, 1993: A1; "Judge to rule on Homolka trial ban," *Toronto Star*, July 5, 1993: A1; "Public barred from trial, Judge also excludes U.S. media in Homolka case," *Globe and Mail*, July 6, 1993: A1; "Homolka judge bars public, curbs media," *Toronto Star*, July 6, 1993: A1; "Homolka found guilty, Judge says he understands public's 'righteous outrage,'" *Globe and Mail*, July 7, 1993: A1; "Karla Teale gets 12 years for slayings, 'Not worst offender,' judge says," *Daily News*, July 7, 1993: 10; "Tearful Teale convicted, Sex slaying earns 23-year-old 12-year term," *Halifax Herald*, July 7, 1993: A2; "Homolka gets 12 years," July 7, 1993: A1; "Tears for Kristen, tears for Leslie," *Globe and Mail*, July 9, 1993: A18; "Homolka sentencing has rumours swirling," *Toronto Star*, July 11, 1993: A1.

10. "Star joins Globe to fight court ban," *Toronto Star*, June 22, 1993: A2; "Dubin seeks transcript of reasons for ban," *Toronto Star*, July 22, 1993: A5; "Media seek Homolka ban justification," *Toronto Star*, October 7, 1993: A12; "Media 'have no right' to appeal Teale ban," *Daily News*, January 1, 1994: 10; "Gag orders challenged today in Supreme Court; Teale case ban up next," *Daily News*, January 24, 1994: 8; "When rights collide: Top court hears ban cases," *Daily News*, January 25, 1994: 10; "Senior panel of judges stepping into Homolka ban breach," *Globe and Mail*, January 29, 1994: A1; "Appeal court justices set to hear crown, media argue over Homolka ban," *Toronto Star*, January 30, 1994: A1; "The Homolka Ban," *Maclean's*, January 1994: 2, editorial; "Media appeal of Teale ban starts today," *Daily News*, January 31, 1994: 9; "Court urged to reject appeal of media ban," *Toronto Star*, February 1, 1994: A2; "Reject media's bid to appeal Teale ban, court urged," *Halifax Herald*, February 1, 1994: A9; "Court of Appeal lets media fight Homolka ban, But final decision must await ruling by Supreme Court," *Toronto Star*, February 2, 1994: A3; "Gag order threatens system's integrity, court told," *Globe and Mail*, February 2, 1994: A3; "Media lawyers protest 'black box' of Teale ban," *Halifax Herald*, February 2, 1994: A7; "Media fights for right to appeal Teale ban," *Daily News*, February 2, 1994: 10; "Lawyers in ban hearing 'roasted,'" *Toronto Star*, February 3, 1994: A2; "Media face judges in Teale case gag challenge," *Daily News*, February 3, 1994: 8; "Lawyers, judges spar over Teale ban," *Halifax Herald*, February 3, 1994: A19; "Press mocked Teale's rights to fair trial, Crown says: Judgment reserved on media challenge of publication ban," *Globe and Mail*,

February 4, 1994: A7; "Judges reserve decision in Teale murder trial ban," *Daily News*, February 4, 1994: 11; "Media lawyers always thought chances slim," *Halifax Herald*, February 5, 1994: A1.

11. "Media hails 'dawn of new era' with court ruling," *Halifax Herald*, December 9, 1994: C23; "Top court decision 'a great victory,'" *Daily News*, December 9, 1994: 26; "Top court tips scale to freer speech, Publication bans harder to impose," *Globe and Mail*, December 9, 1994: A1; "Rock reconsiders ban law," *Daily News*, December 10, 1994: 10, Brief; "Raising the hurdle on publication bans," *Globe and Mail*, December 10, 1994: D6, editorial; "Publication bans? Nothing has really changed," *Globe and Mail*, December 13, 1994: A21, opinion.

10

The Westray Mine Explosion:
Covering a Disaster and a Failed Inquiry

"Pack journalism" describes a process whereby the media takes a uniform convergent line on a story, a line from which stories seldom deviate. In her talk, Deborah Woolway recounts stories about how the media covered the Donald Marshall inquiry in Nova Scotia, a wrongful conviction case where an Aboriginal person was jailed for eleven years for a murder he didn't commit. Through her talk we are exposed to the idea that the media are not always as critical as they should be and often unwittingly take the line lawyers and politicians want them to.

In "Reading the news," we look at a tragedy and the inquiry which followed—the Westray mine disaster at Plymouth, Nova Scotia, where a methane explosion occurred deep in a mine, killing twenty-six men. The media initially covered the explosion as a human tragedy story, and the coverage was an overwhelming example of "pack journalism." Many of the critical issues Deborah Woolway identifies from the Marshall inquiry are similar: how to get a story and get it right, covering the legal issues while also reporting a human tragedy.

What subsequently came to light after the initial blanket coverage was that there had been warning signs that an explosion at Westray was likely to occur, that safety standards were not adhered to at the mine and that the provincial department of labour had issued warnings about safety that were ignored. This part of the chapter is heavily footnoted, in part because it is important to illustrate how the coverage of this disaster was so massive, but also to enable an examination of the legal ins and outs of a very complex case.

In the "Analyzing the news" section the adequacy of media coverage of the explosion, the subsequent criminal investigation and the inquiry is examined. What were the consequences of the line the media took on the tragedy? Has the media coverage itself become part of the story of the Westray disaster?

The talk—Deborah Woolway

It seems it was a long time ago now when the news director of the day came into the station and said, "Does anyone want to cover this Marshall inquiry thing? It's probably going to last about three weeks." No one had any idea what we were getting ourselves in for, but I leapt at the chance. I could see, even then, that it was going to be probably the biggest story to hit these parts in many, many years, and I wanted in, I was excited by it. So that's how I got involved.

And from the very beginning, CBC [radio] news did this in a very calculated way. They decided there would be one person who would stay with the inquiry for the duration, and that person would handle both the local and national requirements. That person would also do documentary work, and debriefs with Information Morning, or wherever they were required. What was stressed over and over, my editors kept telling me over and over, and I strived to do it over and over was context.

My problems were different from other media problems. There were a number of private stations covering the story that I used to call sausage machines because they'd just churn out the stories. I mean it was unbelievable: thirty-second hits every hour on the hour, where they'd synthesize what they'd just heard into a succinct little package. But it offered nothing beyond a headline. And that's clearly what I was not to do. I was to provide context. To that end I strived to do that within the limitations of my one minute and thirty, plus my debriefs and so forth and the other work that I did.

But all the media was different. There was also the drop-in approach of the Sunday morning team, which would come in and do the big hit, the big splash, and do a pretty good job picking the brains of everybody who'd been involved in the thing, and then get out. They'd parachute in and parachute out. And then there were the colour commentators and the columnists who were there to provide context and flavour. And then there was TV. This was an especially difficult thing for TV to cover, I think, because TV is pictures. I don't deal with TV, I don't actually know a lot about TV, and I think TV really had a lot of problems covering this inquiry.

Needless to say it was a demanding assignment, and I'm giving you a personal look at what I was doing at the time, so what I say is purely anecdotal. It was pretty demanding filing stories all day, every day: 12:30 news, 1:00 news, "Canada at Five," the afternoon regional run, "World at Six." Then turning around, rewriting the whole thing again for the morning for "World Report," and for the local stations and so forth. So like a lot of people, we all worked very long hours and became quite obsessed, quite frankly, with this whole thing.

You can well imagine, some very interesting and possibly very unhealthy relationships developed between the media and the people they were covering, specifically the lawyers. While as journalists we talk about objectivity, it is a myth. There is no objectivity, but what you strive to do is to be fair. I mean, of course you have a perspective and a point of view. You try and control it, and assess it, and clear it in your own head, so when you're dealing with controversial information you can assess it as coolly as you can and try and be fair. And that, I think, is what we're striving for, not to be objective but to be fair. That's the best you can hope for.

Again, back in the inquiry hall what was required was stamina as well. There was an enormous amount of reading to do. I had a problem of synthesis: I had to compile down everything I'd heard into a minute-thirty, two-minutes-max news story, using clips and so forth. And there was always the temptation to go for the juicy clip, and we almost always did. It seemed there were very few days when the clip did not match, that I felt I was taking anything out of context. Nobody's perfect, of course, but I think what I was trying to do was convey the sense and the context of what was happening, using the voices that were available.

Often I'd get up in the morning, I'd look at the *Globe and Mail*'s reams of stuff and I'd think "Oh God, if only I had that time and space," you know. But then they'd say to me, "Oh, Debbie, you know, I wish we had the immediacy and the power to put the voices on the air and to convey the sense." Anyway, we all had different problems is my point.

But certainly some days my biggest challenge became just writing a lead that did not contain the phrase "Donald Marshall, the Micmac who spent 11 years in prison for a murder he did not commit." That became his name, and it was difficult. That was part of the job, part of the problem. It was a struggle to remain objective as it became so overwhelmingly obvious that the wave of the system had crushed an innocent person.

But to get back to the relationships that developed. It became pretty obvious that certain reporters and certain lawyers felt more at ease with each other and would be sharing information. Some journalists would have their pet lawyers, and maybe lawyers had their pet journalists, I don't know, but it seemed to work that way. And at every break you'd often find the same couple of journalists caucused around a lawyer and saying what did this mean and what did you think of that, and speculating and becoming almost part of the story. I didn't think that was a terribly healthful sort of pattern to get into, and for the most part I tried to distance myself from that and tended to rely more heavily on commission counsel, which was another set of problems, because their version of what they were hearing, or the truth, was an interpretation.

My job, inasmuch as we all like to talk about truth, was information as much as anything. And you hear different things from different sources. It was an interesting time. To give you an illustration of the cozy and somewhat unhealthy relationship that can develop, I'll tell you this story. We'd finished a very grim day at the inquiry, I forget the testimony now, it was something to do with Marshall's suffering at Dorchester and the lousy compensation package that he got the first time out. And a journalist who shall remain nameless went over to a couple of Donald Marshall's lawyers at the end of the day and was kind of chewing the fat with them, and they were sort of laughing grimly about the evidence they'd heard, and they said to him, "Yeah, and that money didn't include the $30,000 payback Marshall had to give Dorchester for room and board." And the journalist, who in every other respect is a very astute person—he had a deadline and was probably past it, he had to do a live debrief—he turned around and walked out of the room, walked straight onto the air and talked about a $30,000 payback.

First thing I heard about it is when I get a screaming phone call from my editor saying, "Debbie what's this about a $30,000 payback?" Actually this was the next morning, as it transpired, when I got the call. I said, "I don't know. What are you talking about? I don't think that's right." So I went down to the inquiry and I walked straight up to commission council and I said, "What's all this about this payback?" I drew blanks there, so turned around and walked down to Donald Marshall's lawyers and said, "What is this all about, this payback?" Her face turned as white as this sheet, and she said "Debbie, he said that on the air?" I said, "Yeah." She said, "We were just joking."

Well, I didn't know lawyers actually joked. My point is he had no reason to doubt these lawyers, they'd dealt with him. And the lawyers hadn't done anything wrong, you know, it was just because of the relationship that had developed, the sort of informal chatter that went on, and they assumed that he realized they were joking, and he didn't, and he went straight to air with that.

Anyway, we all had problems, and I'll tell this one on myself. There was a day when in a live debrief I referred to a judge, live, on the air, as deceased. Well, the gentleman wasn't deceased, and the switchboard lit up, or at least a couple of people called in. I honestly thought that the judge was dead; he has subsequently died, and without being crass, I was right eventually. Anyway, there were a lot of facts, figures, names, personalities, and we all made mistakes. I spent a weekend in hell twitching nervously from that one, but we all recovered. The joke was I happened to have lunch with a lawyer on the following Monday and told her my tale of woe, and she said, "It's OK, Debbie, I thought he was dead too." So I felt a little better about that.

To get back to a couple of comments about pack journalism, because it's the thing that journalists are always afraid of, and often get accused of, whether it's a group of journalists covering the legislature or doing anything intensely for a long period of time. I was busy doing what I was doing, we watched and read and talked to each other and read each other's work and listened to each other, but there was a fair degree of cooperation that happened among the journalists that I wouldn't characterize as pack journalism at all.

Now maybe I'm being a Pollyana here, but I didn't see it at play the way I've seen it at other places, especially the legislature, where there are certain rules to play by, and if you don't play by them, you get left out in the cold. Generally there was a fair degree of cooperation. I recall one day a private radio guy filing a story, and in the midst of all the chaos of the media room—the working conditions were abominable—he made an error in his report, and there was a chorus around him saying, "No John, Sandy Seal was sixteen years old. You said he was twenty years old," or something. So there was a certain amount of helping out that went on.

Couple of points, in no particular order, while I wrap up. I disagree from my own perspective about the role of the media being to get the sexiest, juiciest clip or lead right off the top. I mean I saw my goal anyway as personally quite different. I don't know if I succeeded, but that's what I worked toward, to do a more interpretive explaining kind of thing within the confines. And I'll just wrap up by saying some of us didn't go home. There has been some work done. I know I did a documentary piece and news stories one year to date, trying to analyze where the recommendations have gone. So, I think in our defence, a lot of it has been largely forgotten, but I've done some stuff, and I know some other people have too.

Reading the news

On May 9, 1992, at 4:47 a.m. Saturday morning, methane alarm warnings sounded in the Westray mine at Plymouth, Nova Scotia; twenty-five seconds later another alarm went off. These proved to be false alarms, although the *Globe and Mail* published an allegation that the alarms had been ignored, a story it later retracted under threat of lawsuit.[1] Thirty-three minutes later, at 5:20 in the morning, an explosion occurred.

Twenty-six men were killed underground: no one was found alive and many of the bodies were not recovered. There was speculation that the cause of the explosion was methane combustion. The reaction to the disaster was swift and massive: police and rescue teams left for the scene immediately and "hordes of media" descended on the mine to cover the disaster.

The "marathon" news coverage of the Westray mine disaster was extensive, yet not necessarily intensive. The explosion happened on a Saturday morning and the first stories appeared in print on Monday the eleventh. Then, between Monday and Saturday, more than one hundred stories were published by the *Halifax Herald*. Article 10.1 details the extensive effort on the part of the media to cover the disaster.

Many of the stories focused on the families of the fallen miners and the meaning of the tragedy to the community. More than half of the 503 "Westray—disaster" stories published in 1992 came out in the first month after the explosion, between May 11 and June 12. In 1992 more than seven hundred newspaper articles were published in the Halifax *Chronicle-Herald* and *Mail-Star* alone under the topic of "Westray" and, again, 503 articles were indexed specifically under "Westray—disaster."

Article 10.1
Explosion triggers media marathon
(*Halifax-Herald*, May 11, 1992: A14 and A16)

1 **By Paul MacNeill TRURO BUREAU—PLYMOUTH**—A media marathon was in place
2 early Saturday morning as a shocked community struggled to grasp a disaster which
3 trapped 26 of their neighbors deep in the bowels of the Westray mine.
4   Just an hour after the accident was reported at 5:20 a.m. Saturday, local television,
5 print and radio reporters were on the scene.
6   But as news of the mine explosion seeped out, hordes of media and their support
7 crews converged on the mine area. Gradually, reporters from provincial news agencies
8 and across Canada drifted in. They were immediately directed to a community centre,
9 located just up the road from the mine site.
10   The heart of the centre, located in a former school, was abuzz with activity 24 hours
11 a day. Modern lap-top computers sat on wobbly tables, under the shadow of dart boards
12 located around the main media room. The dirty floor was strewn with miles of cable,
13 which eventually snaked into phones, microphones, computers and satellite dishes.
14 Initially, telephone service was limited to one pay phone and a regular unit. However,
15 thanks to a group of local residents, who gave up their own telephone lines for the
16 media, and some quick installation work by MT&T, service quickly improved.
17   Local volunteers from the Stellarton fire department kept the media supplied with
18 coffee and sandwiches. More than 50 media representatives—the most in this area
19 since Brian Mulroney's election in 1983 as a member of Parliament for the federal riding
20 of Central Nova—were on hand for the event, which was beamed live to households
21 across Canada by various television networks.
22   International media also showed a keen interest in the story. The disaster was the
23 lead story Saturday on the Atlanta-based Cable News Network as well as other major
24 United States television networks.

Many of the articles, especially in the early stages, just tried to detail what had happened in the explosion and what was involved in the rescue effort, providing updates of the sort illustrated by Article 10.2. The "Chronology" is itself a construction, for it reflects a particular way of looking at the event. The article begins with the explosion (lines 1–2), details to the minute the actions of the police, firefighters and rescue teams (lines 2–8), and the presence of the media (lines 4–6, 8–9, 11–17 and 20–23). Explanations are offered to account for what happened (lines 15–18). Together, these elements form a textual reconstruction of events.

Article 10.2
Chronology
(*Halifax Herald*, May 11, 1992: A14 and A16)

1   **By Wilkie Taylor NEW GLASGOW BUREAU**—SATURDAY MORNING 5:18
2   Underground explosion, power failure rock Westray Coal mine. 5:20 Emergency response
3   under way. 5:30 Traffic barriers erected. Aberdeen Hospital staff alerted. Firefighters
4   on scene. 6:30 ATV's Dan MacIntosh, first reporter outside security fence. 6:35
5   Reporters from The Chronicle-Herald, radio station CKEC and New Glasgow Evening
6   News arrive. 7:40 Westray setting up media centre. 8:00 Canadian Press reports 17
7   miners trapped. 8:30 Rescue team from Pugwash arrives. 9:00 Truck load of lumber
8   drives to pithead. 9:15 Reporters told media centre being set up in Plymouth Community
9   Centre. 10:15 First press briefing conducted by Cst. Ivan Baker of Stellarton RCMP
10 detachment. Twenty-three believed trapped 1.5 kilometres underground.
11   SATURDAY AFTERNOON 12:15 Photo opportunity at minesite. 3:15 Second
12 press briefing by RCMP and Westray officials. Number trapped revised to 26, families
13 gathering in fire hall. 7:08 Third press briefing by RCMP and Westray officials. Mine
14 officials decline to speculate how long it will take to reach miners. 10:00 Fourth press
15 briefing by Westray officials aiming at 3:30 deadline for reaching trapped men. Cite
16 gas as probable explosion cause.
17   SUNDAY MORNING 12:15 Fourth press briefing by Westray officials. Gas
18 monitoring program defended by mine officials. Rescue workers within 600 metres of
19 goal.
20   SUNDAY AFTERNOON 1:15 Fifth press conference. Deaths of 11 miners announced.
21 4:30 Sixth press conference. Premier Donald Cameron says it will be a long time, if ever,
22 before Westray mine reopens. 5:30 Seventh press conference. Westray official outlines
23 continuing rescue operations.

This chronology is not simply a listing of the progression of events, although that certainly seems plausible given the time annotations. It is also not simply a construction in the sense of a made-up story, for it reflects the organized work of people and appears obviously factual. The chronology is a recursive display of the work of the media, however, because it emphasizes the presence of the media at the disaster as a witness, setting up camp, taking photo opportunities and attending press briefings. The disaster is defined here prominently in terms of the presence of the media.

The *Toronto Star* filed stories from Plymouth the very next day, and for the rest of the week its lead stories appeared on page one.[2] The first day of reporting on Sunday, the day after the explosion, was about tragedy, as were most of the stories. But by Tuesday, in a story filed in Ottawa, it was pointed out that in 1987 the federal regional development minister, Robert de Cotrêt, responsible for the Cape Breton Development Corporation (Devco), had said the Plymouth mine was neither economic nor safe because of methane deposits. Another article pointed out that the mine was located in the former federal riding of Brian Mulroney and in the provincial riding of Premier Don Cameron. It was made to seem as if politics had played a hand in where the mine was built.

Cameron was industry minister when the project was announced and former Tory MP Elmer MacKay, who gave up his seat for Mulroney, helped put together the project before becoming the federal Public Works Minister and head of the Atlantic Canadian Opportunities Agency (ACOA). Cameron endorsed the mine and lobbied Mulroney to approve a financing deal which saw Curragh Inc. get a $12 million loan from the province and a federal loan guarantee of $85 million. Curragh was also able to negotiate a fifteen-year contract with Nova Scotia Power Corporation to buy $200 million worth of coal over fifteen years.[3] It seemed like a deal too good to be true, especially given the volatile nature of the coal seam.

Stories like this that stressed the economic and political side of the disaster were few and far between, perhaps because the emotional, family angle was so obvious, but also because it is so difficult to research and document corporate crime (Jobb 1994; McMullan 1992; Snider 1993).

Most of the coverage followed a line like that established in Article 10.3, where we are told that we can find stories on the draegermen who risked their lives to help those trapped underground (line 8), stories on the explosion (lines 11 and 12), safety (lines 4, 5, 9 and 13) and other disasters (lines 14 and 15). They are essentially updates on the tragedy and the progress made in trying to reach the underground miners, if any were still alive. Only a few of the stories listed attempted to offer explanations of what had occurred (lines 5 and 9).

Article 10.3
Inside on Westray mine disaster
(*Halifax-Herald*, May 11, 1992: A1)

1   **SPECIAL REPORT**: See our extended, four-page report on the Westray mine disaster
2   on pages A14, A15, A16 and A17. The Chronicle-Herald and The Mail-Star sent a team
3   of four reporters and three photographers to cover the dramatic story in Plymouth.
4   -Premier Cameron calls for inquiry into disaster/A2
5   -Critics predicted disaster for Westray mine/A16
6   -Explosion triggers media marathon/A16
7   -NSPC to seek another coal supply/A16
8   -Draegermen risk their lives to save others/A17

The initial articles overwhelmingly focused on the tragedy of the explosion, the attempt to rescue the miners and the effect on the families.[4] A few articles compared the explosion to other mining disasters in the province, such as the one at Springhill on October 23, 1958, and made references to the 244 miners who had died in the history of mining coal in Pictou County.

Although most of these articles simply tried to come to grips with what had happened and to portray the tragedy affecting the families, only a few articles raised claims that the mine was unsafe. Inspection records from the provincial department of labour were said to reveal that the mine's owners were cautioned about the unstable structure of the coal seam, high methane gas levels, improper storage of flammable materials, and the use of unauthorized equipment.[5] Equipment was said either to have no gas-monitoring equipment or to have been turned off. Two miners on the last crew to work before the explosion said methane levels had exceeded 3.5 percent even though the law required evacuation after it reached 2.5 percent.

Premier Donald Cameron immediately called for an inquiry into the explosion. Announcing that "no one would escape scrutiny," he appointed Justice Peter Richard, a fourteen-year veteran of the Nova Scotia Supreme Court trial division to lead an inquiry.[6] The terms of reference for the inquiry are important for they set the limits and boundaries of what could be investigated:

> The Commissioner, Mr. Justice K. Peter Richard, may inquire into, report findings and make recommendations respecting:
> (a) The occurrence, on Saturday, the 9th day of May, A.D., 1992, which resulted in the loss of life in the Westray Mine at Plymouth, in the County of Pictou;
> (b) whether the occurrence was or was not preventable;
> (c) whether any neglect caused or contributed to the occurrence;
> (d) whether there was any defect in or about the Mine or the modes of working the Mine;
> (e) whether the mine and its operations were in keeping with the known geological structures or formations in the area;

(f) whether there was compliance with applicable statutes, regulations, orders, rules or directions; and

(g) all other matters related to the establishment and operation of the Mine which the Commissioner considers relevant to the occurrence.

The order further stipulates that the Commissioner will pay for all reasonable expenses; staff, legal counsel, and technical experts and allows the Commissioner to make rules to regulate proceedings of the inquiry and conduct its business.[7]

Of particular importance are items (c) and (f), for they can be read to give the inquiry authority to establish criminal responsibility, something in fact it cannot do, which became a problem later.

On September seventeenth, four months after the explosion, the RCMP took control of the mine and seized documents and equipment to determine if there was a basis for charges of criminal negligence causing death. A separate trial, subject to a media ban, heard whether the inquiry or the RCMP could view seized documents Curragh maintained were privileged communication between the firm and its lawyers. Eighty-five of the 125 documents in question were subsequently ruled confidential. In both September and December the RCMP also seized documents from the inquiry itself.[8]

Initially it seemed that the provincial labour department had no knowledge of safety problems or of the risk of methane buildup in the mine, and inspectors in the mine found evidence of a second explosion and cave-in at the end of May that had not been reported.[9] However, although the province could not find federal reports that cautioned against mining the Foord seam, provincial labour department inspectors had issued four different orders to clean up dangerous working conditions between December 1990 and April 29, 1992, a week before the explosion. And the province's department of natural resources had approved unauthorized changes to the mine even though it was apparent that worker safety was at risk.[10]

In October, Curragh and four of its managers were charged with fifty-two violations of the provincial Occupational Health and Safety Act, charges which had to be laid within six months of the infractions.[11] The charges included failure to prevent the accumulation of coal dust, improper use and storage of flammable materials and tampering with monitoring devices for methane detection. The maximum penalty for any of these offences was $10,000 and a year in jail. It also came to light that previous warnings had been given by inspectors to the mine managers, a fact that caused the labor minister some embarrassment. Three weeks before the safety violations charges, the provincial cabinet had finally formally transferred responsibility for enforcing the Coal Mines Regulation Act from the department of natural resources to the department of labour, six years after that responsibility had been transferred in practice.

Meanwhile, the Supreme Court of Nova Scotia heard arguments late in September 1992 for an injunction against the inquiry on the grounds that it was delving into criminal matters. The inquiry's mandate was under provincial jurisdiction but appeared also to involve questions of criminal responsibility, a federal matter. The provincial attorney general said the mandate of the inquiry could be changed so it would not conflict with the criminal investigation, but that would require cabinet approval and the head of the inquiry was himself reluctant to request such a change. But in October the Supreme Court of Nova Scotia ruled that the inquiry should be postponed until a formal legal challenge could be heard, in order to protect the constitutional rights of the managers to a fair trial. In November the inquiry was struck down on the basis that its terms of reference involved assigning criminal responsibility. This could have been foreseen, as it had been an issue in the inquiries into baby deaths at Toronto's Hospital for Sick Children in 1984, and into the fund-raising activities of Patricia Starr in 1990. In June 1993 the United Steelworkers of America appealed the Nova Scotia decision to the Supreme Court of Canada.[12] A decision was expected in late 1994 but was unavailable at the time of writing. The trial of Curragh and the mine managers began in February 1995.

In December 1992, thirty-four of the fifty-two charges under the Occupational Health and Safety Act were stayed by the director of public prosecutions to avoid interfering with criminal charges that were anticipated to be laid by the RCMP. In March 1993 the remaining eighteen charges were stayed as well, a decision which led to questions about the competence of the director of public prosecutions.[13] But it wasn't until April 1993, almost a year after the explosion, that criminal charges were laid.[14] The charges read that Curragh Inc. and two mine managers had committed criminal negligence causing death and manslaughter, both carrying a maximum penalty of life imprisonment. The charges were quickly criticized as flawed because they did not specify exactly what "unlawful acts or omissions" on the part of Curragh or the mine managers had led to the deaths of the miners. The first charges were thrown out and charges were refiled. These were then criticized on the basis that the prosecutors were not specifying how failing to comply with provincial statutes was connected to the criminal charges of negligence and manslaughter. There were also allegations that insufficient staff and funds were allocated for the Crown investigation and that officials from government departments possibly implicated in the disaster attended meetings with government prosecutors.[15]

Spreading blame around, in April 1993 the new labour minister (the minister at the time of the explosion had been removed) revealed the results of a report that showed the department of labour was disorganized and had failed to follow up on safety orders. The independent report criticized the department for unplanned and reactive inspections, for incomplete file documentation, inadequate identification of violations in order to ensure compliance, and lack of follow-up to see if orders had been carried out.[16]

While the inquiry was barred from holding public sessions until the criminal charges were heard, it requested federal documents on Westray. The Mulroney government initially refused to hand over "thousands of pages" of documents.[17] This withholding pointed to further questions about the involvement of the federal and provincial governments in the financing and sponsorship of the Westray mine.

The most recent danger of explosive methane in the Foord seam had been known in 1986, and in 1988 Clifford Frame, the chairman of Westray, had pointed out the hazards of mining the seam in a letter to the government requesting funds. The politics of the disaster were further evidenced by the fact that the contract for coal negotiated with the Nova Scotia Power Corporation attached to the loan agreement was better than that held with the Cape Breton Development Corporation. In 1989 the vice-president of mining for Curragh had met with then-premier John Buchanan and then local MLA Don Cameron, after previous meetings between Clifford Frame and former Defence Minister Robert Coates, advisers from the Prime Minister's Office, local MP and future head of ACOA Elmer MacKay, and Robert de Cotrêt, the minister responsible for the Department of Regional Industrial Expansion (DRIA). The next year, in May 1990, more than $100 million in loans and guarantees were extended to the mine.

Between 1989 and 1992 there had been eight cave-ins and numerous safety violations, but no charges were ever laid. In 1992, three weeks after the explosion, a Cape Breton MLA made the allegation that the premier had called him in 1990 and threatened him after he was critical of the government sponsorship of the mine, an allegation the premier denied. After the explosion, the U.S. expert brought in to advise on the disaster was alleged to have participated in a coverup of government responsibility in a mine explosion in Kentucky. Two days after the explosion, the federal government set up a Westray task force at the federal industry department, and $400,000 was allocated to explain the federal role at Westray. At the provincial level, it passed unremarked that the media relations officer for the department of justice was moved to the labour department.[18]

Needless to say, the facts on the politics of the disaster received little attention in the press, even though Dean Jobb, one of the staff reporters at the *Herald* eventually was nominated for several awards for his investigative reporting on Westray which later appeared in book form.

Analyzing the news

The coverage on Westray was massive: the coverage was almost the story. In the first week, 14 percent of the total citations indexed under "Westray—disaster" for two years were published; in the first month, 36 percent. This massive coverage provided smothering detail of the tragedy: the explosion, the attempt to rescue the trapped miners, discovering the bodies, flooding the mine and the suffering of the families. It was the human interest story next door, a tragedy in a primary industry in a traditional economy.

However, much of the reporting is not critical or informative but emotional, containing phrases such as "the price of mining coal has been measured in human lives."[19] An editorial abridged from the *Halifax Herald* of May 11, 1992, entitled "Tragedy at Westray," is not only full of sentimental phrases but unfortunately comes across as an apologetic for the disaster:

> Underground coal mining in Nova Scotia . . . has long been a story of *great human courage* pitted against *great natural hazards.* . . . too often, it has also been a history of hope and fortitude and *heartbreak* in the face of unbearable tragedies. So it was again in Plymouth, Pictou County, this weekend, when a methane bump early Saturday buried 26 miners underground. The scene was the Westray mine . . . sunk last year into one of [the] most *treacherous* troves of coal. . . . The dimension of the tragedy . . . was *truly heart-rending.* . . . shifts of draegermen continued to work *tirelessly* to reach the 15 others still trapped underground . . . all of Nova Scotia is now waiting and praying . . . we share the pain and grief of the families and friends of the men who have perished. . . . [This] is a terrible reminder of the *enormous sacrifice* made by generation after generation of *brave men* to mine Nova Scotia's deep coal seams. . . . [This is] *an awesome testament* to the *courage* of those who go down to the deeps. It's a reminder, too, that advanced technology . . . hasn't changed the equation. It is still *brave men* toiling in the face of *unseen danger* in the dark. The risks are still there; the men still go knowingly to meet them. And our hearts still mourn when the danger claims these finest of men (italics added).[20]

The sentiment behind this editorial is admirable, but abridging it makes the consequences of such a depiction more obvious: brave men courageously working underground, knowing the risks, sacrificing themselves to mine the coal which can turn on them capriciously despite the best of technology. In such a depiction we do not get a sense that people most often work out of necessity rather than courageous decision, that occupational safety standards might not be followed or that workers often have no choice about working in unsafe conditions; there is no analysis of the politics involved in establishing Westray, or acknowledgement that it was not run perfectly.

The image readers get from such an editorial is individualistic and romantic, of courageous men working on the frontier, pitted against capricious nature. The difficulty with such a portrayal is that it gives us no way to understand the disaster as anything other than an accident. This explosion was about as much an accident as the grounding of the *Exxon Valdez*, or the release of gas from the Union Carbide plant in Bhopal, India (Mokhiber 1988).

Similar misconceptions that mystify the disaster are exhibited in the following quotations. In an article entitled "Call of the coal," an academic expert who was a former provincial deputy minister of development said that coal mining is engrained in the culture of Nova Scotia: "There's always that thing in the back of every Nova Scotian's mind—I think they grew up with it in their mother's milk—that coal once paid for everything and maybe someday it'll do it again. . . . When people die in an accident like this, it just reinforces that this is the price we've got to pay and just keep pluggin' on."[21]

In an article entitled "Nova Scotian coal mining fuelled by politics of need," another academic expert attributed the acceptance of the disaster to fatalism: "We really are a region of the country where there are horrendous disasters, whether it's people lost at sea or in a mine. You just accept it because it's there. That may be the reason we accept coal mining, because it's just part of the culture. . . . Yeah, coal mines are dangerous. You could lose your life doing it. But you could lose your life fishing, too. We just accept it.[22]

The problem with these explanations is that they romanticize and justify the disaster, offering no critical insight into why the tragedy occurred and how it might have been prevented.

Figure 10.1 shows the type and progression of coverage of the Westray explosion in the *Halifax Herald*. This chart links the amount of coverage to major events as the story unfolded. During 1992–93, about seven hundred articles were indexed under "Westray—disaster" for the *Halifax Herald*, and this includes articles, editorials, commentaries and letters to the editor. The articles are shown broken into fifty-unit blocks, with the average number of articles per day represented on the line. So, for example, the first fifty citations were published in the first two days and represent an average of about twenty-five per day. During the first month, 250 articles are published, 36 percent of the total coverage for two years.

During the first week the promise to establish an inquiry was announced. The number of citations published per day quickly dropped to about an average of seven at the end of the first month. During June, one month after the explosion, the coverage increased slightly during the discussion over whether to flood the mine. By the time safety charges were laid in October, the number of citations had dropped to an average of about one and a half a day. The inquiry was quashed in November, and in April criminal charges were finally laid by the RCMP.

Figure 10.1
Westray disaster coverage, *Halifax Herald*, 1992–93

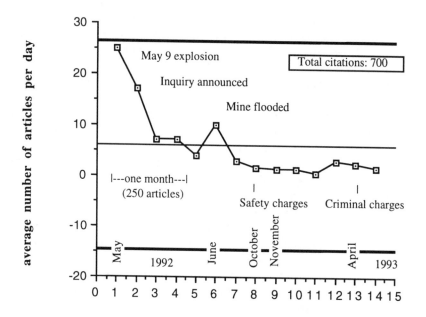

The consequence of massive coverage at the beginning and its subsequent drop is that the amount of information published declined as the legal and criminal issues came to the fore. Initially, when the topic was "the Westray disaster," the coverage of human suffering and tragedy was massive and overwhelming. When the topic became "the Westray case," the coverage was minimal in comparison. There are, of course, several possible reasons for this: after saturation coverage, interest in the case declined; reporters lack the ability to understand and communicate the legal technicalities; or new topics have captured public attention and the Westray story's "shelf life" had expired.

Whatever the explanation, the consequence in terms of the textual construction of the disaster, is that readers were exposed to information on tragedy, but not to information which would increase their understanding of the legal, criminal, economic and political issues involved in the case. Reporting that emphasizes the emotional side of the disaster, instead of the crime, ignores or mystifies the conditions that led to the explosion in the first place, making it likely that in the long run these conditions will be reproduced.

The tendency of reporters to cover similar stories in the same way has been called "pack journalism." (Ericson, Baranek and Chan 1991). This term has often been used to describe how different media "converge" in their news content. Pack journalism results in part from the organization of the news media, their need to maximize resources, and the reliance of reporters on the work of others to gain a sense of the newsworthiness of stories. The ideological consequence of pack journalism is a uniform, homogeneous, lowest-common denominator type of coverage where orthodoxy rules. Instead of a heterodoxy of opinion, readers are exposed to a uniform world view.

The convergence in the news about Westray meant that not many media stories were critical of how they covered the explosion. The media seemed overwhelmed by the disaster and struggled to put it into context, but they seemed unsure about the technology and terminology of mining, and there was both complaint and praise for their role.[23] As estimated two hundred journalists descended on Plymouth with the modern technology of communication at their disposal. However, they were quickly separated from the families and told the latter did not wish to speak to them. Instead of seeing this as information control, the media focused on the rescue effort and the explosion. It was patronizing to say that "all most viewers really needed or wanted was to know whether [the miners] had survived."[24]

Furthermore, the media missed the story about safety concerns at the mine before the explosion occurred. The extreme danger had become routine. Safety regulations were not observed or were flagrantly violated, and miners were often ordered to work in unsafe conditions and verbally abused when they protested. Day after day the danger became almost banal, as the workers anticipated they could be killed at any time. Miners even told their relatives that if there was an explosion to make sure that somebody got to the bottom of what happened (Comish 1993). The fact that Curragh was going to operate Westray was certainly no secret; safety had also been known to be a concern at its Yukon mine; and the political manoeuvring to establish the mine at Plymouth merited more investigation. Investment in mining is a risky business and companies are going to go where the red tape is minimal.[25] One columnist wrote how he had learned that a miner had called a local paper to complain about rockfalls in the mine, suggesting they contact the mine inspector, but the newspaper had failed to follow up on the lead.[26]

Mining is a risky business. In general, the risk of being killed at work is higher than that of being murdered. In the primary industries of forestry and mining the risk is greatest. The Law Reform Commission (1986) says the occupational fatality rate around mines, quarries and oil wells is the second highest in Canada at 83.6 deaths per 100,000 people, surpassed only by the rate for work in forestry. Between 1989 and 1991, the number of injuries in mining in Canada went down by 25 percent, and was down 16 percent in all occupations. In Nova Scotia, however, the number of time-loss injuries in mining went up by 28 percent, even though the overall provincial occupational injury rate went down 9 percent. Mining was certainly not getting safer in Nova Scotia.

The Worker's Compensation Board routinely collects information on the number of people killed by occupation in Canada and passes it on to Statistics Canada, but the last year that survey was published was 1986. Injuries and fatalities are highest in the primary occupations and, because these industries are located in certain regions, it can be argued that occupational danger is part and parcel of economic inequality in Canada. This danger is part of Maritime history, whether on the water or in the mines. This story is all the more shocking because of its familiarity.

The Westray disaster could be a story about political interference in the way grants are given to the mining business. It could also be a story of laxity and ineffectiveness in the provincial department of labour. While the inspectors have been cleared, we still do not know enough about why safety standards were not in place or not enforced. It could also be a story about the political economy of death and how risk is part of the calculation of profit. But it is also a story about how the media contributed to a climate where the explosion was able to happen in the first place. The media was part of the story, and perhaps part of the crime.

Summary

A summary of hundreds of articles have been looked at in this chapter. The Westray explosion has been called a tragedy and a disaster; it has led to an inquiry and a court case; it is a story about safety, politics, economics and the media. In reading the news, we have had to look beneath the surface of an incredible drama of life and death, of families coping with the loss of brothers, sons, fathers and husbands. It has been necessary to stand back from the tragedy and look at the overall pattern of reporting. In this way we can come to see how when it came time to cover the legal issues of the Westray case, news coverage dwindled to a trickle.

We could use a similar methodology to "unpack" many other cases in the news. Two were alluded to above: the grounding of an oil tanker, the *Exxon Valdez*, off the coast of Alaska on March 24, 1989, which released

41 million litres of crude oil into Prince William Sound and polluted more than two-thousand kilometres of coastline; and the release of forty tons of methyl isocyanate gas from the Union Carbide factory in Bhopal, India, which killed 2,000 to 5,000 people and injured 200,000 more. The initial media approach to such events is to treat them simply as disasters and then, at some point when emotions have been rubbed raw, to begin to see the political and economic conditions that underlay these tragedies. The trick is to see how the textual construction of the event in the news overlays the event and conditions our understanding, creating the risk of a reproduction of the very conditions that made the disaster possible in the first place.

Notes

1. "Alarm preceded Westray explosion," *Globe and Mail*, March 27, 1992; "Gas alarms sounded before blast, report says, Westray printout showed dangerous methane level," *Halifax Herald*, March 27, 1993: A1; "Curragh will sue Globe for millions over story," *Halifax Herald*, April 1, 1993: A16; "Apology to Curragh Inc.," *Globe and Mail*, April 9, 1993: A1; "Globe apologizes for Westray story," *Halifax Herald*, April 9, 1993: A1.

2. "Rescuers race to reach 26 trapped in mine," *Toronto Star*, May 10, 1992: A1; "'Everybody here is very, very stricken,'" *Toronto Star*, May 10, 1992: A10; "Ear-splitting boom alerted residents to disaster," *Toronto Star*, May 10, 1992: A10; "Just 'never give up hope,' Survivor of 1958 Springhill 'miracle' relives his 8-day ordeal," *Toronto Star*, May 10, 1992: A10; "Safety stations provide haven for miners in disasters," *Toronto Star*, May 10, 1992: A10; "Mine town 'aches' as 11 bodies found, Rescuers continue search for 15 miners," *Toronto Star*, May 11, 1992: A1; "Miners knew they could die, They were used to dangers of working thousands of feet underground," *Toronto* Star, May 11, 1992: A8; "Deafening blast fired ex-miner's worst fears," *Toronto Star*, May 11, 1992: A9; "Steel-nerved draegermen seek survivors," *Toronto Star*, May 11, 1992: A9; "Coal-miner buddies buried side by side," *Toronto Star*, May 14, 1992: A1; "When all hope had gone, Search for miners called off," *Toronto Star*, May 15, 1992: A1; "Sympathy, donations flow into Plymouth," *Toronto Star*, May 15, 1992: A13; "PM to attend miners' service," *Toronto Star*, May 15, 1992: A13.

3. "Ottawa knew of blast risk at coal mine Epp admits," *Toronto Star*, May 12, 1992: A1; "Key minister opposed aid for Westray, ex-official says," *Toronto Star*, May 14, 1992: A2; "Nova Scotian coal mining fuelled by politics of need," *Toronto Star*, May 16, 1992: A1.

4. "Westray facts," *Halifax Herald*, May 11, 1992: A21; "Inside on Westray mine disaster," *Halifax Herald*, May 11, 1992: A1; "Mining tragedy, 11

bodies pulled from Westray pit, rescuers hunt for, 15 men," *Halifax Herald*, May 11, 1992: A1; "Families' dread turns to anguish," *Halifax Herald*, May 11, 1992: A1; "Tragedy at Westray," *Halifax Herald*, May 11, 1992: C1; "Rescuers inch closer to 15 miners," *Halifax Herald*, May 12, 1992: A1; "Westray mine disaster victims," *Halifax Herald*, May 12, 1992: A1; "Rescuers delayed in search for miners," *Halifax Herald*, May 12, 1992: A1; "Methane likely explosion cause—expert," *Halifax Herald*, May 12, 1992: A15; "Families hold tight to hope," *Halifax Herald*, May 12, 1992: A15; "Rallying to the families at Plymouth," *Halifax Herald*, May 12, 1992: C1; "Family of Springhill miner offers support," *Halifax Herald*, May 13, 1992: A1; "Rescuers 'progress remains slow,'" *Halifax Herald*, May 13, 1992: A1; "Wait beginning to wear on families," *Halifax Herald*, May 13, 1992: A1; "Crew set to break through last barrier," *Halifax Herald*, May 13, 1992: A1; "Crews turn back after two tries," *Halifax Herald*, May 13, 1992: A1; "Victims' families to be compensated," *Halifax Herald*, May 13, 1992: A2; "Draegermen clear rock by hand, squeeze through tiny gaps," *Halifax Herald*, May 13, 1992: A8; "Canadians east to west share deep sadness," *Halifax Herald*, May 13, 1992: A8; "Explosion victims mourned," *Halifax Herald*, May 14, 1992: A1; "Rescuers continue search for missing 11," *Halifax Herald*, May 14, 1992: A1; "A community bears its tragedy," *Halifax Herald*, May 14, 1992: C1, editorial; "Search suspended, four bodies removed," *Halifax Herald*, May 15, 1992: A1; "Long wait ends, deep sorrow begins," *Halifax Herald*, May 15, 1992: A1; "A heartbreaking conclusion," *Halifax Herald*, May 15, 1992: C1, editorial; "Tearful draegermen describe their ordeal," *Halifax Herald*, May 15, 1992: A2; "First 11 died quick, painless deaths, says medical examiner," *Halifax Herald*, May 15, 1992: B3; "Victims' funerals: Antigonish miner remembered," *Halifax Herald*, May 15, 1992: B2; "Aid for families pours in, Tragedy strikes chord around world," *Halifax Herald*, May 15, 1992: B2; "Westville miners," *Halifax Herald*, May 16, 1992: A2; "Black ribbons symbolize mining tragedy," *Halifax Herald*, May 16, 1992: A5; "Westray victims," *Halifax Herald*, May 16, 1992: A1; "Cards of comfort: Students send families support," *Halifax Herald*, May 16, 1992: A1; "Westville man recalls loss of friend, fellow coal miner," *Halifax Herald*, May 16, 1992: A2.

5.   "Westray unsafe, say two miners who quit jobs," *Halifax Herald*, May 11, 1992: A2; "Methane a lethal threat to miners," *Halifax Herald*, May 11, 1992: A1; "Westray miner says he'd return to pit," *Halifax Herald*, May 11, 1992: A14; "Rescuer convinced mine was not safe," *Halifax Herald*, May 11, 1992: A15; "Devco warned of Pictou mine danger, Pit blast victim planned to quit due to danger," *Daily News*, May 12, 1992:

4; "Westray rejects allegations that worker safety ignored, Rescuers still trying to reach missing miners," *Globe and Mail*, May 12, 1992: A1; "Westray victim planned to quit," *Halifax Herald*, May 12, 1992: A2; "Report reveals warnings ignored; N.S., Ottawa told mine not safe or economic," *Halifax Herald*, May 12, 1992: A13; "Lid kept on past probes at mine," *Halifax Herald*, May 12, 1992: A15; "Methane likely explosion cause—expert," *Halifax Herald*, May 12, 1992: A16; "Records show 'concern' over safety; Inspection reports finger steep coal dust, methane levels," *Halifax Herald*, May 14, 1992: A16; "Former miners slam Westray's safety practices," *Halifax Herald*, May 16, 1992: A2; "Minister alarmed by charges of mine's safety violations," *Halifax Herald*, May 16, 1992: A2; "Mining industry's image darkened by disaster," *Halifax Herald*, May 16, 1992: B1; "Safety a relative term in mining," *Globe and Mail*, May 18, 1992: A4; "Miners say probe to be eye-opener, Westray crew complains of high methane levels," *Halifax Herald*, May 19, 1992: A1; "Westray explosion dominates debate," *Halifax Herald*, May 21, 1992: A1; "Blast blamed on coal dust," *Halifax Herald*, May 22, 1992: A1; "Westray warned before disaster, Company cautioned on coal dust dangers," *Halifax Herald*, May 22, 1992: A1.

6. "Premier orders mine disaster inquiry," *Halifax Herald*, May 11, 1992: A2; "Inquiry to have broad mandate—Cameron," *Halifax Herald*, May 13, 1992: A1; "'No person' will escape mine probe—Cameron," *Daily News*, May 16, 1992: 5; "Mine's fate on hold, Judge to head probe into Westray disaster," *Halifax Herald*, May 16, 1992: A1; "Richard to head mine inquiry, Supreme Court judge to have wide-ranging powers," *Halifax Herald*, May 16, 1992: A4; "Judge no stranger to high-profile cases," *Halifax Herald*, May 16, 1992: A4;

7. "'No person' will escape mine probe—Cameron," *Daily News*, May 16, 1992: 5.

8. "RCMP eyes charging Westray, Documents seized in criminal negligence probe," *Halifax Herald*, September 12, 1992: A1; "RCMP seizes records in Westray investigation," *Halifax Herald*, September 14, 1992: A1; "Westray memos, computer data among records seized by RCMP," *Globe and Mail*, September 14, 1992: A6; "RCMP will enter Westray mine alone because of risks," *Halifax Herald*, September 16, 1992: C16; "Mounties take control of Westray," *Daily News*, September 18, 1992: 3; "RCMP enter Westray mine, Police seek cause of explosion," *Globe and Mail*, September 19, 1992: A7; "Mounties remove evidence from mine," *Daily News*, September 26, 1992: 6; "Westray owners in court today, Judge to decide whether documents stay confidential," *Halifax Herald*, October 15, 1992: C17; "Scorched helmets, notebooks among evidence seized," *Halifax Herald*, October 15, 1992: C17;

"Inquiry to get unprotected Curragh papers," *Daily News*, October 20, 1992: 4; "RCMP seize mine probe documents," *Halifax Herald*, December 14, 1992: A1.

9. "Little evidence of methane woes in reports," *Daily News*, May 14, 1992: 4; "Second cave-in at Westray coal mine revealed; Delayed announcement heightens concern about safety of investigators, work crews," *Globe and Mail*, June 4, 1992: A4; "Volume of charges shows safety ignored—critics," *Halifax Herald*, October 6, 1992: A2.

10. "Province searches records," *Halifax Herald*, June 6, 1992: A13; "Westray repeatedly ordered to clean up," *Globe and Mail*, May 29, 1992: A4; "McDonough says province ignored study," *Daily News*, June 5, 1992: 5; "Federal Westray review noted dangers; Government guilty of gross negligence, Dingwall charges," *Daily News*, June 5, 1992: 4; "Government acts as Westray mine's 'compliant partner,'" *Halifax Herald*, July 16, 1992: A2.

11. "Westray officials, company charged; 52 offences cited over explosion," *Globe and Mail*, October 6, 1992: A1; "Labor department charges Westray; Probe results in 52 charges against mining company, managers," *Halifax Herald*, October 6, 1992: A1; "Action very gratifying, says Westray family spokesman," *Halifax Herald*, October 6, 1992: A2; "Mine safety goes to court," *Halifax Herald*, October 7, 1992: C1, editorial; "Legere defends timing of charges," *Halifax Herald*, October 7, 1992: A1; "Curragh, mine bosses in court Dec. 10 on safety allegation," *Halifax Herald*, October 7, 1992: A2; "Coal mine order passed one day before Westray charged," *Halifax Herald*, October 27, 1992: A4; "Any Westray charges restricted by time," *Daily News*, June 4, 1992: 20, editorial.

12. "Westray official seeks to ground inquiry," *Halifax Herald*, September 19, 1992: A1; "Mine probe could be altered, AG says; RCMP conflict will be avoided," *Daily News*, September 25, 1992: 4; "Court challenge seeks to ban Westray inquiry," *Halifax Herald*, September 26, 1992: A1; "Judge wants more info on Westray proposal, Richard reluctant to get involved in firm's bid to scale down probe," *Halifax Herald*, September 28, 1992: A10; "Judge postpones Westray inquiry; Trio likely to be charged, lawyer says," *Daily News*, October 1, 1992: 3; "The law's delay," *Halifax Herald*, October 2, 1992: C1, editorial; "Ruling today on challenge to mine probe, Westray inquiry's fate hangs on decision," *Halifax Herald*, November 13, 1992: A1; "Westray inquiry derailed, Glube pulls plug on constitutional grounds, appeal launched to save mine probe," *Halifax Herald*, November 14, 1992: A1; "N.S. didn't see legal storm coming," *Globe and Mail*, November 14, 1992: A5; "Inquiry quashed, Taking the sting out of Westray," *Globe and*

Mail, November 21, 1992: D3; "No more excuses on Westray," *Globe and Mail*, November 30, 1992: A20, editorial; "Court raises families' hopes for Westray mine disaster probe," *Toronto Star*, December 10, 1993: A15; "Westray miners pin job hopes on restarting halted inquiry despite legal, political obstacles," *Halifax Herald*, June 11, 1993: A5; "Westray probe seeks speeded-up inquiry," *Daily News*, June 11, 1993: 4; "Ex-mine bosses fight bid to revive inquiry," *Halifax Herald*, June 16, 1993: A7; "Westray inquiry asking highest court to end delay," *Daily News*, June 29, 1993: 8; "Westray inquiry asks top court to rule on future of hearings," *Halifax Herald*, June 29, 1993: A5; "Supreme Court to hear Westray inquiry appeal," *Globe and Mail*, December 10, 1993: A3; "Top court to hear Westray appeal, Families hope ruling will clear way for public hearings," *Halifax Herald*, December 10, 1993: A1; "Court gives fresh hope to early inquiry start," *Daily News*, December 10, 1993: 3; "Families 'want to see justice done,' Westray probe shouldn't jeopardize criminal cases," *Halifax Herald*, June 1, 1994: A12.

13. "34 Westray charges dropped," *Halifax Herald*, December 11, 1992: A1; "Westray charges stayed, AG withdraws 18 charges under labor safety laws," *Halifax Herald*, March 4, 1993: A1; "'An unacceptable risk' to any criminal case; Excerpts, transcripts, reports, studies, etc.," *Daily News*, March 5, 1993: 19; "Pearson's 'competence' questioned," *Daily News*, March 5, 1993: 4; "Mr. Pearson's big gamble," *Halifax Herald*, March 5, 1993: C1, editorial; "Westray widows shaken by decision, Victims' families pin hopes on RCMP investigation," *Halifax Herald*, March 5, 1993: A1; "N.S. drops charges in Westray explosion, Chief prosecutor fears potential criminal trial would be jeopardized," *Globe and Mail*, March 5, 1993: A5; "Pearson answers critics," *Halifax Herald*, March 6, 1993: A4; "Nova Scotia's legal system is a laughingstock—again," *Daily News*, May 15, 1994: 2, commentary.

14. "RCMP decision 'likely' in 30 days, Westray investigation winds down," *Halifax Herald*, March 29, 1993: A1; "Decision on charges within 30 days; Westray probe 'winding down,' Mountie says," *Daily News*, March 29, 1993: 3; "RCMP promises word on Westray this month, Globe retracts story citing high-methane levels," *Daily News*, April 10, 1993: 4; "'Upset Curragh calls it quits, RCMP to lay manslaughter charges," *Daily News*, April 16, 1993: 4; "Westray mine to be charged," *Toronto Star*, April 16, 1993: A1; "2 managers at Westray to be charged over deaths," *Toronto Star*, April 18, 1993: A12; "Families cheer Westray charges, 'No evidence' of Labor 'criminality,'" *Daily News*, April 21, 1993: 4; "Charges could take years to be heard," *Daily News*, April 21, 1993: 4; "RCMP lay charges in mine blast," *Toronto Star*,

April 21, 1993: A9; "Westray probe clears two mine inspectors," *Toronto Star*, April 22, 1993: A13.

15. "Westray charges flawed—Curragh lawyer, Mention of acts or conduct causing deaths said missing from wording," *Halifax Herald*, June 15, 1993: A4; "Westray challenge premature—Crown," *Halifax Herald*, July 9, 1993: A4; "Charges still flawed—Curragh, Judge expected to rule Oct. 26 on refiled allegations," *Halifax Herald*, September 29, 1993: A7; "N.S. Liberal seeks review of Westray prosecution," *Globe and Mail*, September 11, 1993: A3; "Province a 'suspect' in Westray," *Halifax Herald*, April 5, 1993: A1; "Prosecutors accuse N.S. of endangering mine probe," *Globe and Mail*, May 5, 1993: A18; "Top prosecutor downplays Westray memo," *Daily News*, May 6, 1993: 3.

16. "N.S. report reveals mine safety flaws, Labour Department apparently failed to follow up on many safety orders," *Globe and Mail*, April 30, 1993: A4; "Labor Department laxity lashed; Aftermath of Westray explosion 'paralysing' staff, report finds," Daily News, April 30, 1993: 4; "All downhill at labor offices," *Daily News*, April 30, 1993: 26; "Labor Department rapped; Auditors expose years of mismanagement, sloppy work," *Halifax Herald*, April 30, 1993: A1; "Report attacks inspections at Nova Scotia coal mines," *Toronto Star*, April 30, 1993: A12; "Westray and a better way," *Halifax Herald*, May 1, 1993: B1, editorial.

17. "Ottawa broke Westray vows, lawyer charges; Counsel says inquiry staff still waiting for some files," *Daily News*, March 31, 1993: 4; "Inquiry threatens legal action; Release all Westray documents, feds urged," *Halifax Herald*, March 31, 1993: A1; "Westray inquiry threatens Ottawa, Commission says it would go to court in bid for documents," *Globe and Mail*, March 31, 1993: A1; "Ottawa stands firm on Westray papers," *Halifax Herald*, April 1, 1993: A16; "The Westray disgrace," *Halifax Herald*, April 1, 1993: C1, editorial; "Inquiry may get censored memo; Westray document classified as 'advice to ministers,' Hockin says," *Globe and Mail*, April 1, 1993: A3; "Grits seek Westray link to Campbell," *Daily News*, April 2, 1993: 14; "PM backs Campbell in Westray controversy," *Halifax Herald*, April 2, 1993: A1; "N.S. public inquiry to receive remaining Westray files," *Halifax Herald*, April 7, 1993: A5; "Feds promise 11,000 Westray papers tomorrow," *Daily News*, April 7, 1993: 3; "Ottawa accused of censoring data on Westray blast," *Toronto Star*, April 20, 1993: A9.

18. "Cameron made threat over coal mine—Boudreau," *Halifax Herald*, May 29, 1992: A1; "'86 study noted explosive potential of Foord seam," *Halifax Herald*, June 4, 1992: A14; "Mine expert's objectivity disputed," *Halifax Herald*, June 4, 1992: A14; "Financial facts prove mine result

of politics—Boudreau," *Halifax Herald*, June 6, 1992: A13; "The road to Westray," *Globe and Mail*, September 30, 1992: A22, editorial; "Is N.S. actually interested in solving Westray mystery?" *Daily News*, December 2, 1992: 2, commentary; "Ottawa sets $400,000 to explain Westray role," *Halifax Herald*, December 8, 1992: A2; "Politics' role in Westray queried; Public needs to know, official says," *Globe and Mail*, March 29, 1993: A1; "What's revealed is trivial; what's concealed is scary," *Daily News*, March 31, 1993: 2, commentary; "'88 letter outlined Westray hazards," *Halifax Herald*, April 3, 1993: A1; "Paper trail in Westray case leads to PMO," *Halifax Herald*, April 5, 1993: A1; "NDP MP calls for fed inquiry into Ottawa's role in Westray," *Daily News*, April 8, 1993: 5; "Parliament misled about Westray, says NDP critic," *Halifax Herald*, April 8, 1993: A4; "Westray's dealmakers," *Halifax Herald*, April 10, 1993: B1; "The Westray factor," *Daily News*, June 9, 1993; "Westray paid Coates's son to compile manual," *Halifax Herald*, June 30, 1994: A3.

19. "Tragedy triggers memories in Springhill," *Halifax Herald*, May 11, 1992: A17, A19; Rich coalfields exact heavy toll; Explosions, floods, asphyxiation have claimed hundreds of lives in Pictou County coal mines," *Halifax Herald*, May 11, 1992: A17, A19.

20. "Tragedy at Westray," *Halifax Herald*, May 11, 1992: C1, emphasis added.

21. "Call of the coal," *Halifax Herald*, May 16, 1992: B1.

22. "Nova Scotian coal mining fuelled by politics of need," *Toronto Star,* May 16, 1992: A1.

23. "Our coverage," *Halifax Herald*, May 11, 1992: A2; "Explosion triggers media marathon," *Halifax Herald*, May 11, 1992: A14; "The '56 explosion and '58 bump: A veteran newsman looks back," *Halifax Herald*, May 12, 1992: A13; "TV integral to Westray coverage," *Halifax Herald*, May 15, 1992: M37, Mayflower; "Families, media worlds apart," *Halifax Herald*, May 13, 1992: A2; "Volunteer's marathon: People from across country go extra mile to help out," *Halifax Herald*, May 14, 1992: A15; "Westray's Benner runs the show, Mine exec picture of grace under pressure," *Halifax Herald*, May 15, 1992: A2; "Media should do soul-searching over Westray mine disaster role," *Daily News*, May 17, 1992: 2, commentary; "Newsworld's quality in hands of CRTC," *Halifax Herald*, May 19, 1992: M3, Mayflower; "Blaming someone natural part of grieving," *Halifax Herald*, May 21, 1992: A7, commentary; "Seeking shelter from bad-news bombardment," *Halifax Herald*, May 23, 1992: A8, commentary; "Westray: People deserve truth," *Halifax Herald*, June 5, 1992: B2; "Journalists should reveal biases—MP," *Halifax Herald*, July 24, 1992: A3; "Curragh

twists truth with crafty PR practices," *Daily News,* September 3, 1992: 21, commentary; "Mine probe could be scaled back—Cameron," *Halifax Herald,* October 2, 1992: A1; "Westray inquiry offers in-camera hearings," *Halifax Herald,* November 3, 1992: A1; "Media, families have it wrong, Westray owner," *Halifax Herald,* January 26, 1993: A5; "Mining disaster worst tragedy—Mountie," *Halifax Herald,* May 8, 1993: B2.

24. "Mine tragedy in pictures," *Halifax Herald,* May 12, 1992: M37, Mayflower.
25. "How Canada has dug itself into a miner role," *Globe and Mail,* June 29, 1993: A9.
26. "Media should do soul-searching on Westray mine disaster role," *Daily News,* May 17, 1992: 2, column.

Conclusion

Conclusions are always difficult. A conclusion is often read first, and it is often the one written first, because usually it's not only where the writer ended up but where they wanted to arrive. However, individual topics can take on a life of their own, and the writer must then face the task of genuinely summing up underlying themes and issues that have revealed themselves.

The method used in this book was eclectic, drawing techniques and articles from many sources. The media has been used as a resource and topic—as a source of materials and a site of analysis. The sampling has been systematic, but the point has been to focus on some key problems, to use the strongest examples possible and then reconstruct an analysis to interpret the issues. For that reason, my conclusions here are ultimately the result of analysis, not simply the result of method.

The analysis developed here is built upon the idea that crime in society is as much a matter of a general attitude as any person's individual actions. Crime is not simply an act of violence, for example; as people have to react to that act and define it as a problem. But crime is also not simply an act of labelling because the law itself sets the context for how people react to crime. Taken together, the motivation and commission of a crime, the reaction of others and the passing and repeal of legislation, all create an interwoven moral drama.

In this sense, crime is socially constructed—it is not absolute or universal. People rely upon and create a web of meanings for understanding action, and it is this active sense-making that is the condition for taking crime for granted in the first place. The news media is an integral part of this process because it affirms and confirms the meaning of crime in a textual discourse. The media does not simply create a consensus but participates in debating the dissensus over the significance of crime in modern society to our communities.

"Crime" is not found in the act, or even in the label, but in its legal and social construction. And the media has become an inextricable part of this construction. To simply accuse the media of sensationalism is to create a red herring—being excited is not the problem. To improve crime reporting, more in-depth, far-reaching changes are needed. What follow are comments and suggestions on how news reporting on crime could be improved. These comments are general because the issues are quite different in the reporting of sexual assault from those in the reporting on arson, for example. However, some major points can be made, based on the idea that there is a "typical crime narrative" which mis/constructs crime.

Issues and recommendations

1. *Moralism*: Writing about crime tends to be reactionary. Although the news media has often been on the forefront in breaking scandals and exposing corruption, when it comes to crime the critical edge seems lost. News articles often adopt a moral point of view when reporting on crime, trading upon easy stereotypes and reproducing off-the-shelf labels, whether writing about prostitution, sexual assault or infanticide. This moralism can result in blaming the victims, misunderstanding the act and failing to see the deeper reasons behind the commission of the crime in the first place. To overcome this, editors, reporters and columnists will need to become schooled in the various myths our society perpetuates about crime and deviance.[1] This seems especially important in crimes dealing with gender and sexuality where it is very easy to project morality into legislation.

2. *Independence*: The news media needs to be more critical of the role of the police and the workings of the criminal justice system. It is difficult to be critical of the police when they are a main source of information on crime for reporters. However, the tendency to be dependent on the police is linked to reporters' general ignorance of the criminal justice system; as reporters learn more about the nature of the criminal justice process, they will be better able to form independent interpretations. This will also require being less dependent on lawyers, government and other authorities, who are not above trying to manipulate the press in favour of their own interests.[2] It may mean being more patient and avoiding the compulsion to beat out the competition by publishing the quick story first or by using anonymous sources. Readers do not switch papers easily, and they are motivated by the desire for more information. Taking the time to develop a better story ultimately leads to more control of the story.

3. *Interpretation*: Reporting still trades on the idea that the only thing important is to "get the facts." But what do we mean when we use the word "fact"? (Heidegger 1968) Do we mean indisputable, not a matter of opinion, reputable, authorized by expert advice? When seeking balance, experts are

often used to show opposing points of view, which simply shows just how contestable "facts" are. A "fact" is a very malleable thing; it depends on whose point of view is represented, on what sources are consulted, on what slant is taken, on what is left out and what is left in. Reporters need to trust less in this naive dictum and more in the idea of investigative reporting, digging deeper, going for the more difficult story. A reporter doesn't want to become part of the story, of course, but needs to be more critical of the easy story, for the easy story often reflects a dominant point of view that simply reproduces the status quo, particularly when reporters rely on sources who have their own axes to grind.

4. *Fragmentation*: The news media tends to report on crime in fragments, as incidents, reflecting how crime is treated institutionally. Focusing on the initial crime and the subsequent arrest, readers get a sense of isolated bizarre incidents committed by individuals. Such treatment, paradoxically, leads to a feeling of alienation. The more crimes reported, and the more random and unconnected they seem, the more people feel crime is out of control.[3] This individualistic treatment of crime ironically feeds into the conservative point of view that there is a need to return to a law and order agenda, with stronger laws and stricter punishments. The media needs to focus more on the larger picture and to be more responsible in reporting trends. Stories should follow cases through to the end, so readers can develop a more realistic sense of the reality of crime, how the system works and that criminals are punished.[4]

5. *Sensationalism*: The sensationalistic tendency to focus on the unusual creates illusions and delusions about the nature of social life.[5] Horrific crimes do occur in society, but to focus on them contributes to an overwhelming fear of others among the public and caters to the worst instincts of gossip and voyeurism. The media can actually contribute to an escalation of problems by drawing attention to and exaggerating them.[6] It is not simply a matter of avoiding the sensational but of balance and proportion because, in the process, much more mundane and serious crime goes unreported. Domestic violence is largely invisible in the media, as is corporate crime— yet both affect society far more than armed robberies do. Celebrity crime is part of this phenomenon as well, but why is there so much interest in Michael Jackson's friends, the Menendez brothers' dysfunctional family, O.J. Simpson's problems and John Bobbitt's sex life?[7]

6. *Context*: Discussing legislative changes is dry stuff and portraying the larger context is hard. Going for the sensational and the quick soundbite is just too easy.[8] The feeding frenzy that accompanies violent crime or a whiff of conspiracy in the upper echelons can lead all too easily to creating a story where there is none or to losing perspective and missing the real crime. From Whitewater to the savings and loan scandal, it is easy to resort to pack

journalism in the drive for ratings and to miss the more mundane crimes that happen every day. In covering court trials, it is easy to take the point of view of the prosecution—for after all, if a person has been charged with a crime, they must be guilty, right? It is also easy to downplay some crimes out of a sense of political correctness or embarrassment, forgetting that the community the media serves is a complex and diverse one.[9]

7. *Integrity*: Public confidence in the media sags when reporters and journalists are perceived as opportunistic and willing to do anything for a story. Exaggeration and sensationalism are just some of the most obvious faults in a business where there is a lot of pressure to get the story and beat out the competition. The seamier side involves doctoring photographs, exploiting tragedy, staging crime and faking events.[10] It need not be anything as spectacular as NBC creating the GM exploding truck; spinning the truth can be as simple as selecting an expert for their willingness to support a particular point of view.

However, when all is said and done, I still enjoy reading the news.

Notes

1. "News to them: Prostitution story reveals a media crime," *Daily News*, September 21, 1992: np; "Human-rights chairman regrets remarks," *Globe and Mail*, November 16, 1991: A7.

2. "The case against litigation journalism," *USA Today*, March 1994: 72–73; "U.S. military has iron grip on war coverage—professor," *Halifax Herald*, January 25, 1991: A1; "Quebec TV, radio shows are monitored by police," *Globe and Mail*, March 17, 1989: A1; "Substitute for truth: Despite the TV pictures, we aren't seeing the war," *Daily News*, January 20, 1991: 11; "How to win: 32 examples of the press on a leash," *Village Voice*, March 26, 1991: 17-18; "The use and abuse of anonymous sources," *Globe and Mail*, November 1, 1994: A21; "The media on trial: guilty or not guilty," *Globe and Mail*, May 31, 1994: A19; "The Steinberg gambit: Defense takes media," *Village Voice*, December 6, 1988: 11; "Litigation journalism is a scourge," *New York Times*, February 15, 1993: A15.

3. "9 Florida hotels blacking out a TV station's crime reports," *New York Times*, June 3, 1994: A16; "Bus murders unfairly linked to frustrations over peace talks," *Globe and Mail*, July 21, 1993: A18.

4. "Views on crime distorted, study says; Random incidents called chief factor," *Globe and Mail*, December 31, 1994: A1.

5. "UnNews: A post-Watergate meditation on how the media blew it," *Globe and Mail*, May 30, 1992: D1; "Some have heard enough about O.J.," *Halifax Herald*, November 24, 1994: D12.

6. "Media blamed for inciting rowdies," *Halifax Herald*, August 22, 1991:

A8; "After gunfire dies down, questions arise on newspaper's role," *New York Times*, March 2, 1993: A16; "Public interest wasn't served by police attack on The Star," *Toronto Star*, April 16, 1994: B3, editorial; "Aussie police slam press for 'glorifying' gunmen," *Daily News*, April 2, 1993: 20.

7. "Media messages fuel new school for scandal," *Toronto Star*, January 2, 1994: E3, editorial; "Frontline documentary to explore how media covered Jackson scandal," *Halifax Herald*, January 15, 1994: A14; "Courts here neuter the sensationalism of any Bobbittisms," *Toronto Star*, January 17, 1994: A7; "For 20%, he sells scandal, keeping Britain agog," *New York Times*, March 21, 1994: A4; "News media torn two ways in debate on privacy," *New York Times*, April 30, 1992: B11; "Tabs losing sight of fundamentals," *Globe and Mail*, August 5, 1994: A11; "A killing in Hollywood," *Village Voice*, May 24, 1994: 50; "There's nothing new about media voyeurism," *Toronto Star*, July 26, 1994: A17; "In tabloid times, justice can still be blind," *Toronto Star*, August 27, 1994: C5.

8. "Toronto after dark: It's a tame town," *Globe and Mail*, September 15, 1993: A26; "Whitewater and the press," *New York Times*, April 10, 1994: 18, editorial; "What the media didn't tell the American public," *Daily News*, March 25, 1993: 23; "Media show distorted picture," *Daily News*, February 17, 1993: 18; "Oh, brother," *Village Voice*, December 28, 1993: 53; "TV coverage of unrest in Moscow: a blurred reception," *New York Times*, May 9, 1993, section 4: 5; "Theatre of the absurd (1)," *Globe and Mail*, February 11, 1993: A14; "Theatre of the absurd (2)," *Globe and Mail*, February 12, 1993: A16.

9. "Journalists' malpractices," *Village Voice*, November 24, 1992: 20–21, column; "Media crime coverage under fire as alarmist," *Halifax Herald*, April 1, 1993: A2.

10. "Media outlets split over graphic photos," *Halifax Herald*, November 9, 1994: A15; "When photographs lie," *Newsweek*, July 30, 1990: 44–45; "Bad press: Why don't people trust the media anymore?" *Daily News*, April 30, 1993: 25; "The tale of the tape: Fighting the propaganda war in Mogadishu," *Village Voice*, August 24, 1993: 23–24; "Pay-per-interview," *Globe and Mail*, March 7, 1994: A21; "How CNN jumped the gun," *Globe and Mail*, July 28, 1994: A9; "Lights! Camera! News!" *New Republic*, February 28, 1994: 11–12; "Tuning Out: Saying no to the right to know," *Globe and Mail*, October 3, 1994: A10; "TV crew gets shooting on film," *Daily News*, January 20, 1993: 18; "Forces commander raps media handling of Somalians' deaths," *Daily News*, May 3, 1993: 8; "USA Today says photograph on gangs was 'misleading,'" *New York Times*, March 2, 1993: A14.

Bibliography

Adelberg, Ellen, and Claudia Currie, eds. (1987). *Two Few to Count: Canadian Women in Conflict with the Law*. Vancouver: Press Gang.

Apple, Michael W. (1986). "National Reports and the Construction of Inequality." *British Journal of the Sociology of Education* 7, no. 2: 171–90.

Atkinson, J. Maxwell. (1978). *Discovering Suicide: Studies in the Social Organization of Sudden Death*. Pittsburgh: University of Pittsburgh Press.

Becker, Howard S. (1973). *Outsiders: Studies in the Sociology of Deviance*. New York: Free Press.

Bell, Laurie, ed. (1987). *Good Girls/Bad Girls: Feminists and Sex Trade Workers Face to Face*. Seattle: Seal.

Bembenek, Lawrencia. (1992). *Woman on Trial*. Toronto: Harper Collins.

Benedict, Helen. (1992). *Virgin or Vamp: How the Press Covers Sex Crimes*. New York: Oxford University Press.

Benett, Lance. (1988). *News: The Politics of Illusion*. New York: Longman.

Berger, Arthur Asa. (1988). *Media U.S.A.: Process and Effect*. New York: Longman.

Berger, Peter L., and Thomas Luckmann. (1966). *The Social Construction of Reality: A Treatise in the Sociology of Knowledge*. New York: Doubleday Anchor.

Best, Joel. (1990). *Threatened Children: Rhetoric and Concern about Child-Victims*. Chicago: University of Chicago Press.

———, and Gerald T. Horiuchi. (1985). "The Razor Blade in the Apple: The Social Construction of Urban Legends." *Social Problems* 32, no. 5: 488–99.

Boyle, Christine. (1991). "Sexual Assault: A Case Study of Legal Policy

Options" In Margaret A. Jackson and Curt T. Griffiths (eds.), *Canadian Criminology: Perspectives on Crime and Criminality*. Toronto: Harcourt Brace Jovanovich.

Carriere, Kevin D., and Richard V. Ericson. (1989). *Crime Stoppers: A Study in the Organization of Community Policing*. University of Toronto: Centre of Criminology.

Chomsky, Noam. (1989). *Necessary Illusions: Thought Control in Democratic Societies*. Toronto: CBC.

Clow, Michael, with Susan Machum. (1993). *Stifling Debate: Canadian Newspapers and Nuclear Power*. Halifax: Fernwood.

Cohen, Stanley. (1972). *Folk Devils and Moral Panics: The Creation of the Mods and Rockers*. St. Albans, U.K.: Paladin.

Comish, Shaun. (1993). *The Westray Tragedy: A Miner's Story*. Halifax: Fernwood.

Craft, Christine. (1988). *Too Old, Too Ugly, and Not Deferential to Men*. Rocklin, Calif.: Prima.

Davey, Frank. (1994). *Karla's Web: A cultural investigation of the Mahaffy-French murders*. Toronto: Viking.

Davis, F. James. (1973). "Crime news in Colorado newspapers." In S. Cohen and J. Young (eds.), *The Manufacture of News: Social Problems, Deviance and the Mass Media*. London: Constable.

DeKeseredy, Walter S., and Ronald Hinch. (1991). *Woman Abuse: Sociological Perspectives*. Toronto: Thompson Educational Publishing.

Denham, Donna. (1990). "Wife assault and the criminal justice system." *Vis à Vis* 8, no. 2: 1. Canadian Council on Social Development.

Doern, G. Bruce. (1967). "The Role of Royal Commissions in the General Policy Process and in Federal-Provincial Relations." *Canadian Public Administration* 10, no. 4: 417–33.

Ericson, Richard V. (1991). "Mass Media, Crime, Law, and Justice: An Institutional Approach." *British Journal of Criminology* 31, no. 3: 219–49.

Ericson, Richard V., Patricia M. Baranek and Janet B.L. Chan. (1987). *Visualizing Deviance. A Study of News Organization*. Toronto: University of Toronto Press.

———. (1989). *Negotiating Control: A Study of News Sources*. Toronto: University of Toronto Press.

———. (1991). *Representing Order: Crime, Law, and Justice in the News Media*. Toronto: University of Toronto Press.

Fairstein, Linda A. (1993). *Sexual Violence: Our War Against Rape*. New York: William Morrow.

Faith, Karlene. (1987). "Media, Myths and Masculinization: Images of Women in Prison." In Ellen Adelberg and Claudia Currie (eds.), *Too*

Few to Count: Canadian Women in Conflict with the Law. Vancouver: Press Gang.

Fasiolo, Raffaele, and Steven Leckie. (1993). *Canadian Media Coverage of Gangs: A Content Analysis.* No. 1993—14. Solicitor General of Canada. Ottawa.

Fawcett, Brian. (1986). *Cambodia: A book for people who find television too slow.* Vancouver: Talonbooks.

Fishman, Mark. (1978). "Crime Waves as Ideology." *Social Problems* 25, no. 5: 531–43.

Forcese, Dennis P. (1992). *Policing Canadian Society.* Scarborough: Prentice-Hall Canada.

Garofalo, James, and Maureen McLeod. (1993). "Improving the use and effectiveness of Neighborhood Watch programs." In Chris W. Eskridge (ed.), *Criminal Justice: Concepts and Issues.* Los Angeles: Roxbury.

Gartner, Rosemary, and Anthony N. Doob. (1994). *Trends in Criminal Victimization: 1988—1993.* Juristat Service Bulletin. Canadian Centre for Justice Statistics Catalogue 85—002, vol. 14, no. 13.

Gebotys, Robert J., Julian V. Roberts and Bikram DasGupta. (1988). "News Media Use and Public Perceptions of Crime Seriousness." *Canadian Journal of Criminology* 30, no. 1: 3–16.

Goffman, Erving. (1963). *Stigma. Notes on the Management of Spoiled Identity.* Englewood Cliffs, N.J.: Prentice Hall.

Gomme, Ian McDermid. (1993). *The Shadow Line: Deviance and Crime in Canada.* Toronto: Harcourt Brace Jovanovich.

Grenier, Marc, ed. (1992). *Critical Studies of Canadian Mass Media.* Toronto: Butterworths.

Gunn, Rita, and Rick Linden. (1993). "Evaluating the Impact of Legal Reform: Canada's New Sexual Assault Laws." In Joe Hudson and Julian Roberts (eds.), *Evaluating Justice. Canadian Policies and Programs.* Toronto: Thompson.

Hailey, Arthur. (1990). *The Evening News.* New York: Doubleday.

Hall, Stuart, Chas Critcher, Tony Jefferson, John Clarke and Brian Roberts. (1978). *Policing the Crisis: Mugging, the State, and Law and Order.* London: Macmillan.

Harris, Michael. (1990a). *Justice Denied: The Law Versus Donald Marshall.* Toronto: Harper Collins.

———. (1990b). *Unholy Orders: Tragedy at Mount Cashel.* Harmondsworth: Penguin.

Heidegger, Martin. (1968). *What is Called Thinking?* New York: Harper and Row.

Herman, Edward S., and Noam Chomsky. (1988). *Manufacturing Consent: The Political Economy of the Mass Media.* New York: Pantheon.

Herman, Edward S., and Gerry O'Sullivan. (1989). *The 'Terrorism Industry': The Experts and Institutions that Shape Our View of Terror.* New York: Pantheon.

Hickey, Eric W. (1991). *Serial Murderers and their Victims.* Pacific Grove, Calif.: Brooks/Cole.

Holmes, Helen, and David Taras, eds. (1992). *Seeing Ourselves: Media Power and Policy in Canada.* Toronto: Harcourt Brace Jovanovich.

Holmes, Ronald M. (1988). *Serial Murder.* Newbury Park, Calif.: Sage Publications.

Hornick, Joseph P., Barry N. Leighton and Barbara A. Burrows. (1993). "Evaluating Community Policing: The Edmonton Project." In Joe Hudson and Julian Roberts (eds.), *Evaluating Justice: Canadian Policies and Programs.* Toronto: Thompson Educational.

Jackson, Margaret A., and Curt T. Griffiths. (1991). *Canadian Criminology: Perspectives on Crime and Criminality.* Toronto: Harcourt Brace Jovanovich.

Jenkins, Philip. (1992). *Intimate Enemies: Moral Panics in Contemporary Great Britain.* London: Aldine de Gruyter.

Jessome, Phonse. (1994). *Murder at McDonald's: The Killers Next Door.* Halifax: Nimbus.

Jobb, Dean. (1994). *Calculated Risk: Greed, Politics, and the Westray Tragedy.* Halifax: Nimbus.

Juristat. (1991a). *Children as Victims of Violent Crime.* Canadian Centre for Justice Statistics catalogue 85—002, vol. 11, no. 8.

———. (1991b). *Homicide.* Canadian Centre for Justice Statistics catalogue 85—002, vol. 12, no. 18.

Kelling, George L. (1993). "Police and communities: The quiet revolution," In Chris W. Eskridge (ed.), *Criminal Justice: Concepts and Issues.* Los Angeles: Roxbury.

Kelly, Liz. (1988). *Surviving Sexual Violence.* Minneapolis: University of Minnesota Press.

Kinsella, James. (1989). *Covering the Plague: AIDS and the American Media.* New Brunswick: Rutgers University Press.

Kitsuse, John I. (1962). "Societal Reaction to Deviant Behaviour." *Social Problems* 8, no. 3: 247–56.

Kramarae, Cheris, and Paula A. Treichler. (1985). *A Feminist Dictionary.* London: Pandora Press.

Kurtz, Howard. (1994). *Media Circus: The Trouble with America's Newspapers.* New York: Random.

Law Reform Commission of Canada. (1986). "Workplace Pollution." Working paper no. 53. Ottawa: Law Reform Commission of Canada.

Lee, Martin A., and Norman Solomon. (1990). *Unreliable Sources: A Guide to Detecting Bias in News Media.* New York: Lyle Stuart.

Leyton, Elliott. (1986). *Hunting Humans: The rise of the modern multiple murderer.* Toronto: McClelland and Stewart/Hickey.

———, William O'Grady and James Overton. (1992). *Violence and Public Anxiety: A Canadian Case.* St. John's: ISER.

Linden, Rick, ed. (1987). *Criminology: A Canadian Perspective.* Toronto: Holt, Rinehart and Winston.

Lippert, Randy. (1990). "The social construction of Satanism as a social problem in Canada." *Canadian Journal of Sociology* 15, no. 4: 417–39.

Loseke, Donileen R. (1987). "Lived Realities and the Construction of Social Problems: The Case of Wife Abuse." *Symbolic Interaction* 10, no. 2: 229–43.

———, and Spencer E. Cahill. (1984). "The Social Construction of Deviance: Experts on Battered Women." *Social Problems* 31, no. 3: 296—310.

Lowman, John. (1988). "Street prostitution." In Vince Sacco (ed.), *Deviance. Conformity and Control in Canadian Society.* Scarborough: Prentice Hall.

Lowman, J., M.A. Jackson, T.S. Palys and S. Gavigan, eds. (1986). *Regulating Sex: An Anthology of Commentaries on the Findings and Recommendations of the Badgley and Fraser Reports.* Vancouver: Simon Fraser University School of Criminology.

MacLeod, Linda. (1987). "Criminal Justice Initiatives: The Law as a Symbol of Change." In *Battered But Not Beaten: Preventing Wife Battering in Canada.* Ottawa: Canadian Advisory Council on the Status of Women.

Maggio, Rosalie. (1988). *The Nonsexist Word Finder: A Dictionary of Gender-Free Usage.* Boston: Beacon Press.

Manette, Joy, ed. (1992). *Elusive Justice: Beyond the Marshall Inquiry.* Halifax: Fernwood.

Manitoba. (1991). *Report of the Aboriginal Justice Inquiry of Manitoba.* Winnipeg.

Manoff, Robert Karl, and Michael Schudson, eds. (1986). *Reading the News: A Pantheon Guide to Popular Culture.* New York: Pantheon.

Mastrofski, Stephen D. (1993). "What does community policing mean for daily police work?" In Chris W. Eskridge (ed.), *Criminal Justice: Concepts and Issues.* Los Angeles: Roxbury.

McKibben, Bill. (1992). *The Age of Missing Information.* New York: Random House.

McLuhan, Marshall. (1964). *Understanding Media: The Extensions of Man.* New York: Signet.

———, and Quentin Fiore. (1967). *The Medium is the Massage: An Inventory of Effects.* Toronto: Bantam.

McMullan, John L. (1992). *Beyond the Limits of the Law: Corporate Crime and Law and Order*. Halifax: Fernwood.

Mills, Kay. (1990). *A Place in the News: From the Women's Pages to the Front Page*. New York: Columbia.

Mokhiber, Russell. (1988). *Corporate Crime and Violence: Big Business Power and the Abuse of the Public Trust*. San Francisco: Sierra Club Books.

Naffine, Ngaire. (1987). *Female Crime: The Construction of Women in Criminology*. Sydney: Allen and Unwin.

Newfoundland and Labrador. (1991). *The Royal Commission of Inquiry into the Response of the Newfoundland Criminal Justice System to Complaints*. St. John's.

Nova Scotia. (1989). *Royal Commission on the Donald Marshall, Jr. Prosecution*. Halifax.

Nova Scotia. Attorney General. (1992). "Spousal assault directive update." News release, April 7, 1992. Halifax.

Pfohl, Stephen J. (1977). "The Discovery of Child Abuse." *Social Problems* 24, no. 3: 315–21.

Postman, Neil, and Steve Powers. (1992). *How to Watch TV News*. New York: Penguin.

Raffel, Stanley. (1979). *Matters of Fact: A Sociological Inquiry*. London: Routledge and Kegan Paul.

Reiner, Robert. (1992). *The Politics of the Police*. Second edition. Toronto: University of Toronto Press.

Ressler, Robert K. (1992). *Whoever fights monsters*. New York: St. Martin's Press.

Roberts, Julian V. (1994). *Criminal Justice Processing of Sexual Assault Cases*. Juristat Service Bulletin. Canadian Centre for Justice Statistics catalogue 85—002, vol. 14, no. 7.

Rodgers, Karen. (1994). *Wife Assault: The Findings of a National Survey*. Juristat Service Bulletin. Canadian Centre for Justict Statistics, vol. 14, no. 9.

Romanow, Walter I., and Walter C. Soderlund. (1992). *Media Canada: An Introductory Analysis*. Toronto: Copp Clark Pitman.

Rosenbaum, Dennis P. (1993). "Community crime prevention: A review and synthesis of the literature" In Chris W. Eskridge (ed.), *Criminal Justice: Concepts and Issues*. Los Angeles: Roxbury.

Sabato, Larry J. (1991). *Feeding Frenzy: How Attack Journalism has Transformed American Politics*. New York: The Free Press.

Schutz, Alfred. (1967). *The Phenomenology of the Social World*. Chicago: Northwestern University Press.

Sears, Donald J. (1991). *To Kill Again: The Motivation and Development of Serial Murder*. Wilmington, Del.: SR Books.

Shaver, Frances M. (1985). "Prostitution: A Critical Analysis of Three Policy Approaches." *Canadian Public Policy* XI, no. 3: 493—503.

Sheriff, Peta E. (1983). "State Theory, Social Science, and Government Commissions." *American Behavioural Scientist* 26, no. 5: 669–80.

Shilts, Randy. (1987). *And the Band Played On: Politics, People, and the AIDS Epidemic*. New York: Penguin.

Smith, Dorothy E. (1987). *The Everyday World as Problematic: A Feminist Sociology*. Toronto: University of Toronto Press.

———. (1990). *Texts, Facts, and Femininity: Exploring the Relations of Ruling*. London: Routledge.

Snider, Laureen. (1993). *Bad Business: Corporate Crime in Canada*. Scarborough: Nelson Canada.

Sontag, Susan. (1990). *Illness as Metaphor: AIDS and its Metaphors*. New York: Anchor.

Soothill, Keith, and Sylvia Walby. (1991). *Sex Crime in the News*. London: Routledge.

Soothill, Keith, and Debbie Soothill. (1993). "Prosecuting the Victim? A Study of the Reporting of Barristers' Comments in Rape Cases." *Howard Journal* 32, no. 1: 12—24.

Statistics Canada. *Crime in Canada*. Ottawa.

———. (1993). "Violence Against Women Survey Highlights." *The Daily*, November 18, Catalogue 11—001E. Ottawa.

Stephens, Mitchell. (1988). *A History of News: From the Drum to the Satellite*. Harmondsworth: Penguin.

Surette, Ray. (1990). *The Media and Criminal Justice Policy: Recent Research and Social Effects*. Springfield, Ill.: C.C. Thomas.

———. (1992). *Media, Crime and Criminal Justice: Images and Realities*. Pacific Grove: Brooks/Cole.

Tierney, Kathleen J. (1982). "The Battered Women Movement and the Creation of the Wife Beating Problem." *Social Problems* 29, no. 3: 207–20.

Treichler, Paula. (1987). "AIDS, Homophobia, and Biomedical Discourse: An Epidemic of Signification." In Douglas Crimp (ed.), *AIDS: Cultural Analysis/Cultural Activism*. Cambridge: MIT.

Trudeau, G.B. (1994). "Doonesbury," July 10, 1994. Universal Press Syndicate.

Turner, Roy, ed. (1974). *Ethnomethodology: Selected Readings*. Harmondsworth: Penguin.

Vallee, Brian. (1986). *Life with Billy*. Toronto: McLelland/Bantam.

Valverde, Mariana. (1991). *The Age of Light, Soap, and Water: Moral Reform in English Canada, 1885—1925*. Toronto: McClelland and Stewart.

Voumvakis, Sophia E., and Richard V. Ericson. (1984). *News Accounts of Attacks on Women: A Comparison of Three Toronto Newspapers.* University of Toronto: Centre of Criminology.

Walker, Lenore E. (1989). *Terrifying Love: Why Battered Women Kill and How Society Responds.* New York: Harper Collins.

Warshaw, Robin. (1988). *I never called it rape: The Ms. report on recognizing, fighting, and surviving date and acquaintance rape.* New York: Harper & Row.

Watney, Simon. (1989). *Policing Desire: Pornography, AIDS, and the Media.* Minneapolis: University of Minnesota Press.